Social Causes of Health and Disease

Second Edition

Praise for *Social Causes of Health and Disease*

"In this revised edition William Cockerham develops a strong and challenging case for the role of social factors in health and disease. Drawing on the latest and most important research, *Social Causes of Health and Disease* will stimulate debate and discussion in equal measure - essential reading for students and researchers alike."
Michael Bury, Royal Holloway, University of London

"This second edition of William Cockerham's acclaimed book updates his argument about the social causes of disease, drawing on the latest research from both the US and UK. His argument about the direct causal effects of social factors on health and disease is compelling and will be of considerable interest to students and researchers of both sides of the Atlantic."
Jonathan Gabe, Royal Holloway, University of London

Social Causes of Health and Disease

Second Edition

William C. Cockerham

polity

First edition published in 2007 by Polity Press
This edition first published in 2013 by Polity Press
Reprinted 2013, 2014

Polity Press
65 Bridge Street
Cambridge CB2 1UR, UK

Polity Press
350 Main Street
Malden, MA 02148, USA

ISBN-13: 978-0-7456-6119-3
ISBN-13: 978-0-7456-6120-9 (pb)

A catalogue record for this book is available from the British Library.

Typeset in 10.5 on 12 pt Times New Roman
by Servis Filmsetting Ltd, Stockport, Cheshire
Printed in the USA by Edwards Brothers Malloy

The publisher has used its best endeavors to ensure that the URLs for external websites referred to in this book are correct and active at the time of going to press. However, the publisher has no responsibility for the websites and can make no guarantee that a site will remain live or that the content is or will remain appropriate.

Every effort has been made to trace all copyright holders, but if any have been inadvertently overlooked the publisher will be pleased to include any necessary credits in any subsequent reprint or edition.

For further information on Polity, visit our website: www.politybooks.com

Contents

Preface

For more than half a century, medical sociology has evolved as a sub-discipline of mainstream sociology. At times it was more beholden to medicine than sociology for its support, even though the field became one of the most popular sociological specialties. Time invariably brings change and medical sociology has indeed changed since its inception. For example, the old claim that medical sociology is atheoretical has been definitively quashed; there is now even a specialized journal (*Health and Social Theory*) on the topic. Sociological theory, in fact, has become one of the most important and distinctive research tools in the field. Moreover, medical sociology has positioned itself to provide even more precise and extensive analyses of the social aspects of health and disease. The first edition of this book represents one of the first treatises of the twenty-first century describing a new direction for research that will likely be commonplace in the not-to-distant future: the social causation of health and disease. This edition follows up on that argument. The book begins with the notion that society can make you sick and then explains the ways in which this happens.

The revised book is a further extension of a lecture I presented at the University of Montreal on a cold, grey, slushy, wet Canadian afternoon in January, 2006. This presentation was part of the university's "Alexis de Tocqueville: Questions on American Society" lecture series. Arnaud Sales of the sociology department and Andrée Demers of Groupe de recherche sur les aspects sociaux de la santé et de la prevention (GRASP) were wonderful hosts. In preparing for this lecture,

I wanted to look forward in discussing medical sociology and focus on the future rather than the present or past. It seemed clear that the current state of theory and developments in statistics for multilevel analyses will allow medical sociologists to better assess the effects of different layers of social structure on the health of individuals. This not only forecasts a greater concern with structure in our future work, but will also permit us as a community of scholars to uncover the social mechanisms that cause health and disease. This book represents an early step in that direction.

I would like to acknowledge the assistance of several people, although the conclusions expressed are my own. Emma Longstaff, the sociology editor for Polity in Cambridge, England, provided many helpful suggestions and a high level of professionalism in her work concerning this manuscript, as did her replacement Jonathan Skerrett. Their influence led to producing a manuscript that will hopefully bridge the Atlantic as it relies heavily on both North American and British research literature. I would also like to acknowledge the contributions of Ann Bone and Belle Mundy in the production and copy-editing of the manuscript.

Mike Bury, Emeritus Professor of Sociology at Royal Holloway College London, was a stalwart critic as a reviewer for Polity on the first edition. His detailed comments helped sharpen the book's thesis and he went beyond reviewing to make many cogent and thoughtful suggestions that proved to be extraordinarily helpful. I would like to additionally thank an anonymous American reviewer for her comments and reminders to make the book appealing to students. Brian Hinote and Jason Wasserman, both doctoral students in medical sociology at the University of Alabama at Birmingham, were an especially competent sounding board when working through some of the issues discussed in the first edition. Carrie Betcher was an efficient replacement for the second edition. I would like to thank Olena Hankivsky (Simon Fraser University) for a clarification and three anonymous reviewers for Polity who provided helpful comments. Ferris Ritchey and Mark LaGory, in their former positions as sociology department chairs at UAB, made sure that I had the time and support to work on the manuscript. Finally, I would like to thank my wife, Cynthia, for her continued support. Time and time again, she has proven herself to be an intelligent, insightful, and wry observer of the human social condition.

William C. Cockerham

Schopenhauer's saying, that a human can very well do what he wants, but cannot will what he wants, accompanies me in all of life's circumstances . . .

Albert Einstein – in a 1928 speech to the German League for Human Rights and repeated in his "My Credo," 1932

1

The Social Causation of Health and Disease

The capability of social factors to make people ill seems to be widely recognized by the general public. Ask people if they think society can make them sick and the probabilities are high they will answer in the affirmative (Blaxter 2010). Stress, poverty, low socioeconomic status, unhealthy lifestyles, and unpleasant living and work conditions are among the many inherently social variables typically regarded by lay persons as causes of ill health. However, with the exception of stress, this view is not expressed in much of the research literature. Studies in public health, epidemiology, behavioral medicine, and other sciences in the health field typically minimize the relevance of social factors in their investigations. Usually social variables are characterized as distant or secondary influences on health and illness, not as direct causes (Link and Phelan 1995, 2000; Phelan et al. 2004). Being poor, for example, is held to produce greater exposure to something that will make a person sick, rather than bring on sickness itself. However, social variables may be more powerful in inducing adversity or enrichment in health outcomes than formerly assumed. Society may indeed make you sick or conversely, promote your health.

It is the intent of this book to assess the evidence indicating that this is so. It is clear that most diseases have social connections. That is, the social context can shape the risk of exposure, the susceptibility of the host, and the disease's course and outcome – regardless of whether the disease is infectious, genetic, metabolic, malignant, or degenerative

(Holtz et al. 2006). This includes major afflictions like heart disease, Type 2 diabetes, stroke, cancers like lung and cervical neoplasms, HIV/AIDS and other sexually-transmitted infections, pulmonary diseases, kidney disease, and many other ailments. Even rheumatoid arthritis, which might at first consideration seem to be exclusively biological, is grounded in socioeconomic status, with lower-status persons having significantly greater risk of becoming arthritic than individuals higher up the social scale (Bengtsson et al. 2005; Pederson et al. 2006). Consequently, the basic thesis of this book is that social factors do more than influence health for large populations and the lived experience of illness for individuals; rather, such factors have a *direct* causal effect on physical health and illness.

How can this be? Just because most diseases have a social connection of some type, does not necessarily mean that such links can actually cause a disease to occur – or does it? Social factors such as living conditions, lifestyles, norms, social values, and attitudes are obviously not pathogens like germs or viruses, nor are they cancer cells or coagulated clots of blood that clog arteries. Yet, quarantined in a laboratory, viruses, cancers, and the like do not make a person sick. They need to be exposed to a human host and assault the body's physiological defenses in order to be causal. However, assigning causation solely to biological entities does not account for all of the relevant factors in a disease's pathogenesis, especially in relation to the social behaviors and conditions that bond the person to the disease in the first place. Social factors can initiate the onset of the pathology and in this way serve as a direct cause for a number of diseases. One of many examples is smoking tobacco.

Smoking

Smoking is associated with more diseases than any other health-related lifestyle practice (Cockerham 2006b; Jarvis and Wardle 1999). Autopsies on heavy smokers show lung tissue that has been transformed from a healthy pink to gray and brownish white in color. Smoking also affects the body in other ways, such as damaging the cardiovascular system, causing back pain, and producing increased risk of loss of cartilage in knee joints through osteoarthritis. The physiological damage caused by smoking cigarettes is due to the irritant and carcinogenic material ("tar") released by burning tobacco into smoke that is inhaled in the lungs and enters the blood stream where it is spread throughout the body. Persons who die from lung cancer are increasingly less able to breathe and feel suffocated as their lungs lose the capacity to transfer oxygen to the blood.

In Britain, some 120,000 people die annually from smoking. In the United States, with its much larger population, about 440,000 Americans die each year from smoking-related causes, including some 200,000 dying from lung cancer and another 200,000 from adverse effects on the cardiovascular system. Smoking promotes heart attacks and strokes, narrows and hardens arteries, damages blood vessels and causes them to rupture (aneurysms), and brings on high blood pressure. Habitual smoking regularly results in premature death, with a man in the US losing 13 years of life on average and a woman 14.5 years (Centers for Disease Control and Prevention 2002; Pampel 2009).

How do social variables enter into this disease pattern in a causal role? At one level it looks like the causal factors are all biology: tar in smoke causes cancer and impairs blood circulation. But tar by itself is not causal. It has to enter the human body to have any effect. What is ultimately causal is the human being – both as a host inhaling the smoke and as a manufacturer of a smoking-prone social environment. There is a social pattern to smoking that indicates tobacco use is not a random, individual decision completely independent of social structural influences.

However, smoking and other risky behaviors have not been viewed in a broad social context by researchers as much as they have been characterized as situations of individual responsibility. If people wish to avoid the negative effects of smoking on their health, it is therefore reasoned that they should not smoke. If they choose to smoke, what happens to them is no one's fault but their own. This victim-blaming approach, argue Martin Jarvis and Jane Wardle (1999), is not helpful, because it does not explain why people, especially those from socially disadvantaged circumstances, are drawn to poor health habits like smoking and the types of social situations that promote this behavior. Today, smoking is unusual among persons at the higher and middle levels of society and is concentrated among people toward the bottom of the social ladder. Persons in higher socioeconomic groups were the first to adopt smoking in the early twentieth century and other social classes followed, but growing publicity about the harmful effects of cigarettes in the 1960s led to a shift in smoking patterns over time as better educated and more affluent groups began avoiding the practice (Antunes 2011; Narcisse et al. 2009; Pampel 2009).

The social process of becoming a smoker is described by Jason Hughes (2003) who determined that confirmed smokers pass through five stages in their smoking career: (1) becoming a smoker, (2) continued smoking, (3) regular smoking, (4) addicted smoking, and, for some, (5) stopping smoking. Based on interviews with both smokers and ex-smokers in Great Britain, Hughes determined that the first experience people have with smoking cigarettes in the initial stage of *becoming a smoker* is typically unpleasant. The smoker usually feels nauseated. One respondent told Hughes (2003: 148) that she really did not like her first cigarette, describing it as "foul." This raises a crucial question: If the first experience is unpleasant, why do people continue? Hughes's answer is that people learn how to smoke by having other individuals interpret the experience for them and tell them how to distinguish the desired sensations from the undesirable. Specifically, they are taught how to inhale properly and pull the smoke into their lungs. One woman in the Hughes (2003: 149) study reported on what it was like being a smoker when she first started: ". . . it was quite exciting. I thought I'd grown up! It was something new. And it is a skill that you have to learn to do it properly so that people don't say, 'she's not inhaling properly, she's not smoking.' You have to learn how to do it."

Hughes explains that, initially, smoking is a social activity carried out with other people. It typically has its origins in adolescent peer groups, in which teens imitate adult or older teen behavior. Teens smoke to "connect with," "fit in," and "impress" their friends. Joy Johnson and her colleagues (Haines, Poland, and Johnson 2009; Johnson et al. 2003) studied teen smoking in Canada and found that adolescents are more socially than physically dependent on cigarettes in the beginning.

The social setting, namely relaxing with peers, caused smoking more than wanting to inhale tobacco smoke. Often the teen did not smoke when friends were not around. But when friends were present, new smokers used cigarettes primarily to connect with them socially, project an image of being "cool," and express solidarity. Three teenagers in the Johnson et al. (2003: 1484–6) study analyzed smoking in their peer groups this way:

> Like it [smoking] is a social aspect of their life that they have become dependent on, as much as the nicotine, you know. I think almost the social setting of it is something that is somewhat addictive itself. (17-year-old female)

> People don't really have to smoke, but they do it anyways to like fit in, or whatever, and they smoke to put out an image to people. (17-year-old male)

> It's more what you will do to fit in, not what you will do to smoke, because you may not actually want to smoke. (16-year-old male)

Reports such as these support Hughes's (2003) contention that the beginning stage of becoming a smoker is principally a social experience. Not only are the techniques learned within peer groups, but the act of smoking is used to promote social relationships, reinforce personal bonds, and express group affiliation. Soon the adolescent smokers also learn to recognize the effect of nicotine on their emotions. Smoking helped them feel calm and reduced anxiety; it could also ease depression, sadness, fear, loneliness, and anger. Some novice smokers found they could like the taste and others felt smoking was a sign of transition to an adult identity. While most adolescents likely try smoking at some point in growing up, the majority do not continue. For those that do, however, they enter the second stage of smoking described by Hughes, that of *continued smoking*. Here the beginning smoker starts smoking more frequently as part of a consistent pattern of behavior. These smokers continue to use cigarettes to socialize, but also for other reasons like relaxation, pleasure, alleviating stress, or helping their concentration. They also smoke when they are alone, instead of just when they are with other people. They begin recognizing themselves as smokers and find they have a growing sense of dependence on the addictive qualities of nicotine as they move into the third stage of *regular smoker* in which smoking becomes a lifestyle habit that leads to the fourth stage of *addicted smoking* in which the smoker has to smoke a cigarette just to feel "normal." As one addicted smoker (Johnson et al. 2003: 1488) put it: "It's gone beyond maybe wanting it or enjoying it, but at this point, your body is addicted to it, and no matter what, you couldn't get through the day without either thinking about it or feeling you need a cigarette" (19-year-old female).

The causal chain leading to a smoking-related disease in this scenario would look like the following: social interaction among peers leads to smoking which, when continued over time, results in regular smoking and addiction to cigarettes that has a high probability of eventually producing health problems. While perhaps not all smokers begin smoking with someone else's assistance, it appears that almost all do. Moreover, even when smoking is self-taught, the novice smoker confirms the practice in the company of other smokers (Haines, Poland, and Johnson 2009). Growing up in a household where one or both parents smoke, having a spouse who smokes, and regularly socializing with smokers are other social situations promoting smoking. In practically all cases, smoking is behavior initially acquired in the company of other people (Cockerham 2006b). The origin of this causal chain is social. Removing the social element breaks the chain and prevents the disease process from occurring. Since smoking typically begins in social networks, it is logical that such networks can also curtail its use. This possibility was considered by Nicholas Christakis and James Fowler (2008) who investigated smoking patterns in densely inter-connected social networks in the Framingham, Massachusetts, heart study. They found that whole clusters of closely connected people had stopped smoking more or less together. This was due to to collective pressures from their network, coming mainly from spouses, siblings, other family members, and co-workers who were close friends. As a social and therefore shared behavior, Christakis and Fowler deter-mined that smokers were more likely to quit when they ran out of people with whom they could easily smoke. They (Christakis and Fowler 2008:2256) concluded "that decisions to quit smoking are not made solely by isolated individuals, but rather they reflect choices made by groups of people connected to each other both directly and indirectly." Those who remained smokers were pushed to the periph-ery of the networks as the networks themselves became increasingly separated into smokers and non-smokers. Consequently, to minimize or deny the role of social processes in the onset and continuation of health problems stemming from smoking renders any other explana-tion incomplete. In this scenario the social is clearly causal.

Smokers also typically have less healthy lifestyles across many related behaviors, such as poorer diets, less regular exercise, and more problem drinking (Cockerham 2005; Edwards et al. 2006; Laaksonen, Prättälä, and Lahelma 2002). This is in addition to the powerful influence of other social variables like class and gender that influence health-related behavioral practices like smoking positively or nega-tively. To minimize or deny the role of social processes in the onset of health problems stemming from such practices renders any other explanation incomplete.

The Biomedical Model

Every disease specific
The relegation of social factors to a distant supporting role in studies of health and disease causation reflects the pervasiveness of the bio-medical model in conceptualizing sickness. The biomedical model is based on the premise that every disease has a specific pathogenic origin whose treatment can best be accomplished by removing or controlling its cause using medical procedures. Often this means administering a drug to alleviate or cure the symptoms. According to Kevin White (2006), this view has become the taken-for-granted way of think-ing about sickness in Western society. The result is that sickness has

come to be regarded as a straightforward physical event, usually a consequence of a germ, virus, cancer, or genetic affliction causing the body to malfunction. "So for most of us," states White (2006: 142), "being sick is [thought to be] a biochemical process that is natural and not anything to do with our social life." This view perseveres, White notes, despite the fact that it now applies to only a very limited range of medical conditions.

The persistence of the biomedical model is undoubtedly due to its great success in treating infectious diseases. Research in microbiology, biochemistry, and related fields resulted in the discovery and development of a large variety of drugs and drug-based techniques for effectively treating many diseases. This approach became medicine's primary method for dealing with many of the problems it is called upon to treat, as its thinking became dominated by the use of drugs as "magic bullets" that can be shot into the body to cure or control afflictions (Dubos 1959). As historian Roy Porter (1997: 595) explained: "Basic research, clinical science and technology working with one another have characterized the cutting edge of modern medicine. Progress has been made. For almost all diseases something can be done; some can be prevented or fully cured." Also improvements in living conditions, especially diet, housing, public sanitation, and personal hygiene, were important in eliminating much of the threat from infectious diseases. Epidemiologist Thomas McKeown (1979) found these measures more effective than medical interventions on mortality from water and food-borne illnesses in the second half of the nineteenth century.

However, as a challenge to the biomedical model, McKeown's thesis is considered rather tame since a rise in living standards naturally improves health and reduces mortality. Moreover, McKeown has been criticized for his focus on the individual when an analysis of social structural factors would have been more informative (Nettleton 2006). For example, David Blane (1990) subsequently investigated changes in mortality in Britain between 1870 and 1914 in relation to the purchasing power of workers and the quality of their work environment. He found that the increased capability to purchase goods and services, along with better work conditions, had a stronger effect on reducing mortality than improvements in nutrition and sanitation. In this instance, the decisive variable was ultimately structural, namely, the collective actions of workers in obtaining higher wages and an improved work situation.

The general improvement in living standards and work conditions combined with the biomedical approach to make significant inroads in curbing infectious disease. By the late 1960s, with the near eradication of polio and smallpox, infectious diseases had been severely curtailed in most regions of the world. This situation led to longer life spans which were reflected in the change in the pattern of diseases, with chronic illnesses – which by definition are long-term and incurable – replacing infectious diseases as the major threats to health. This epidemiological transition occurred initially in industrialized nations and then spread throughout the world. It is characterized by the movement of chronic diseases such as cancer, heart disease, and stroke to the forefront of health afflictions as the leading causes of death. As Porter (1997) observed, cancer was familiar to physicians as far back as ancient Greece and Rome, but it has become exceedingly more prevalent as life spans increase.

As for heart disease, Porter notes the comments of a leading British medical doctor who observed in 1892 that cardiac deaths were "relatively rare." However, within a few decades, heart disease had become the leading cause of death throughout Western society as people lived longer. New diagnostic techniques, drugs, and surgical procedures including heart transplants, by-pass surgery, and angioplasty were developed in response. Porter (1997: 585) also finds that greater public awareness of risk factors like smoking, poor diet, obesity, and lack of exercise along with lifestyle changes made a fundamental contribution to improving cardiovascular health.

The transition to chronic diseases meant medicine was increasingly called upon to confront the health problems of the "whole" person, which extend well beyond singular causes of disease such as a virus that fit the biomedical model. As Porter pointed out, even though the twentieth century witnessed the most intense concentration of attention and resources ever on chronic diseases, they have nevertheless persisted. "It can be argued," states Porter (1997: 594), "that one reason why there has been relatively little success in eradicating them is because the strategies which earlier worked so well for tackling acute infectious diseases have proved inappropriate for dealing with chronic and degenerative conditions, and it has been hard to discard the successful 'microbe hunters' formula."

Consequently, modern medicine is increasingly required to develop insights into the social behaviors characteristic of the people it treats. According to Porter, it is not only radical thinkers who appeal for a new "wholism" in medical practice that takes social factors into consideration, but many of the most respected figures in medicine were insistent that treating the body as a mechanical model would not produce true health. Porter (1997: 634) states:

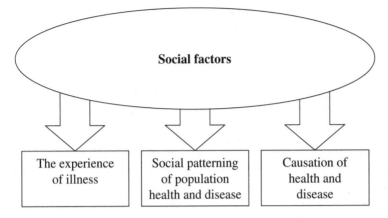

Figure 1.1 The direct effects of social factors on health and disease

Disease became conceptualized after 1900 as a social no less than a bio-logical phenomenon, to be understood statistically, sociologically, and psychologically – even politically. Medicine's gaze had to incorporate wider questions of income, lifestyle, diet, habit, employment, education, and family structure – in short, the entire psychosocial economy. Only thus could medicine meet the challenge of mass society, supplanting laboratory medicine preoccupied with minute investigation of lesions but indifferent as to how they got there.

Contemporary physicians now treat many health maladies that are aptly described as "problems of living," dysfunctions that may involve multiple sources of causation, including those that are social in origin and part of everyday life. This includes social structural factors like class, living conditions, and social capital that can cause health or illness. These factors are causal because good or bad health originates from their influence. Consider, for example, the problem of low birth-weights among newborn babies. Such babies are more likely to have health problems than infants with normal birth-weights and less likely to survive the postnatal period. In researching this situation, Dalton Conley, Kate Strully, and Neil Bennett (2003) determined that if there are two groups of couples – one with high incomes and the other with low incomes – and each group has the same 20 percent biological pre-disposition toward having a low-birth-weight baby – the high-income group has a very high probability of counteracting their biological predisposition with better nutrition and prenatal care. In this instance, social factors – namely, income and how it translates into better edu-cation, living situations, jobs, quality medical care, and a good diet and other healthy lifestyle practices – reverse the biological risk. In the low-income group, the biological risk proceeds unimpeded. In both groups, social factors are causal in that biological predispositions are blunted in the high-income group and do not allow the biological risk to be countered in the low-income group. In fact, it could be argued that low income and how it signifies poor education, less healthy living situations, inadequate employment, less quality medical care, and poor diets along with less healthy lifestyle practices like smoking and alcohol abuse, promotes the biological risk into reality.

Social factors not only can determine whether or not a person becomes sick, but also shape the pattern of a population's health and disease, as well as how people experience illness. The direct effects of social factors on health and disease are depicted in figure 1.1. First, social factors can mold the illness experience, for example, in helping or hindering adaptation, alleviating or exacerbating symptoms by making remedies more or less accessible, providing therapeutic or detrimental environments, or in causing good or poor health care to be available. Second, social factors determine the social patterning of health, disease, and mortality at the population level. All societies have social hierarchies and within those hierarchies health and longevity invariably reflect a gradient in health that is better at the top than at the bottom, while most diseases are also concentrated at earlier ages at the bottom. Third, is the topic of this book: the social causation of health and disease that will be discussed in this and forthcoming chapters.

Elements of Proof

However, as biostatistician Ronald Thisted (2003) points out, assembling convincing evidence about the social determinants of health is a challenge because of difficulties in linking the social with the biological. Although social factors are associated with various causes of mortality, he states that the mere association of such factors with health or a disease does not necessarily prove causality. Since the concept of a determinant requires a mechanism for action, finding social mechanisms at the aggregate level that affect health and disease at the individual level is a necessary element of proof that social factors are causal. Thisted suggests that a strategy for locating such mechanisms is the use of the traditional epidemiological triad of agent, host, and environment. Agents are the immediate or proximal cause of a particular disease and can be biological, nutritional, chemical, physical, or social. Hosts are the people susceptible to the agent, and the environment consists of factors external to the person, including agents, which either cause or influence a health problem.

The relevance of this strategy is apparent from the different roles social factors perform in the agent–host–environment triad. Agents can be social as seen in the health effects generated by class position, occupations, neighborhoods, and lifestyles; human hosts reflect traits that are both social (habits, customs, norms, and lifestyles) and biological (age, sex, degree of immunity, or other physical attributes that promote resistance or susceptibility); while features of the environment are not only physical but social with respect to poverty and unhealthy living conditions, as well as the social relationships, norms, values, and forms of interaction in a particular social context. Health-related lifestyles are of particular relevance as a social mechanism producing positive or negative health outcomes. As Anthony Giddens (1991: 81) points out, lifestyles can be defined as a more or less integrated set of practices that fulfill utilitarian needs and give material form to particular narratives or expressions of self-identity, such as class position. Everyone has a lifestyle, even the poor. When it comes to health, lifestyles have multiple roles in that they function as a collective or shared pattern of behavior (agent) that is normative in particular settings (environment) for the individual (host). As will be discussed in chapter 3, health lifestyles can be decisive in determining an individual's health and longevity. Some 40 percent of premature deaths in the US have been linked to unhealthy lifestyle practices such as smoking, alcohol abuse, overeating, and a lack of exercise (Mokdad et al. 2004).

Thisted, however, does not focus on lifestyles, but examines the preconditions for cholera. He notes the link between the biological agent (*Vibrio cholerae* bacteria) and poor sanitation, observing that poor sanitation is often a consequence of social conditions like poverty and a lack of infrastructure. In this case, the environment could serve as the social mechanism, while social factors might also be important for the host with respect to the availability of modern vaccines. Except for the agent, Thisted concludes that many of the preconditions for cholera may indeed result from social rather than biological factors. He comes to a similar conclusion for the noninfectious problems of hypertension and homicide, suggesting each can be understood through the model of agents and hosts interacting in a suitable environment.

Yet he maintains that the validity of social mechanisms has not been proven beyond a doubt and seriously questions whether the effects of such mechanisms can account for much of the variation in health. He compares differences in the percentages of deaths in the black and white population in the United States in 2000 and, while noting the higher

Table 1.1 Age-adjusted death rates for selected causes of death, according to race, United States, 2007 (deaths per 100,000 resident population)

	Non-Hispanic whites	Non-Hispanic blacks	Hispanics	American Indian/ Alaska Natives	Asians/Pacific Islanders
All causes	749.4	958.0	546.1	627.2	415.0
Cardiovascular diseases	244.1	335.0	181.0	169.7	147.1
Cerebrovascular diseases	40.5	60.3	32.7	29.8	34.3
Cancer	177.5	215.5	116.2	117.8	106.7
Pulmonary diseases	43.0	28.1	17.5	30.9	13.4
Pneumonia and influenza	16.0	18.4	13.1	13.8	13.6
Liver disease and cirrhosis	9.4	7.4	13.8	24.8	3.3
Diabetes	20.5	42.8	28.9	37.2	16.2
Accidents	41.5	36.6	30.1	55.7	17.0
Suicide	12.5	5.0	6.0	11.5	6.1
Homicide	3.7	21.1	6.9	6.5	2.3
AIDS	1.9	17.3	4.1	2.6	0.5

Source: National Center for Health Statistics 2010.

percentages in deaths for blacks, nonetheless finds the differences are not extreme for mortality from diabetes and homicide in particular. While a disadvantaged social situation may cause many blacks to have greater exposure than most whites to these afflictions and bear some responsibility for the differences, Thisted states that most individuals of both races do not die from diabetes and homicide, and therefore social determinants are likely to have a low level of causation.

In order to put this critique in perspective, the age-adjusted mortality data for all races in the United States in 2007 (the most recent year available as this book goes to press) are shown in table 1.1. For mortality from all causes, table 1.1 shows that non-Hispanic blacks have the highest death rates of 958 per 100,000 persons, followed by non-Hispanic whites (749.4), American Indians/Alaska Natives (627.2), Hispanics (546.1), and Asians/Pacific Islanders (415.0). Non-Hispanic blacks have the highest rates for each specific cause of death in table 1.1, except for pulmonary disease and suicide that is greater among non-Hispanic whites, and liver disease/cirrhosis and accidents that are higher among American Indians/Native Alaskans. Particularly striking are the exceptionally high death rates for non-Hispanic blacks for heart disease, cerebrovascular diseases (strokes), cancer, diabetes, homicide, and AIDS. While most individuals do not die from diabetes and homicide, they do die from heart disease, cancer, and cerebrovascular diseases and blacks are clearly well ahead of whites in these causes of mortality.

If we compare the 2007 mortality rates for diabetes and homicide shown in table 1.1 to the 2000 results used by Thisted, we see the pattern is virtually the same. In 2000, there were 42.5 deaths per 100,000 persons from diabetes for blacks and 22.8 for whites. In 2007, there were 42.8 deaths for blacks compared to 20.5 for whites – which is almost identical to 2000, except for some slight improvement among whites. Black rates for diabetes are more than twice as high as those for whites for both periods. For homicide, there were 20.5 deaths for blacks in 2000 and 21.1 in 2007, compared to 3.6 and 3.7, respectively, for whites. Overall, black rates for homicide are more than five times higher than white rates. Consequently, the differences are not slight as suggested, but extreme. Heart disease, cancer, and stroke show similar outcomes. These death rates are clearly unequal which points toward some important differences in the lives of non-Hispanic blacks and whites in relation to mortality. These health outcomes cannot all be blamed on biology. In fact, very little of it can be attributed to biological differences between the races (Holtz et al. 2006). What is decisive in many cases are social factors, as seen in the examples of diabetes and HIV/AIDS.

Diabetes

Diabetes is of growing importance in the United States and it is clear that race is a key variable in this development, despite claims that race is simply a social label that by itself should not have any effect on health. What makes race most important with respect to health in American society is its close association with being affluent or poor. Even though members of all races are in each socioeconomic category and many whites are poor, blacks and Hispanics are over-represented among lower-income groups (Hattery and Smith 2011; D. Williams and Sternthal 2010). As for diabetes, both the Type 1 and Type 2 versions are diseases in which excess amounts of sugar (glucose) in the blood damage the body's organs – promoting kidney failure, heart disease, stroke, blindness, amputations of limbs, and other problems. Type 1 typically appears in childhood when the pancreas quits producing insulin that controls blood sugar levels because the body's immune system has destroyed the cells that make it. Type 2 or adult onset diabetes is the most common form of the disease and usually develops in people after the age of 40. Some 90 percent of all diabetics are Type 2. This type features the ability to make insulin, but the inability of the cells to use it to control blood sugar levels. Type 2 diabetes is often controlled through diet and exercise, but if this fails then oral medications and/or insulin injections are required.

The *New York Times* published a series of investigative articles on diabetes in New York City in 2006. The *New York Times* cited Centers for Disease Control and Prevention (CDC) figures indicating that 20.8 million Americans nationwide had diabetes and 41 million more were in a prediabetic stage. One in three children born at the time could expect to become diabetic; for Hispanics, it may be as high as one in every two children – thereby suggesting a future explosion in the numbers of diabetics in the United States. In New York City, the percentage of diabetics has already increased 140 percent in the last decade (Kleinfield 2006a). The number of diabetics in the city is about 800,000 or one in every eight residents. In East Harlem, the epicenter of the city's diabetes crisis, the ratio is one in every five residents. Diabetes is the only major disease in New York City that is *increasing* with respect to both the number of new cases and the number of people who die from it. *New York Times* reporter N. R. Kleinfield (2006a: A1) describes the situation in one hospital in the Bronx when observing that nearly half of the patients there on any given day were admitted for some health problem due to diabetes.

Genetics plays a critical role in that diabetes is more prevalent in certain families and groups than others. A variant gene (TCF7L2) has been discovered that increases the risk of Type 2 diabetes and is carried by more than a third of the American population (Grant et al. 2005). Since people carry two copies of each gene, one inherited from each parent, the extent of the risk depends on whether one or two copies of it have been inherited. The estimated 38 percent of Americans with only one copy are 45 percent more likely than the unaffected population to come down with the disease, while the 7 percent who have inherited two copies are 141 percent more likely than those without the gene to develop diabetes. This gene has existed in the American gene pool for generations and its presence in the body does not guarantee its activation; rather, it enhances the risk. However, the rapid acceleration of new cases in recent years cannot be explained by genetics alone since the human gene pool does not change that fast.

Instead, the culprit appears to be social behavior and is inextricably linked to race and income (Kleinfield 2006b). Low income is significant because of what it signifies with respect to diet (sugar and high fats), exercise (little or none), and medical care (inadequate). Race is important because blacks and Hispanics are twice as likely as whites to become diabetic and more than half of New York City's population is comprised of people in these two racial categories. Affluent and predominately white neighborhoods like the Upper West Side, Brooklyn Heights, and the Upper East Side have low rates of diabetes. Working-class areas like Ridgewood in Queens have moderate rates, while largely black and Hispanic low-income areas like East Harlem have a virtual diabetes epidemic. Some 16–20 percent of all adults in East Harlem have diabetes (Kleinfield 2006b).

In this situation, the host is genetically-predisposed individuals, the agent is negative health lifestyles, and the environment is socially and economically disadvantaged neighborhoods in New York City. The social mechanism triggering the disease is the agent: negative health lifestyles, notably poor eating practices and an absence of exercise. Many more grocery stores selling healthy foods are available, for example, in the Upper East Side than in East Harlem, although the two areas border each other. Also many of the residents of East Harlem expressed a pervasive fatalism about coping with the disease. They reported being stressed or depressed, or both. They got tired of checking their blood sugar levels and taking medications, and would give in to the desire to smoke, drink heavily, or simply eat sweets or high-fat foods that they needed to avoid, in order to obtain a momentary pleasure. One diabetic woman said she had too much to worry about, such as having a job and paying the rent, so she was not going to also worry about eating a piece of cake. Some had other health problems, including asthma or HIV, that they believed were more serious and required more attention. Since diabetes is a silent and unobtrusive disease unaccompanied by pain as the high blood sugar levels it produces damage the body, dealing with diabetes was often thought of as something that could be put off until another day.

The *New York Times* team also found that Asians, New York City's fastest growing racial minority, were especially susceptible to Type 2 diabetes and 60 percent more likely to get the disease than non-Hispanic whites (Santora 2006). Additionally, Asians developed diabetes at far lower body weights than people of other races. For the large influx of Chinese immigrants into the city, the social mechanism for diabetes was also a negative health lifestyle. They often rejected traditional Chinese foods in favor of high-calorie processed foods, large food portions, and a sedentary lifestyle that seemed consistent with American culture. Children in particular were immersed in an environment of fast-food restaurants, television ads for junk food, high-sugar drinks at school and few opportunities for exercise, and snacks loaded with fats and sugar.

The extent of diabetes in New York City is the highest of any metropolitan area in the country (nearly a third higher than in the nation as a whole). The city is in the vanguard of a surge in diabetes that may be extended nationally, as negative health lifestyles increasingly trigger the disease in susceptible people – especially racial minorities. This *New York Times* investigative reporting not only reveals how powerful social structural factors like class and ethnicity can be in relation to health, but also how the influence of these structural variables is mediated and expressed through culture. For example, the Chinese children opted for the high-sugar and high-fat foods they associated through television advertising with American culture, while devaluing the traditional foods of their homeland. The grocery stores in the affluent Upper East Side stocked fresh produce and healthier foods consistent with the tastes of their customers than the food outlets in East Harlem, whose customers had less money, wanted cheaper foods, and were less discriminating about the food they consumed. Thus class boundaries were also cultural boundaries and in a very real sense constituted health boundaries as well.

HIV/AIDS

HIV/AIDS is another example of how race (and class) serves as a social determinant of health in the United States. In the beginning (the mid-1980s), HIV/AIDS was a disease most characteristic of white homosexual males. But gay men, many of whom are affluent and well-educated, were the first to change their social behavior by adopting safe sex techniques in large numbers and the pattern of the disease changed dramatically. By the 1990s, the magnitude of the epidemic – even though it began to decline after 1995 – had shifted especially to non-Hispanic blacks and also to Hispanics. Mortality rates for HIV/ AIDS for 2007 show that non-Hispanic blacks have the highest rates by far of any race for both males and females. Black males had a mortality rate of 4.5 per 100,000 compared to 6.3 for Hispanics and 2.5 for non-Hispanic whites. For females, the death rate was 11.3 for non-Hispanic blacks, 1.8 for Hispanics, and 0.5 for non-Hispanic whites. Most women – some 85 percent in 2009 – contract HIV through sexual intercourse with infected men.

There are no known biological reasons why racial factors should enhance the risk of HIV/AIDS. Simply being poor and living in economically disadvantaged areas is not the entire answer as many Hispanics and whites are poor, but have lower rates. In addition to poverty, joblessness, minimal access to quality medical care, and a reluctance to seek treatment because of stigma, social segregation is also a factor. Edward Laumann and Yoosik Youm (2001) conclude that blacks have the highest rates of sexually-transmitted diseases because of the "intra-racial network effect." They point out that blacks are more segregated than other racial groups in American society and the high number of sexual contacts between an infected black core and a periphery of yet uninfected black sexual partners act to contain the infection within the black population. Laumann and Youm determined that even though a peripheral (uninfected) black has only one sexual partner, the probability that partner is from the core (infected) group is five times higher than it is for peripheral whites and four times higher than for peripheral Hispanics. In this instance, the core is the agent, the periphery the host, and the intra-racial network the environment.

Social Determinants of Disease: Fundamental Cause Theory

The seminal work on the role of social factors in disease causation in medical sociology is that of Bruce Link and Jo Phelan (1995, 2000; Carpiano, Link, and Phelan 2008; Phelan et al. 2004; Phelan, Link, and Tehranifar 2010). Link and Phelan maintain that social conditions are *fundamental* causes of disease. In order for a social variable to qualify as a fundamental cause of disease and mortality, Link and Phelan (1995: 87) hypothesize that it must (1) influence multiple diseases, (2) affect these diseases through multiple pathways of risk, (3) be reproduced over time, and (4) involve access to resources that can be used to avoid risks or minimize the consequences of disease if it occurs. They define social conditions as factors that involve a person's relationships with other people. These relationships can range from ones of intimacy to those determined by the socioeconomic structure of society.

Link and Phelan conclude that there is a long and detailed list of mechanisms linking socioeconomic status with mortality. In addition to stratification variables such as class, race, and gender, stressful life events and stress-process variables like social support qualify as social factors. Also included is a sense of control over one's life because people with such control typically feel good about themselves, cope with stress better, and have the capability and living situations to adopt healthy lifestyles. This situation may especially apply to people in powerful social positions. "Social power," states Link and Phelan (2000: 37), "allows one to feel in control, and feeling in control provides a sense of security and well-being that is [health-promoting]." Persons at the bottom of society are less able to control their lives, have fewer resources to cope with stress, live in more unhealthy circumstances, and face powerful constraints in adopting a healthy way of life, and die earlier. Consequently, Link and Phelan argue that broad-based societal interventions may be able to produce more substantial health benefits than individually-based intervention strategies in many situations.

Of particular interest as a structural variable is social class or socioeconomic status (SES). A person's class position influences multiple diseases in multiple ways and the association has endured for centuries. Numerous studies have for years linked low SES with worse health and higher mortality throughout the life course (Link and Phelan 1995; Lutfey and Freese 2005; Robert and House 2000). Even accounts of the black or bubonic plague (*Yersina pestis* bacteria) in Europe in the fourteenth century describe how the poor were more heavily afflicted than the rich and note that the common people suffered the most (Tuchman 1979). In advanced societies like the US and Britain, people generally live 30 more years on the average than they did in 1900. Over 80 percent of all deaths occur past the age of 65, with poor people living longer today than the wealthy did in past historical periods. But the gap remains the same in that while everyone typically lives longer today, people in the upper social strata usually live the longest. Consequently, Link and Phelan argue that the level of socio-economic resources a person has or does not have, such as money, education, status, power, and social connections, either protects his or her health or brings on sickness and premature mortality. Phelan et al. (2004: 267) state:

> These resources directly shape individual health behaviors by influencing whether people know about, have access to, can afford and are motivated to engage in health-enhancing behaviors. Current examples include knowing about and asking for beneficial health procedures; quitting smoking; getting flu shots; wearing seat belts and driving a car with airbags; eating fruits and vegetables; exercising regularly; and taking restful vacations. In addition, resources shape access to broad contexts such as neighborhoods, occupations, and social networks that vary dramatically in associated profiles of risk and protective behaviors. For example, low-income housing is more likely to be located near noise, pollution, and noxious social conditions and less likely to be well served by police, fire, and sanitation services; blue-collar jobs tend to be more dangerous and stressful than white-collar and to carry inferior health benefits; and social networks with high status peers are less likely to expose a person to second-hand smoke, more likely to support a health-enhancing lifestyle, more likely to inform a person of new health-related research, and more likely to connect him or her to the best physicians.

Phelan et al. confirmed their thesis that socioeconomic status is a fundamental cause of mortality by finding a strong relationship between SES and deaths from preventable causes in a 2004 study. For deaths from less preventable causes about which little is known in terms of prevention and treatment, the relationship was less strong. However, people with higher SES had significantly higher probabilities of survival from preventable causes of death because they were able to use their greater resources to that end. Their enhanced access to and effective use of resources (money, knowledge, etc.) served as the social mechanism allowing them to obtain greater longevity. Such resources also shape broader contexts affecting health like jobs, neighborhoods, and social networks that vary dramatically in promoting protection or risk.

When fundamental cause theory is reduced to its most basic proposition, it is the idea that resources consisting of money, knowledge, power, prestige, and social connections are vital to maintaining a health advantage (Phelan et al. 2010: S31). Conversely, an absence or shortage of these resources causes poor health outcomes and earlier deaths. People with resources have less risk of exposure to preventable diseases in the first place and are better able to achieve positive out-comes when they occur by employing their resources. Persons with lower income, education, and social status lacking such resources not only have greater exposure to risk and more likelihood of the risk being realized, but also a diminished capacity for preventing negative consequences. This is seen in a study by Virginia Chang and Diane Lauderdale (2009) who observed how people in higher socioeconomic groups embraced the widespread use of statin drugs to reduce cho-lesterol levels and lower the risk of heart attacks. Statins have been credited with helping reduce cardiovascular mortality and while there has been an overall reduction in such deaths in the United States, the highest burden of mortality has shifted away from the top of society to the bottom. Although the polio vaccine in the 1950s quickly leveled disparities between the classes because it was administered universally, statins have not done likewise for heart disease because high-income persons are far more likely to use them compared to people with less income and knowledge about heart ailments, and others who only visit physicians for care when they are sick and not for prevention. Only recently have generic, lower-cost statin drugs become available to the public.

Another study by Karen Lutfey and Jeremy Freese (2005) of patients at two diabetes management clinics in a large Midwestern American city set out to confirm the role of SES as a fundamental cause in health outcomes as suggested by Link and Phelan. One clinic (Park Clinic) had a primarily white, upper and upper-middle-class clientele, while the other clinic (County Clinic) served a largely racial minority, working-class, and uninsured population. The study focused on the control of blood sugar levels that is essential for the survival of diabetics, since high glucose levels as previously noted damage the body. The high SES patients had their own physicians that they saw regularly at Park Clinic and they joined health clubs for exercise, ate healthily, and made other lifestyle adjustments to effectively manage their diabetes. Not surprisingly, the high SES patients had significantly better blood glucose management, health, and survivability.

The patients at County Clinic saw whatever doctor was on duty at the time, had significantly longer waiting times to see a physician, lacked the financial resources to buy needed diabetic supplies, had jobs that interfered with medication schedules, and had to take time away from their jobs to have their prescriptions filled at the clinic pharmacy since the medications there were subsidized by the state. Some of the patients needed an insulin pump but could not afford to buy one. Getting prescriptions filled was time-consuming. One doctor at County Clinic called the long waits a travesty, saying a business-man would fire any doctor who made him leave work, take a bus, and then wait 30–40 minutes in line to fill a prescription, before getting on another bus to be transported back to work. As one physician (Lutfey and Freese 2005: 1349) said:

> It's like the legal profession. . . . If you have endless money, you can buy the best of lawyers and get out of the jam. Not that money buys you understanding in diabetes or allows you to negate your responsibilities, but money can put you in a position where you either have more time to devote to it or you have more resources to devote to it. . . . How much difference does it make in patients? It varies from patient to patient, but I think there's no question. People that are financially strapped are going to be in trouble.

By comparing patients in two clinics that served two very different social clienteles, Lutfey and Freese found several mechanisms by which SES influenced the design and implementation of diabetic control pro-grams. These mechanisms included the organizational features of the clinics (e.g., staff specialties, diabetic education services, continuity of care), structural constraints on patients (e.g., incomes, job demands, types of occupations, availability of private health insurance, loca-tion of pharmacy), and influences on patient motivation (e.g., waiting times, need to refill prescriptions, benefits and costs to compliance, lifestyle adjustments) and cognitive abilities (e.g., patient communica-tion skills and ability to follow a regimen).

Lutfey and Freese also noted that even possible compensatory factors like insulin pumps and medical interviews that might have evened the odds of survivability between the higher and lower SES diabetics favored the high SES patients instead. The cost of the insulin pumps, which were not subsidized by the state, made them unafford-able to the lower SES patients, while the affluent could pay the $5,000 price or the initial deductible after which their insurance paid the remainder. As for the medical interviews, Lutfey and Freese (2005: 1363) determined that: "Lower-SES patients may be the least skilled at articulating their problems to physicians and so would seem to gain the most from experienced medical interviewers, but, instead, the bulk of the interviewing of low SES patients was conducted by inexperi-enced [physician] residents." Park Clinic also had vastly better in-clinic diabetic education services that were unavailable to the County Clinic patients who might have benefited more, since their need for improve-ment was greater and their predilection for self-education outside the clinic was less.

The finding that a large number of mechanisms reflecting differences in SES either enhanced or harmed the enactment of a successful diabetic control regimen was consistent with the social causation thesis. Some of the critics of this thesis claim that class or SES cannot be a causal factor because it is too difficult to determine a specific social mechanism causing the problem (Hedström and Swedberg 1998). However, Link and Phelan (1995) indicate that SES qualifies as a "fundamental cause" of health outcomes for the very reason that it causes disease and mortality in multiple – not singular – ways. Therefore, as Lutfey and Freese (2005: 1327) point out, the fundamental cause concept does not imply a theory of specific proximate mechanisms responsible for a persistent association; rather, the theory is one of *meta-mechanisms* responsible for how several specific and varied mechanisms that affect health are generated over time. Consequently, the overall direction of the enduring association is maintained even though the potency of some specific social mechanisms may change or disappear over time due to medical innovations, social change, or some other factor.

Lutfey and Freese did not study the origin of diabetes, genetic or otherwise, in their respondents. But they made a major contribution to understanding the social causation thesis by demonstrating the multiple effects of SES on diabetes regimens. These effects shaped the capacity of the diabetics to cope successfully or unsuccessfully with their disease as poor control could end their lives. While it might be argued that the biological pathologies inherent in diabetes are responsible for patient mortality, this argument overlooks the fact that social mechanisms brought the patient much more rapidly to the point that biology ended their life. In this situation, social mechanisms have a causal role not only in the onset of the disease (e.g., unhealthy diets and lack of exercise), but also in the effectiveness of the body's defenses to cope successfully with the affliction.

Measuring Structural Effects

The recognition of social factors inherent in causing sickness or mortality has been late in coming. One reason may be methodological difficulties in specifying the exact underlying explanatory social mechanisms that affect health, since these mechanisms are multiple, complex, and difficult to isolate in order to determine their precise effects. Such difficulties are increased when trying to determine the direct effects of social structures on individuals because of the possible role of other variables that may intervene in the relationship. Nevertheless, the scientific method requires proof that independent variables have specific and measurable effects on dependent variables whether they are structural or not.

Qualitative methods such as participant observation that concentrate on individuals face shortcomings in determining the effects of structure on people. Roger Sibeon (2004) suggests there are limits to what can be achieved by micro-level methods in addressing structural questions, since such methods are not equipped theoretically or methodologically to measure macro-phenomena. However, the Lutfey and Freese (2005) study of diabetic clinics was qualitative, relying on ethnographic data consisting of observations at the clinics; consultations with patients and medical practitioners; video recordings; semi-structured interviews with physicians, nurses, dietitians, social workers, and diabetes educators; and telephone interviews with patients. The study was narrowly focused on capturing the pervasiveness of the causal relationship between socioeconomic status and outcomes for diabetes. Consequently, qualitative studies that are alert to structural influences and the collective origins of those influences on the individual behaviors they observe and monitor do have potential for increasing our understanding.

Determining the effects of structure in quantitative studies requires the construction of independent variables having collective properties indicative of such structures. For example, measuring class effects is a challenge because the usual socioeconomic variables of income, education, and occupational prestige can also be depicted as individual characteristics. One solution is to apply class categories to the family/household rather than the respondent/individual. The status of the person (or perhaps persons) in the family/household with the highest level of labor market participation can be conceptualized as providing a master social status to the household representing its collective position vis-à-vis the marketplace (Erickson and Goldthorpe 1992). This outcome is evident when the parent's social standing is passed to their children and the household as a whole is accorded a particular social standing in the community.

Education can also be measured with respect to the prestige of the institution attended, so that the status associated with an individual's education can be considered a reflection of the institution rather than just the individual. An index of living conditions can be constructed from the value of homes in particular neighborhoods or census tracts and the extent of basic utilities, modern plumbing, heating, air-conditioning, hot water, and the like, as well as the presence of parks, recreational facilities, restaurants, pharmacies, and grocery stores.

Other health-related variables are the ready availability of physicians, clinics, and hospitals, along with crime rates and various measures of public safety. Variables such as these are not the properties of similar individuals, but those of structures that constrain or enable individuals to lead healthy lives.

Recent developments in statistics for estimating hierarchical linear models now provide efficient estimations for a wider range of applications than previously possible. Hierarchical linear modeling (HLM) makes it feasible to test hypotheses about relationships occurring at different levels and also assess the amount of variation at each level (Raudenbush and Bryk 2002). Briefly stated, HLM tests the strength of the interaction between variables that describe individuals at one level (level 1), structural entities (like households) at the next level (level 2), and sequentially higher levels (e.g., neighborhoods, communities, social classes, nations), if necessary, depending on the variable's conceptual position in a structural hierarchy. By comparing changes in the regression equations, the relative effects of each level of variables on health outcomes can be simultaneously determined. As Stephen Raudenbush and Anthony Bryk (2002: 5) point out, "the barriers to the use of an explicit hierarchal modeling framework have now been removed." Therefore, the capability to examine complex social dynamics and the links extending from society to the individual is now possible.

A caveat issued by Thisted (2003) concerning multilevel measures of social settings involving both collectives and individuals is that such measures in the past have often been subject to problems of ecological inference. What this means is that the association of two variables at aggregated levels may not reflect the association between the same two variables at the individual level. However, Thisted suggests that rather than treat structural variables as an aggregation or sum of individual-level variables, problems of ecological inference can be overcome by using structural variables that are a direct measure of the structure itself, such as measures of neighborhood characteristics that reflect the neighborhood not the individuals who reside in it. This way the direct effects of the neighborhood on individuals can be determined since they are not confounded by individual characteristics. Properly employed, multilevel measures can ascertain the effects of higher levels of social organization on individuals.

There are other multilevel statistical techniques like variance component analysis by maximum likelihood (VARCL) and procedures like MLn and MLWIN that can be used. The point is that adequate statistical models now exist that allow sociologists to test hierarchical models that better reflect the reality of everyday situations in which individuals experience the layers of social structures that exist in their lives and affect their health.

Conclusion

A number of factors, including the pervasiveness of the biomedical model in conceptualizing health problems, a research focus on health from the standpoint of the individual, and the former lack of appropriate statistical techniques have all combined to relegate social structural factors to the background in the quest to discover the social connections to health. But this situation is changing in the direction of a more realistic approach in which the relevance of structure is not only being recognized, but endowed with causal properties with regard to health and disease.

In fact, it can be argued that a major paradigm shift toward a neo-structural perspective is now appearing in twenty-first-century medical sociology. This is seen in the greater emphasis upon structure in both theory and research that is stimulated by the need to acquire a more comprehensive understanding of the social causes of health and illness in contemporary society. The work in medical sociology of Link and Phelan (1995, 2000; Phelan et al. 2004; Phelan et al. 2010), Lutfey and Freese (2005), Katherine Frohlich, Ellen Corin, and Louise Potvin (2001), and William Cockerham (2005, 2010a) in the United States and Saffron Karlsen and James Nazroo (2002) and Gareth Williams (2003) in Great Britain is evidence of this paradigm shift. As the old gives way to the new in medical sociology, the field is headed toward a fundamentally different orientation than the one prevailing in the late twentieth century.

We now know that the biomedical model is limited in its application to problems in living and behavioral models emphasizing the individual's failure to connect with structural effects on health. However, hierarchical linear modeling can be used to investigate multiple levels of social life simultaneously and so new ways of explaining the causal effects of structure on health are likely to be forthcoming. Society does act back on individuals and, in doing so, affects their health, diseases, and mortality. This outcome needs to be more fully explained by medical sociologists in their future work.

This does not mean that micro-level methods and theories like symbolic interaction are obsolete. Quite the contrary, qualitative research provides some of the most insightful data available on social relationships and situations. It puts a human face on what would otherwise be only a narrative of numbers. However, a neo-structuralist approach, in turn, allows medical sociologists to more accurately measure the effects of structure on individuals and assess structure's causal qualities. The fact that structure may be able to overwhelm the influence of agency or individual-directed action in some social situations does not negate the need to account for micro-level phenomena. The ultimate goal of medical sociology, and, for that matter, all of sociology, is an accurate assessment of social life at all levels which is only possible by accounting for the interplay of the individual and society in empirical settings. By incorporating methods which span levels of social reality, the new medical sociology should be able to take the field to an even higher level of development. The next chapter will examine the current state of sociological theory in relation to the social causation thesis and the remainder of this book will explore the coming neo-structural component of the field by further examining the causal qualities of structure in relation to health and disease.

Suggested Further Reading

Blaxter, Mildred. 2010. *Health*, 2nd ed. Cambridge, UK: Polity.
Reviews the various definitions of health in medical sociology, how health is linked to social systems, and contemporary changes in the meaning of health.

Phelan, Jo C., Bruce G. Link, and Parisa Tehranifar. 2010. "Social Conditions as Fundamental Causes of Health Inequalities: Theory, Evidence, and Policy Implications." *Journal of Health and Social Behavior* 51(Extra Issue):S28–S40.
Discusses key findings of fundamental cause theory, refinements, limits, and implications for policies to reduce health inequalities.

2

Theorizing about Health and Disease

As background for the forthcoming chapters on the social causation of health and disease, this chapter examines the current state of theory in medical sociology. Sociological theory is particularly important in this project, since theory provides explanatory models of the social processes producing specific health outcomes. Theory allows us to see how sociologists conceptualize social reality and establish modes of analysis accounting for the dynamics of that reality and its outcomes. Whereas many techniques developed by sociologists have been adopted by other disciplines, including particular quantitative (social survey) and qualitative (participant observation) research methodologies, sociological theory remains *the* most important pillar of medical sociology's uniqueness in studies of health and disease. It is the sociological perspective, as exemplified by its theoretical gaze, which gives medical sociology its distinctiveness. Consequently, we will discuss relevant theoretical perspectives before moving to a more detailed examination of various social causes of health and disease in the chapters ahead.

The Rise and Fall of Structural-Functionalism

Theoretical support for the causal role of social factors in health originates in the work of the French sociologist Emile Durkheim, one of sociology's most renowned classical theorists and founding fathers. Durkheim ([1893] 1964) is responsible for the initial formulation of structural-functionalist theory emphasizing the importance of social structures (what he called "social facts") that exist above and beyond the level of individuals influencing or perhaps even determining their behavior. As Durkheim ([1895] 1950: 13) explains, social facts like norms and values were capable of exerting external constraints on the behavior of individuals causing them to act in particular ways. The end result, concludes Durkheim ([1895] 1950: 127–8), is that: "Society is not a mere sum of individuals; rather the system formed by their association represents a specific reality that has its own characteristics." This reality is distinct not only from individuals but from other realities, such as the biological and psychological (Sibeon 2004).

According to Durkheim, societal reality emanates from macro-level social structures constituting a system of interrelated parts functioning together to produce stability, order, and integration. Society itself is held together in a state of dynamic equilibrium by harmonious patterns of norms and values adopted by the people who are part of it. What makes social life possible is the expectation that people will normally behave in accordance with these consensual standards. This process is "functional" because it results in social order. When "dysfunctional" processes arise that create instability, like crime, society counterbalances the potential for disorder by creating restorative and/or punitive institutions like criminal justice systems. Talcott Parsons (1951) later showed how sickness was a dysfunctional social process that society contained by the application of health care delivery systems.

Durkheim's only work having a direct link to medical sociology is his study of suicide. Durkheim ([1897] 1951) applied basic sociological principles (e.g., norms, social values) to the problem of suicide in Western Europe in the late nineteenth century by identifying certain social conditions (anomic, egoistic, altruistic, and to a lesser extent fatalistic) external to the individual that stimulated the taking of one's life. In doing so, Phelan and her colleagues (2004) credit Durkheim with providing a bold model for medical sociology to follow. The boldness in his work is his insistence that social forces outside of an individual's direct control can have a reality affecting people's health and in some situations curtailing their lives. This thesis can be extended to show that a person's health can be negatively affected through stressful conditions requiring responses to social situations not necessarily of the individual's own choosing.

Much of the attractiveness of Durkheim's work for sociologists is that it maintains society exists external to the individual to constitute a reality of its own having a strong capacity to influence individual social behavior. Social reality does not pertain to material objects but is an awareness of social norms, attitudes, and values that are real in the sense that they are standards for behavior that everyone is expected to follow. Deviation from these standards can have serious consequences (social rejection, loss of companionship, and perhaps death or prison) for the person who chooses to ignore them. The structures that project society's influence are reflected through regularities in social interaction (such as that necessitated by roles and institutions), systematic social relationships (such as group affiliations, class standing, and other forms of social stratification), and resources (either human or non-human) that script behavior to be expressed in particular ways as opposed to other possible options (Giddens 1984; Sewell 1992).

During the 1950s and 1960s, when medical sociology was established as an academic specialty in the United States, the structural-functionalist perspective advocated by Durkheim and Parsons was the dominant theory in all of sociology. Parsons' (1951) concept of the sick role was the first contribution by a leading theoretician directly applicable to medical sociology. It specified the normative behavior expected of people who were ill, including the social imperative to try to get well. By drawing upon the ideas of Durkheim and Max Weber, Parsons grounded the sick role concept within the parameters of classical sociological theory consistent with his usual style of theorizing. He demonstrated that the topic of sickness could be embraced by mainstream sociology. More than any other sociologist of his generation, Parsons made medical sociology academically respectable by providing its inaugural theoretical orientation and calling attention to its potential as an important area of sociological inquiry (Cockerham 2012).

The importance of Parsons for medical sociology's early development is seen in the fact that the 1960s were a time of tremendous academic interest in theory. Historian Tony Judt (2005: 398) described the 1960s as "the great age of Theory" in that there was a market for theories of every kind fueled by an insatiable demand on the part of intellectuals and academic journals. At the forefront in the social sciences were theories trumpeting various forms of structuralism. These included the theories of Durkheim and Parsons in sociology, Claude Lévi-Strauss in cultural anthropology, Fernand Braudel and the Annales School in history, Louis Althusser in structural Marxism, and Ferdinand de Saussure and Roland Barthes in structural linguistics. What these theories had in common were notions that minimized or – in certain instances – even denied individuals a role in shaping social processes. In France, home of many of the leading theorists and where theorizing about society was a major feature of public discourse,

French structuralism dramatically displaced existentialism from its formerly dominant intellectual position (Gane 2003).

However, while structuralism was able to explain why social change was needed, Judt (2005) observes that it was inexact about how such change occurred or why individuals choose to facilitate the process. This was a fundamental weakness, especially in relation to decisive political events in which individuals played a key role. The problem in sociology was that structural-functionalism presented a static image of dominant social structures highly resistant to change. Moreover, structural-functionalism's emphasis upon consensus, stability, order, and balance seemed to justify the maintenance of the status quo perpetuating existing social inequalities and the power of already existing elite groups. This perspective was simply unacceptable to conflict theorists, symbolic interactionists, and other sociologists in the 1960s in light of the change-inducing civil rights, women's, Black Power, and anti-Vietnam War movements in the United States, protests against war and social inequality in Western Europe, and various Marxist-inspired rebellions in the Third World. The end result was that conflict theorists overwhelmingly rejected structural-functionalism because it did not adequately consider conflict as a catalyst for social change, especially rapid and revolutionary change.

Symbolic interactionists attacked structural-functionalism on a different front: its diminishment of individual behavioral creativity and micro-level social processes. The problem here was that structural-functionalism lacked a social psychology giving individuals a role in shaping their own behavior. Margaret Archer (1995: 3) refers to this type of theorizing as "downward conflation" in which society unilaterally molds individuals to act in particular ways and has a complete monopoly over causation. In contrast, symbolic interaction theory accords priority to the individual choosing his or her social behavior in opposition to the structural-functionalist view that such behavior is typically determined by structural influences. "As an interpretation of human experience," concludes Judt (2005: 400–1), "any theory dependent on an arrangement of structures from which human choice had been eliminated was thus hobbled by its own assumptions." This shortcoming further fed structural-functionalism's downfall, and ultimately Durkheim's model failed to attract a large following in medical sociology.

The Fall of Conflict Theory and Repackaging of Marxism

Conflict theory gained even less of a foothold in medical sociology than structural-functionalism which could at least point to the significance of Parsons' (1951) concept of the sick role. The basic proposition of conflict theory is that inequality exists in all societies which causes conflict that leads to social change. The norms and values holding society together are not considered a true consensus, but instead are imposed by dominant groups and social classes on the less privileged in order to maintain their advantages. Social processes are essentially viewed as struggles over resources and change results from the outcome of such struggles. Conflict theory, however, like structural-functionalism, accorded the individual little opportunity for creativity. It was another example of downward conflation in which individual behavior is determined more or less exclusively from above. Additionally, the theory was never fully developed and severely criticized for ignoring social order and stability, just as it had earlier attacked structural-functionalism's failure to account for conflict and change (Ritzer 2011).

Nevertheless, Fernando de Maio (2010) takes the position that researchers working in the conflict perspective with a Marxist orientation have been highly influential in medical sociology. He goes back to the 1845 essay of Friedrich Engels, Marx's friend and collaborator, on the *Condition of the Working Class in England*, and describes it as the forerunner of contemporary research on health disparities. A more central contribution to medical sociology is Vicente Navarro's (1976) critique of medicine under capitalism that has been important for studies in the political economy of health. Unfortunately, the limitations in conflict theory generally also extended to work in medical sociology. Moreover while conflict might be important in some health situations, there were many others in which conflict is not relevant. People may stay healthy or become ill, and neither of these outcomes may have anything to do with group or class conflict. Another problem is that conflict theory could be seen as contradictory in its accusations that the medical profession was *both* overly expansionist (taking ever increasing responsibility for treating social problems) and exclusive (discriminating against the poor) at the same time (Lupton 2003).

Furthermore, Marxism, which provided much of the underpinning for conflict theory, began losing influence from the 1970s onward. There were a few notable publications in the conflict tradition with a direct Marxist focus, such as Navarro's (1976) work, along with Howard Waitzkin's (1983) observations on how capitalism affected doctor–patient relationships and shifted responsibility for poor health to the individual rather than the prevailing capitalist social system. However, as Alex Callinicos (1999) points out, political events sank Marxist theory in the universities. First, French scholars turned their back on Marxism as a "theory of domination" in response to Soviet labor camps, the Cold War, Soviet military intervention against revolt in the former Czechoslovakia in 1968, and the Polish government's suppression of the labor union Solidarity in 1981. The French response was followed by similar reactions elsewhere in Europe and Latin America.

"The process of retreat was slower in the English-speaking world," states Callinicos (1999: 261), "but by the beginning of the 1990s, under the impact of postmodernism and the collapse of 'existing socialism' in Eastern Europe and the Soviet Union, Marx was a dead dog for most intellectuals there as well." As an active political doctrine, Marxism also failed to provide healthy social conditions and an effective approach to health care delivery in the former Soviet Union and the East European socialist countries that experimented with it (Cockerham 1997, 1999, 2000b, 2007a, 2009; Cockerham et al. 2006; Meslé et al. 2003; Shkolnikov et al. 1998). Socialist medicine lacked the flexibility administratively and structurally to adjust to chronic health problems like heart disease that could not be handled by the mass measures successful in controlling infectious illnesses (Field 2000). The theoretical and practical failure of Marxism to produce healthy societies substantially undermines the utility of Marxist theories in medical sociology.

Nevertheless, Marxist thought has continued to live on in various forms. First was the appearance of neo-Marxism that used Marx's work as a foundation to frame its own response to fascist, Stalinist, and capitalist ideologies, as in the case of critical theory that originated in the Frankfurt School in the 1930s. Neo-Marxism was replaced by post-Marxism, a term applied to Marxist-oriented theories that evolved in the aftermath of the collapse of communism in the late 1980s and early 1990s (Ritzer 2011). Neither approach secured a leading role for Marxism in medical sociology, although there has been work of both the neo-Marxist and post-Marxist varieties. British medical sociologist Graham Scambler (2002; Cockerham and Scambler 2010) has used the critical theory of Jürgen Habermas to analyze how American health reform has been adversely affected by the transformation of health care into a commodity and the ways in which medicine, as an "expert" system, has been more answerable to system imperatives than to the lifeworlds of patients. Habermas, however, is in retirement and critical theory has yet to attract a sizable following among medical sociologists.

British economist Richard Wilkinson's (1996) income inequality hypothesis in population health represents a post-Marxist approach. Wilkinson argued that once countries make a transition to high living standards and achieve a positive level of health, they can continue to increase their wealth but not be any healthier if class differences do not diminish. His hypothesis was initially greeted with enthusiasm (De Maio 2010); however, controversy arose when other studies failed to replicate his findings and found his analysis flawed (Beckfield 2004; Eberstadt and Satel 2004). Canadian health theorist David Coburn (2004) observes that the income inequality hypothesis does not have the singular importance given to it by Wilkinson and advances a post-Marxist argument that income inequality is part of a broader set of social determinants causing inequities in health that stem from class conflict.

George Ritzer and William Yagatich (2012: 105), however, describe both structural-functionalism and conflict theory in sociology as "zombie theories," or at least dying and transitioning into "a zombie-like state." "The theories," say Ritzer and Yagatich (2012: 105), "seem alive to many, especially supporters and textbook authors, but in fact, if they are not yet dead, there is only the faintest of pulses reflecting a bare minimum of life." The best example of a zombie theory is structural-functionalism that was at one time the most important theory in sociology, but no one seems to be a structural-functionalist today and there is virtually no significant work in this area. Conflict theory can also be considered a zombie theory because it developed largely in opposition to structural-functionalism that has died and there is a lack of recent examples of its importance. With structural-functionalism in a terminal state and the Marxist approach to conflict theory surviving largely in retreat, it fell to symbolic interaction, with its emphasis upon individual and small group behavior, to move into a more influential position in sociological studies of health and set the stage for the dominance of the agency paradigm in medical sociology.

The Rise of the Agency-Oriented Paradigm

Agency is a term referring to the capacity of the individual to freely select his or her behavior, while a paradigm means a shift in orientation. Paradigms can range from virtual revolutions in scientific thinking to new variations of existing ideas, but all paradigms nonetheless represent a definite change in the conceptualization of phenomena (Reynolds [1971] 2007). Agency is embedded in the symbolic interactionist paradigm whose appearance signaled the beginning of the end of the hegemony of structural-functionalism in sociological theorizing. Advocates of agency-oriented approaches in sociology invariably accentuate the ability of individual actors to choose their behavior regardless of structural influences or constraints. Agency is the process by which individuals, influenced by their past but also oriented toward the future (as a capacity to imagine alternative possibilities) and the present (as a capacity to consider both past habits and future situations within the contingencies of the moment), critically evaluate and choose their course of action (Emirbayer and Mische 1998).

Symbolic interaction emerged in the 1960s as the leading agency-oriented theoretical paradigm. It provided a social psychological model of behavior that found its home in sociology because of its theoretical and methodological strengths in investigating and explaining small group behavior. Symbolic interaction was expressly concerned with understanding the individual's stream of consciousness, interior self-conversations, the development of the individual's self-concept in relation to social experiences with other people, self-definitions of social situations, and the merging of individual lines of behavior into collective expressions of joint or group activities with others (Blumer 1969; Denzin 1992; Mead 1934). While it stressed the distinctly social character of everyday group life, the initial focus was deeply lodged in the socialization of individuals and how they came to recognize and adopt as their own the social perspectives of their significant others, groups, communities, and societies (Berger and Luckmann 1967; Mead 1934). The revolutionary aspect of this paradigm was centered on George Herbert Mead's (1934) concept of the development and maintenance of the self (Reynolds [1971] 2007). Thus the starting point for symbolic interactionist theorizing invariably begins with how self-awareness and agency emerge in the individual through the process of social experience.

Mead (1934) and Herbert Blumer (1969) provide the most complete accounts of symbolic interaction's basic parameters. Symbolic interaction theory maintains that individuals interacting with one another construct social reality on the basis of shared meanings. Objects in the social environment do not possess intrinsic meanings of their own, but are what people define them as. A person's concept of self is likewise formed out of social interaction with other people and developed through social experience. The person is able to become an object to him- or herself, just as other people are objects to that person in social situations, and can interpret those situations and organize action on the basis of those interpretations. Humans are credited with the ability to think, define situations, and act out lines of behavior based upon what they decide is appropriate for the circumstances. Social reality is therefore created by people choosing their own behavior and acting accordingly, not by large-scale social processes and structures channeling their activities down more or less option-less pathways.

However, no contemporary theoretical perspective denies that either agency or structure is unimportant; rather, the debate centers on the extent to which one or the other is dominant. Symbolic interaction emphasizes the dominance of agency over structure, but the theory nonetheless recognizes the existence of influences external to the individual. This is seen in Mead's concept of the "generalized other" which refers not to people but to perspectives shared with other people. Mead (1934: 155) defines the generalized other as the organized attitudes of a community as a whole and the social process through which "the community exercises control over the conduct of its individual members." Recognition of the existence of a generalized other in the mind of an individual marks that person as having made the transition from identifying with specific others (e.g., parents) to also identifying with a generality of others (e.g., society). The generalized other thus influences behavior as a consciousness or awareness of a group, community, class, or societal perspective that enters into the thinking of the individual. It provides the individual with knowledge of a collective's perspective that allows that person to be influenced by it, if he or she chooses to do so. Whereas the individual typically is aware of numerous generalized others in his or her decision-making process, usually certain generalized others are more influential than others.

Consequently, symbolic interaction theory does recognize there are external social structures that influence individuals, despite the strong emphasis on agency as the origin of social meanings, reality, and the larger society through the process of social interaction. Even though society and its institutions predate and constrain individuals to the point that they may be required to interact under social conditions not entirely of their own choosing, agency nevertheless is held to outweigh structure because individuals have the ability to decide how they respond and structural constraints can be resisted, circumvented, or ignored (Charmaz 2009).

Symbolic interaction flourished between 1963 and 1970, which Norman Denzin (1992: 12) – a leading participant – described as a period of "creative ferment." The many publications in the field included Howard Becker's (1963) work on the labeling theory of deviance and Erving Goffman's (1963a, 1963b) studies of various aspects of face-to-face interaction that marked him as an important theorist in the interactionist tradition. Barney Glaser and Anselm Strauss (1965, 1967, 1968) produced some of their most important work in medical sociology on death and dying and their methodological treatise on grounded theory, while Blumer (1969) published his collected papers that became a fundamental statement on symbolic interaction theory. The rise of symbolic interaction in sociology brought with it a corresponding increase in the influence of agency in sociology generally, including medical sociology.

Medical Sociology

Medical sociology is the study of the social causes and consequences of health and illness. Early in its development the field was characterized as atheoretical, but, as noted, Parsons influenced a course change consistent with the approach in other sociological specialties. The use of sociological theory eventually became medical sociology's most unique feature in comparison to other health-related sciences. Figure 2.1 depicts the theoretical perspectives that have been most influential in medical sociology along with the most important books expressing those perspectives. Structurally-oriented theories in figure 2.1 are shown to the right and agency-oriented to the left. In the upper right corner of figure 2.1, beginning with Marx, we see Navarro's *Medicine Under Capitalism* (1976) and Waitzkin's *The Second Sickness* (1983) that best represent Marxist thought in medical sociology. Although interest in Marxist theory has waned, its influence lingers, as seen in the arrows continuing into the twenty-first century and also pointing to the intersection of Marx with Durkheim and French structuralism as important influences in the work of Pierre Bourdieu.

Next in figure 2.1 is Durkheim's *Suicide* (1897) which signals the emergence of structural-functionalism that culminates in Parsons' *The Social System* (1951) and Robert Merton et al.'s *The Student Physician* (1957). After Durkheim is Weber whose influence is seen in Bryan Turner's *Body and Society* (2008) that was originally published in 1984. Turner's book is the most difficult to categorize. It focuses on the social control of the body by the wider society – state, religion, and family – in a critical response to Michel Foucault's *History of Sexuality* (1979). The work is not devoid of structural considerations, but it proved to be the seminal work in the sociology of the body – a subspecialty in medical sociology that largely reflects an agency perspective.

Also on the structure side in figure 2.1 is French structuralism that

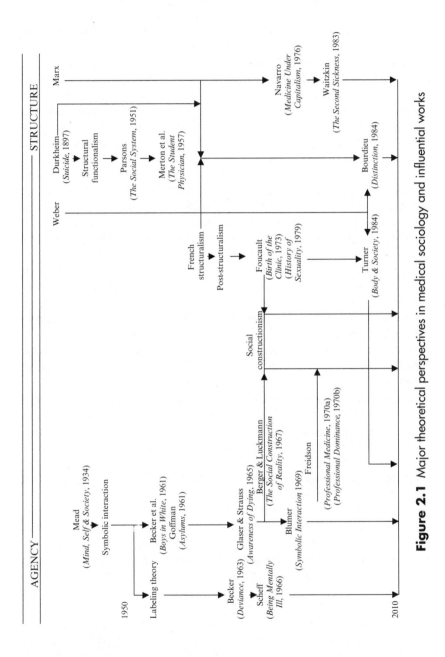

Figure 2.1 Major theoretical perspectives in medical sociology and influential works

influenced Bourdieu and was overturned by post-structuralism in which Foucault occupies the leading role. Bourdieu is only recently attracting the attention of medical sociologists, largely through his book *Distinction* (1984) and its discussion of lifestyles, habitus, and fields. Foucault (1973, 1979) influenced one of the two major strands of social constructionism, as well as work on medicalization and the sociology of the body. The other social constructionist strand comes from Peter Berger and Thomas Luckmann (1967) whose work is grounded in agency by way of symbolic interaction. This approach is also influenced by Eliot Freidson's (1970a, 1970b) landmark work on medical professionalism. Thus, social constructionism has an agency (Berger and Luckmann/Freidson) side and a structural (Foucault) side. Symbolic interaction and its variant labeling theory are shown as agency theories in figure 2.1 with its major theoretical works, such as the basic treatises by Mead (1934), Blumer (1969), and Becker (1963) and the medical sociology classics by Becker et al. (1961), Goffman (1961), and Scheff ([1966] 1999).

There are also various theories not shown in figure 2.1 that are associated with substantive areas in medical sociology. These include theories on the stress process, life course, social capital, medicalization, biomedicalization, health lifestyles, fundamental cause, etc. Some of them have links to the major schools of thought in sociology, such as social constructionism's influence on medicalization theory (Conrad 2007) and the grounding of health lifestyle theory in the work of Weber and Bourdieu (Cockerham 2005). Others do not have these connections. However, all of these substantive theories are designed to explain a particular health-related phenomenon (e.g., stress, medicalization, fundamental cause) in the empirical world and are primarily applicable to those subjects alone. This is the same situation with feminist theories focusing on female-centered perspectives concerning the health problems of women and sexist discrimination in medicine and health care (Annandale 2010). None of these approaches provide a general theoretical orientation in medical sociology that is utilized outside the particular area it addresses, nor do they fundamentally alter or replace any of the major theories. Consequently, they are not included in figure 2.1, although they can provide valuable, though limited, insights concerning certain health situations and problems.

Additional theories not included are postmodern theory, critical realism, actor network theory, and others that have yet to develop an extensive body of literature in medical sociology. Rather, the flow of theory in figure 2.1 depicts the major perspectives influencing the field over the years as the dominant paradigms. None of the theories surviving today that are depicted in figure 2.1 are grand theories or meta-theories explaining total social systems, but all reflect the major "schools of thought" in medical sociology. The manner in which these theoretical orientations have shaped medical sociology and contributed to thinking about the social causation of health and disease will be discussed in the following sections on the development of the sub-discipline in the United States and Britain.

American medical sociology

During its most formative years in the 1960s and 1970s, symbolic interaction was the leading theory in American medical sociology. However, at its inception, medical sociology was influenced more by medicine than sociology. The first use of the term "medical sociology" appeared in 1894 in the *Bulletin of the American Academy of Medicine* in an article written by Charles McIntire, a physician. McIntire (1894: 425) defined medical sociology as "the science of the social phenomena of the physicians themselves as a class apart and separate; and the science which investigates the laws regulating the relations between the medical profession and human society as a whole; . . . and indeed everything related to the subject." This initial definition of medical sociology by a physician thus depicted the field as the study of medical doctors as a social class unto themselves and their relationship with the remainder of society. Elizabeth Blackwell, the first female graduate of an American medical school (Geneva Medical College in New York), used "medical sociology" as the name for a collection of essays she published on health in 1902 and James Warbasse, in a book entitled *Medical Sociology*, published essays on medicine and society in 1909. These early publications were produced by authors with training and interests largely in medicine rather than sociology.

It fell to Bernard Stern to publish the first work from a sociological perspective in 1927, titled *Social Factors in Medical Progress*. As a member of the sociology faculty at Columbia University, Stern went on to publish five books in the years between 1941 and 1945 on topics relevant to medical sociology (Bloom 2002). However, the most important early work is Lawrence Henderson's 1935 paper on the physician and patient as a social system that influenced Parsons, who was one of his students at Harvard. Henderson, a physician researcher, had become interested in the social sciences and made a late-career change to Harvard's sociology faculty when the new department was established in 1931 (Bloom 2002).

Beyond these few publications, there was woefully little research on medical sociology until the late 1940s when ample funding from federal agencies and private foundations became available to promote research opportunities for joint studies by physicians and sociologists on health problems. "It was through the impetus provided by this injection of money," states Malcolm Johnson (1975: 229), "that sociologists and medical men changed their affiliations and embraced the field of medical sociology." Some of the work that resulted from this cooperation included books in the United States like *Social Science and Medicine* (Simmons and Wolff 1954) and the ground-breaking study *Social Class and Mental Illness: A Community Study* (Hollingshead and Redlich 1958). The latter established the conclusive link between class position and specific types of mental disorders and influenced the establishment of community mental health centers throughout the United States in the 1960s. At this time, the trajectory for medical sociology was toward research that could be applied to solving medical problems and answering health questions.

This trajectory was abruptly sidelined, however, when Parsons (1951) included the concept of the sick role in his book *The Social System* and opened the field to theoretical concerns. This development not only called attention to medical sociology and attracted other sociologists to its potential, but also provided, as previously discussed, the academic legitimacy needed to be accepted by sociology faculty in American universities. The importance of this development is seen in the fact that institutional support for sociology in America was in its universities where the discipline was established more firmly than anywhere else in the world. In those countries where medical sociology is largely confined to medical and public health schools, the field is much weaker.

The first sociology department was founded at the new University of Chicago in 1893 and by 1901, 169 American institutions of higher education offered courses in sociology. However, a division began around 1901 in which sociologists "interested in sociological analysis or 'pure sociology' began to separate themselves from their colleagues who were mainly concerned with social problems or 'applied sociology'" (Coser 1979: 293). The American Sociological Association formed in 1905 reflected this orientation. Consequently, at the beginning of the twentieth century, American sociology turned toward research and theoretical development that was to provide the field with the intellectual foundation required of a scientific discipline. Those universities seeking to become leading research institutions paid large salaries for that era to attract faculty, and sociologists with doctorates were in demand. At the top were sociologists that had received training in leading European universities, especially in Germany where they were exposed to the theories of Weber, Georg Simmel, Ferdinand Tönnies, and others. But American sociology did not follow in the German tradition of historical and philosophical speculation. Rather, it took on a distinctive American character that focused on empirical research and analysis of contemporary social life.

Abandoning the role of social reformer for that of social scientist increased the value of theoretical work in sociology. This presented a problem for medical sociology since it evolved much later than sociology's traditional specialties grounded in late nineteenth- and early twentieth-century European social thought. Unlike religion, politics, law, economics, and other fundamental social institutions, medicine did not influence a society's social structure or social behavior and therefore was ignored by sociology's founders. However, as noted, Parsons based his sick role concept on his reading of Durkheim and Weber and thus moved classical theory into a medical sociology previously devoid of such theory.

But Parsons' structural-functionalist theory faltered after a short-lived run in medical sociology. Symbolic interaction theory was a more popular competitor. The leading symbolic interactionist author in medical sociology in the 1960s was Strauss. Strauss joined with Becker and others to produce the now classic study of medical school socialization, *Boys in White* (Becker et al. 1961). This book examined what medical students learned about the professional norms and values expected of a physician other than simply training in technical procedures. Strauss made contributions in a number of other areas, including seminal work on awareness contexts and the social process of death and dying in hospitals (Glaser and Strauss 1965, 1968), the negotiated order of hospital routine (Strauss et al. 1963), and the formulation of grounded theory in which hypotheses are not predetermined but emerge from data during their analysis (Glaser and Strauss 1967).

Another important theorist was Goffman who was neither a symbolic interactionist nor a medical sociologist, but nevertheless made major contributions in both areas. Goffman began his sociology career studying mental patients before expanding his work into topics of general interest. His book *Asylums* (1961) presented the concept of "total institutions" that was an important description of the social situation of people confined by institutions and an insightful depiction of life in mental hospitals. Among his other contributions were his studies of interaction rituals, the presentation of self in everyday life, and impression management, along with the development of the dramaturgical approach in sociology that views "life as theatre" and "people as actors on a stage," and the definitive sociological work on stigma.

With the introduction of symbolic interactionist research into an area previously favorable to structural-functionalism, medical sociology became an important center of debate between two of sociology's major theoretical schools. Symbolic interaction dominated much of the field by the end of the 1960s. One aspect of this domination were the numerous studies employing labeling theory and the controversy this provoked. Labeling theory held that deviant behavior is not a quality of the act a person commits but a consequence of the definition applied to that act by other people (Becker 1963). That is, whether or not an act is considered deviant depends upon how it is labeled (defined) by other people. For example, in a well-known study of jazz musicians, Becker (1963) found marijuana use to be considered normal by the musicians, but labeled as illegal, deviant behavior by the larger society, and subject to sanctions like arrest, fines, and jail terms. Although labeling theory pertained to deviance generally, several studies focused on the mental patient experience in which persons once treated for mental illness found it difficult to shed the label of "former mental patient" even if the experience was in the past and the person supposedly cured (Scheff [1966] 1999).

By the 1980s, however, symbolic interaction entered a period of decline that extended to its use in medical sociology. Labeling theory, despite its merits in accounting for the powerful and often lasting effects of social "labels" placed by others on individuals, could not explain the causes of deviance (other than the reactions of other people), nor whether deviants themselves shared common characteristics like poverty, stress, or social backgrounds relevant to their deviance. Moreover, as Denzin (1992) points out, the larger body of theory represented by symbolic interaction generally seemed to have reached its limits and taken on the image of a "fixed doctrine." Denzin also finds that many of its adherents had been "rebels" intentionally subverting the dominant paradigm of structural-functionalism and giving voices to women and marginal social groups like mental patients, the physically handicapped, children, and the aged and their caretakers by entering their social world and observing it. But once structural-functionalism – the old enemy – had been vanquished, the combativeness of symbolic interaction began to wane.

Additionally, as Denzin observes, between 1981 and 1990, the canonical texts in the field had shifted from Mead to Blumer, and Blumer himself was under attack on several methodological and substantive issues – but most importantly for not advancing the field to meet his own early criticisms. Established practitioners of the perspective were also getting older ("the graying of interactionism") and the number of students espousing interactionism was decreasing, so the ranks of interactionists were becoming smaller. Furthermore, symbolic interaction suffered from a methodological handicap in that studies using the perspective employed qualitative methodologies (e.g., participant observation, focus groups) and most research in American medical sociology and sociology generally was quantitative and based on statistical analyses of survey data. It was sometimes difficult to publish qualitative research outside the few journals that were sympathetic to the approach like *Symbolic Interaction* and the *Sociological Quarterly* in the US and the *Sociology of Health and Illness* in Britain.

Nor was symbolic interaction capable of explaining relationships between institutions and societal-level processes that affect each other, not just individuals. Consequently, it could not be used to account for institutional and higher forms of interaction. Symbolic interaction was also unable to satisfactorily link small group processes at the micro-level to higher macro-level social phenomena. While Mead's concept of the generalized other showed how groups and societies in particular, but also communities and social classes, influenced individual behavior, there was no dialectic exchange by which individuals influenced generalized others or means by which generalized others influenced one another.

In a countervailing view, Archer (2003: 78) goes so far as to call Mead "an almost uncompromising externalist" in that his concept of the internal conversations people have in their mind is not a dialogue with themselves, but in her opinion is a conversation instead with society. In support of her position, she cites Mead's (1982: 155) statement that: "Thinking is the same as talking to other people." However, the structural implications of Mead's work were never developed by his successors, most notably Blumer, and symbolic interactionism has persisted to this day as a theory of agency (Plummer 2000).

Even though much less influential than in the past, symbolic interactionism revived in the late twentieth century with some interactionists moving into postmodern theory and others into the study of emotions. Postmodern theory, despite its early promise of explaining the process of contemporary social change, was unable to account for the structure and character of society after its transition from modernity to postmodernity (Pescosolido and Rubin 2000). It never gained a foothold in medical sociology and is near extinction (Cockerham 2007b). Research on the sociology of emotions, in contrast, has increased as interactionism fills an analytic gap between biological approaches and non-biological social theories like social constructionism (S. Williams and

Bendelow 1996). Interaction between people is paramount in the activation and expression of emotions, as emotions are biological responses to social situations and the interaction between people involved in them.

Despite its currently lessened status, symbolic interaction theory nevertheless played a prominent role in advancing an agency orientation in American medical sociology. And in doing so, it undermined the pursuit of a social causation thesis because of its success in rendering structural-functionalism impotent. The popularity of labeling theory and the work of Strauss and Goffman, along with that of Virginia Olesen and Fred Davis on nursing, Denzin and Thomas Scheff on mental illness, Kathy Charmaz on chronic illness and the physically handicapped, and others laid the groundwork for a medical sociology dominated by a social psychological approach. As the influence of symbolic interaction lessened, studies of stress – utilizing social psychological themes, concepts, and quantitative measures – filled the vacuum. So much research was being published in this area that the *Journal of Health and Social Behavior*, the leading medical sociology journal in the United States, was informally dubbed the "stress journal" by some sociologists even though it published other work as well (Clair et al. 2007). These studies typically focused on interpersonal stressors. Studies of societal-level stressors were rare.

For example, in a major review of stress research in medical sociology in the mid-1990s, Peggy Thoits (1995: 56) observed that: "Despite attributions of the origins of stress to large-scale social structures or processes, few investigators have attempted to examine the links between macro-level factors and micro-level experiences, preferring to assess, for example, status variations in role strains, powerlessness, or lack of control at the individual level only." While there are exceptions, such as research on chronic environmental stressors in disadvantaged neighborhoods that impact downward on individuals (Browning and Cagney 2003; Hill, Ross, and Angel 2005), a review of the relevant literature since the mid-1990s by the author shows the focus on the individual continuing. Most stress studies examine differences among individuals from the standpoint of gender, socioeconomic status, race, marital status, and similar variables in relation to their life events (acute changes), chronic strains (persistent demands over time), and daily hassles (Barrett and Turner 2005; Pearlin et al. 2005; R. Turner and Avison 2003; K. Williams 2003).

These studies are not devoid of structural implications when they consider the social contexts of the lives of the respondents, including their networks of social support as possible intervening variables, and they significantly advance our understanding of the stress process for health as they are intended to do. Yet ultimately what determines the impact of a stressful situation on an individual is that individual's interpretation of and reaction to the situation, along with his or her coping skills and resources. Macro-level factors are seldom the focus. Until Link and Phelan (1995) resurrected the social causation argument, the notion that social structural factors were causal languished. Variables representing the influence of social structures on health and disease were relegated to the background both in and outside of medical sociology.

Studies in public health often followed a similar approach. As Alan Brandt and Martha Gardner (2000) observe, a hostile division between public health and medicine ended after World War II when public health reached an accommodation with the medical profession by adopting a biomedical perspective. Management of individual risk factors, especially for chronic disease, became the primary strategy for most public health initiatives. According to Michael Sweat and Julie Denison (1995), the usual approach in public health prevention programs is to motivate people to abandon or minimize their risk behavior. Education, information, counseling, testing, and other services are used to influence individual psychological processes that will induce behavioral change. Sweat and Denison point out that the major theories of health promotion are primarily psychological theories, including the Health Belief Model, social learning theory, theories of self-efficacy, the Stages of Change Model, the theory of reasoned action, the Common Sense Model of Illness Danger, and others. Research supporting these theories typically examines how the environment is experienced and acted upon by individuals.

As for sociology, Smelser (1997) finds there is a fundamental preference for methodological individualism in our traditions of social thought. Smelser claims that when relating different analytic levels to one another, social scientists appear to be programmed with a bias toward individualism that affects our conceptualization of the social. Smelser (1997: 29) says: "We live in the Western cultural tradition, which has exploited the cultural values of individualism. As children of that tradition, we are most comfortable taking the individual person as the starting point of analysis. Put another way, that cultural tradition 'tilts' us toward assuming that the natural unit for the behavioral and social sciences is the individual."

Smelser continues by pointing out that same tilt tends to discourage recognition of *other* levels of social organization as equally natural, even though they may be analytically as important or more important for some situations. It is his impression that the concept of social structure has experienced a loss of status in sociological thinking over the past several decades and the evidence seems to support him. Smelser (1997: 53) cites three intellectual developments as partially responsible for this outcome: (1) the successful assault on structural-functionalism by the micro-sociological revolution of the 1960s, led by symbolic interaction; (2) the subsequent assault on Marxism resulting from intellectual and political dissatisfaction with it; and (3) revision of the notion of culture to include, among other things, movement away from social structural influences toward more of a psychological emphasis on how culture affects personal identity.

The result for sociology is one in which mainstream theoretical insights have been largely taken over by considerations of agency and individual characteristics. As a subdiscipline of the larger discipline of sociology, medical sociology could be expected to be affected in a similar manner and it has been. However, Smelser (1997: 31) points out that "it is impossible to understand and explain events, situations, and processes of 'lower' units without appealing to some higher order of organization by which they are constrained." He notes that just as physics requires its chemistry, chemistry its biochemistry, and so on, individuals require their social organizations if we are to proceed beyond explaining basic characterizations and understanding more complex behaviors.

British medical sociology

The dominance of agency-oriented paradigms in medical sociology is not just an American phenomenon. It is arguably even more pronounced in Great Britain. Whereas the impetus for the development of medical sociology in the United States came largely from academic sociologists with theoretical orientations, the opposite was true in Britain. Medical sociology first appeared in the 1950s, but did not emerge in strength until the late 1960s (Annandale and Field 2005; Illsley 1975). Prior to this time, the British National Health Service had already been organized (1948) and was functioning without input from sociologists. The British medical profession initially saw sociology as having little to contribute to medicine except for social epidemiology. Nonetheless, as Raymond Illsley (1975) observed, this capability was sufficient to bring sociologists into medical research and, as the wider value of the field became apparent, the teaching of medical sociology spread first to medical schools and later in the 1970s to universities.

Consequently, the stimulus behind the development of medical sociology in Britain did not come from academic sociology, but from medicine and the evolving need for sociological research that could be applied to improving patient care, helping solve health inequities, and contributing to health policy. In 1956, the five sociologists working full time in medicine held their first professional meeting, which led to the formation of the Medical Sociology Group of the British Sociological Association (BSA) in 1969 (Illsley 1975). The BSA had been founded in 1951 and by the mid-1970s, the Medical Sociology Group was the largest in the association. Yet despite its growth, Malcolm Johnson (1975: 229) observed that "in Britain there is no tradition of the early scholarly kind and the grandparents of medical sociology here made their reputations through the medium of applied research within the medical setting."

Therefore, early British medical sociology, like its American counterpart, was more applied than theoretical. The field lacked an indigenous Parsons with the intellectual stature to divert it toward a theoretical emphasis. The same situation existed for general sociology and the development of medical sociology in Britain closely paralleled that of the larger discipline after World War II (Annandale and Field 2005). British sociology had been largely confined to the London School of Economics and Political Science (LSE) for decades. It was not until a major expansion of higher education generally in the 1960s, that sociology significantly increased its presence throughout the university system and eventually carried medical sociology along with it. Sociology's slow start was partially due to opposition at Cambridge and Oxford (Halsey 2004). The roots of this opposition can be traced to the late nineteenth century when the value of political philosophy was so deeply ingrained in the Cambridge and Oxford concepts of a classical education that it was impossible for a rival style of social thought like an emerging sociology to dislodge the prevailing approach.

While sociology was not widely institutionalized until the 1960s and initially received little attention from the public and academics, its level of theoretical achievement was not impressive either. Britain did not produce social theorists of the caliber of Durkheim and Weber, even though these theorists were also without peers in their own countries (Collini 1978). The leading early sociologist was L. T. Hobhouse who literally had the role of sociologist thrust upon him in 1907 when he was offered a chair of sociology at LSE. Hobhouse, a philosopher and journalist with no obvious career in front of him, accepted to become Britain's first professor of sociology and father of British theoretical sociology (Collini 1979; Halsey 2004). The focus of Hobhouse's theoretical work and that of his immediate successors was on the development of non-industrial societies. An insufficient concern with modern societies on Hobhouse's part has subsequently been given as a major rationale for neglecting him in favor of Durkheim and Weber who focused on the rise of twentieth-century modernity (Collini 1978).

Yet British sociology evolved to eventually take a leading role in the development of social theory and criticism, as well making major contributions to historical sociology, Marxist social theory, social stratification, criminology, social constructionism, and social realism theory. According to Anthony Giddens (Halsey 2004), there was a particular reason for the growth of a distinctively British set of theoretical contributions. British sociologists were not only familiar with American sociology, but many of them also became interested in contemporary continental European theorists like Jürgen Habermas and Ulrich Beck of Germany and Michel Foucault and Pierre Bourdieu of France. As a result, they were able to synthesize social thought prevalent on the continent with American perspectives to devise their own concepts. Giddens and Archer ultimately emerged as Britain's foremost theorists in the current generation of sociologists.

Giddens (1984) is noted for his formulation of structuration theory and numerous contributions to the study of critical theory, power, social class, modernity, self-identity, risk, and other topics. Structuration theory is complex and detailed. The theory provides an overview of the relationship between agency and structure, with priority given to agency. It begins with the proposition that social structures and the systems they constitute are created, modified, and reproduced through the recurrent practices of individual agents. The core concepts are structure (consisting of rules and procedures operating as a flow of action), social systems (reproduced social practices), and the duality of structure (in which structure is depicted as both constraining and enabling in relation to action). Giddens (1984: 129) maintains that there is no such entity as a distinctive type of "structural explanation" in the social sciences; rather, all explanations in his view involve at least implicit reference both to the purposive, reasoning behavior of agents and its intersection with the constraining and enabling features of the social and material contexts of that behavior. Although the structured properties of social systems may stretch away in time and space from the control of any individual actors, Giddens (Giddens and Pierson 1998) argues that all social life is generally agent-controlled in the sense that individuals constantly monitor their own behavior in relation to other people and act accordingly.

Archer's (1995) critical realism theory is based on the work of British social philosopher Roy Bhaskar (1998) who advocates the openness of social systems to process and change. People are depicted as agents or actors with the critical capacity, reflexivity, and creativity to shape structure, yet, in turn, are shaped by structure. But the key feature for the critical realist is the ability of the individual to transform structure and produce variable outcomes. That is, individuals are able to withstand or strategically circumvent structure, thereby minimizing its effects. Structure, for its part, is relatively enduring, although it can be modified, and deep structures have generative mechanisms going beyond the superficially observable that influence behavior.

But Archer (2003: 7) finds structural causal powers "at the mercy of two open systems; the world and its contingencies and human agency's reflexive acuity, creativity and capacity for commitment." Thus she ultimately favors the influence of agency on behavior over that of structure. As Archer (2003: 7) puts it: "whether constraints and enablements are exercised as causal powers is contingent upon agency embracing the kinds of projects upon which they can impact." A goal of critical realism is to connect agency and structure in a way that the distinctive properties of both can be realistically accounted for without being reduced to a single entity. Archer concludes that the link between agency and structure is the internal conversation that people have with themselves in their mind in which they reflect upon their social situation and take action based upon their assessment. Neither critical realism nor structuration theory, however, has had a significant impact to date on medical sociology, with the exception of Simon Williams (1999) who has used critical realism to examine how biology, agency, and structure influence sociological concepts of the body, chronic illness, and disability.

Given the slant toward agency in the theories of Britain's two leading contemporary theorists, it is not surprising that medical sociology follows a similar path. This is not to say that structural influences have been neglected, as an extensive research literature exists on health inequalities resulting from structural inequities in British society. These include the assessment of health differences stemming from class divisions (Bartley 2004; Blaxter 1990; Chandola 2000; Popay and Williams 2009; Reid 1998) and the health effects of residence or "place" on people (Macintyre, Ellaway, and Cummins 2002). Such studies have contributed to a materialist explanation that has been described as an "alternative social causation approach" in British medical sociology (Nettleton 2006: 183). The materialist explanation evolved out of the 1980 Black Report on class disparities in health. It maintains that health differences are related to differences in individual income, with income determining diet, housing quality, exposure to polluted environments and dangerous work, and ultimately a person's level of health (Bartley 2004).

Although some studies assign responsibility for poor health to structural influences, others blame the individual for unhealthy behavior, as noted by Mildred Blaxter (1990) and Martin Jarvis and Jane Wardle (1999). Attempts to combine behavioral and materialist explanations have not been helpful because "such theorizing tends to discount any influence of the social and material environment that is not mediated through behavioural patterns" (Davey Smith, Bartley, and Blane 1990: 376). Agency-oriented behavioral studies thus comprise the greatest portion of sociological research on health as seen in major British journals like the *Sociology of Health and Illness*, although there is a body of literature on the effects of structure in this and other journals in the UK (Blane 1990; Jones et al. 2011; Karlsen and Nazroo 2002; Macintyre et al. 2002; G. Williams 2003).

British medical sociologists as late as the 1980s were parasitic on their American counterparts for theory (M. Stacey and Homans 1981). However, this is obviously no longer the case as the British have gone their own way in producing theoretical work and selecting topics for research. The core topics in British medical sociology have become the sociology of the body (Nettleton 2010; Nettleton, Neale, and Pickering 2011; Schilling 2003; B. Turner [1984] 2008; S. Williams 2003), the subjective experience of illness (Bury 2001; Ridge, Emslie, and White 2011), gender, race, and class health inequalities (Annandale 2010; Arber and Thomas 2005; Bartley 2004; Bradby and Nazroo 2010; Dolan 2011; Jones et al. 2011; Karlsen and Nazroo 2002), emotions (James and Gabe 1996), the provision of both formal and informal health care (Benoit et al. 2005; Gregory 2005; McKie, Gregory, and Bowlby 2002, 2004; C. Stacey 2005), and health policy and politics (Macintyre 1997), along with new developments in genetics (Martin and Dingwall 2010; Petersen 2005; Pilnick 2002a, 2002b), pharmaceuticals (S. Williams, Gabe, and Davis 2008; S. Williams, Martin, and Gabe 2011), health risks (Sanders 2004), and Internet medicine (N. Fox, Ward, and O'Rourke 2005; Nettleton, Burrows, and O'Malley 2005).

Arguably, the dominant theoretical perspective is social constructionism (Bury 1986; Nettleton 2006). Social constructionism maintains that scientific knowledge and biological discourses about the body, health, and illness are produced by subjective, historically determined human interests and are subject to change and reinterpretation (Gabe, Bury, and Elston 2004: 130). As Bryan Turner (2004: 40) explains, constructionism is the idea that things are not discovered but socially produced. That is, all facts are social facts because social communities produce them. Things are what they are defined as, even symptoms of illness. An illness, for example, is socially constructed in that the expression of symptoms is shaped by cultural norms and values, experienced through interaction with other people, and influenced by particular beliefs and definitions of health and illness (Gabe et al. 2004). A diagnosis represents the transformation of physiological symptoms into socially appropriate behavior for the person who has been diagnosed and carries with it a changed social status.

Bryan Turner (2004) finds that the classic text of social constructionism is Berger and Luckmann's *Social Construction of Reality* (1967) which is grounded in symbolic interaction. Other works are also important, such as Freidson's (1970a, 1970b) analysis of medical knowledge in his study of the American medical profession and the views of Foucault (1973) depicting the body as a product of power and knowledge (Nettleton 2006). Freidson examined how the medical profession monopolized power and authority in health matters to advance its own interests, while Foucault described how the medical profession defined the human body as an object of study subject to medical intervention and control. Foucault provided social histories of the manner in which knowledge produced expertise that was used by professions and institutions, including medicine, to shape social behavior. Knowledge and power were depicted as being so closely connected that an extension of one meant a simultaneous expansion of the other. In fact, Foucault often used the singular term knowledge/power to express this unity (B. Turner 1995).

Given the extreme differences between Berger and Luckmann in comparison to Foucault, it is obvious that it is a mistake to assume that social constructionism represents a uniform doctrine (Nettleton 2006; B. Turner 2004). "These different types of constructionism," states Turner (2004: 43), "present very different accounts of human agency and thus have different implications for an understanding of the relationship between patients, doctors, and disease entities." The more social constructionist work is influenced by Berger and Luckmann, the more agency-oriented it is; the closer to Foucault, the less agency has a role – as Giddens (1987) observes, Foucault's work is essentially history with agency removed. Foucault, however, is not a strict structuralist. Rather, he is the leading representative of post-structuralism and among those French scholars who rejected the views of structuralists like de Saussure and Lévi-Strauss maintaining there were universal rules organizing social phenomena into compact systems. Foucault shows that the use of knowledge/power is not only constraining as the French structuralists would argue, but also productive and enabling as it is the decisive basis upon which people are allocated to positions in society.

In addition to the lack of doctrinal uniformity in social constructionism, there are other difficulties, such as failing to acknowledge the biological reality of illness, rejecting the possibility that knowledge can be discovered (by insisting that knowledge can only be socially constructed), and adopting a relativist position that no one form of knowledge is more valid than another (which calls the extent of the validity of social constructionism itself into question) (Bury 1986; Gabe et al. 2004; Nettleton 2006; B. Turner 2004). Nevertheless, social constructionism remains popular in studies of the body, use of genetic information and other medical knowledge, women's health, patient–physician interaction, physical disability, aging, and other topics.

According to Ellen Annandale and David Field (2005), medical sociology in Britain has shifted along with society generally from collectivism to individualism. One example they give at the societal level is the rise in service-sector employment and movement away from the production of mass-market goods toward commodities tailored for specialized and changing consumer markets. As for medical sociology, they describe it as shifting away from biomedical models toward topics that reflect individual concerns like the new genetics and health risks in daily living. As Annandale and Field (2005: 247) put it, "a new sociological sensitivity has drawn attention away from a hitherto 'disembodied' conceptualization of the rational individual bounded by collectives such as social class, 'race' and ethnicity toward a self-reflexive individual making an array of life-style choices." Thus the traditional structures of class, gender, and to a lesser extent, race, are considered less relevant for the actions of individuals than in previous historical periods. This is seen in research on health inequalities where Annandale and Field find that British medical sociologists have recently begun to raise questions about the theoretical underpinnings of such research rather than remain steadfastly tied to conventional approaches to the social divisions of class, race, and gender. They (Annandale and Field 2005: 255) conclude: "There is a need to reflect more critically upon sociologically constructed social positions to take account of human agency in the construction of social class, ethnic, gender, and age-related identities and their significance for health status." What this signifies is that British medical sociology, like the American version, is currently influenced more by concepts oriented toward agency than structure – which is seen not only in its journals, but also its textbooks like those of Annandale (1998) and Nettleton (2006).

Conclusion

The dominant orientation in studies of health and disease in medical sociology as seen in this chapter is quite different from that suggested by Durkheim. As followers of Durkheim, medical sociologists would likely be researching the capacity of social structures (as social facts) to cause health and disease. But this has not happened as structural theories like structural-functionalism have been abandoned and agency theories like symbolic interaction and the agency side of social constructionism have moved to the forefront of theorizing. While some social structural variables are correlated with many diseases, such variables are usually considered in current research to be causally related to very few or none of them. As Link and Phelan (1995) observe, these variables are generally regarded as distal (distanced) factors whose effects are undercut by variables more proximate to the individual. Link and Phelan (1995: 80) cite a leading textbook in epidemiology explicitly stating that the "modern" approach views "social conditions such as socioeconomic status as mere proxies for true causes lying closer to disease in the casual chain." Consequently, the direct effects of social structures on health are often ignored, even though social structures and conditions may ultimately be responsible for causing the health problem under investigation (Lomas 1998; Sweat and Denison 1995).

Theories that disregard the effects of structure on the individual are examples of Archer's (1995: 4) notion of "upwards conflation," a term she applies to behavioral models in which individuals monopolize causal power that operates in a one-way, upward direction and seems incapable of acting back to influence individuals. Neither form of conflation, however, either upwards or downwards, captures empirical reality as both agency and structure typically operate in tandem in social settings. Depending on the situation, one may be dominant over the other, but both are nevertheless present. What is obviously needed is a more comprehensive approach to research in medical sociology, epidemiology, and other fields that *also* include a thorough consideration of structural variables as causal factors in health outcomes. The improved capability to measure structural effects forecasts a paradigm shift back to considerations of structure and neo-structural approaches and theories in future studies in medical sociology. The causal properties of social structures for health and disease will be reviewed in the forthcoming chapters.

Suggested Further Reading

Cockerham, William C. and Graham Scambler. 2010. "Medical Sociology and Sociological Theory." In *The New Blackwell Companion to Medical Sociology*, ed. William Cockerham, 3–26. Oxford, UK: Wiley-Blackwell.

An extensive review of the major theories in medical sociology, including work by classical and contemporary theorists.

De Maio, Fernando. 2010. *Health and Social Theory*. New York: Palgrave Macmillan.

A recent book on theory in medical sociology with a Marxist-based, conflict orientation that largely focuses on macro- or large-scale social influences on health.

Scambler, Graham (ed.). 2012. *Contemporary Theorists for Medical Sociology*. London: Routledge.

This is a new edited book with chapters on leading contemporary theorists and the application of their work to health-related topics. The chapters are on Foucault, Habermas, Luhmann, Bourdieu, Merleau-Ponty, World System Theory, Archer, Bauman, Deleuze and Guattari, and Castells.

Turner, Bryan S. 2008. *The Body and Society*, 3rd ed. London: Sage.

The first edition of this book in 1984 established the sociology of the body as a legitimate subfield in medical sociology and contributed to the development of social constructionist theory. The analysis draws heavily on the theories of Foucault and is a classic work in medical sociology.

3

Health Lifestyles

While most of the chapters to follow in this book are about society causing sickness, this chapter begins that discussion by first showing how it causes health. The primary mechanism by which health is socially manufactured is through lifestyles. Lifestyles are integrated sets of practices fulfilling utilitarian needs and giving material form to the expression of a particular social identity (Giddens 1991: 81). This includes sets of lifestyle practices or behaviors that also affect health, either positively or negatively. Health behavior is the activity undertaken by people for the purpose of maintaining or enhancing their health, preventing health problems, or achieving a positive body image (Cockerham 2000a: 159). It is what individuals themselves do to stay healthy. The focus of research in medical sociology, however, is not on the health practices of individuals, which are more appropriately defined as self-care, but rather on the transformation of this behavior into its aggregate form: health lifestyles.

Health lifestyles are collective patterns of health-related behavior based on choices from options available to people according to their life chances (Cockerham 2000a: 160). A person's life chances are the probabilities they have in life to find satisfaction and are largely determined by their socioeconomic or class position, as well as age, gender, race and ethnicity, and other factors that shape the lifestyle choices people make in their lives. This definition is grounded in the classical theory of Weber ([1922: 531–9] 1978: 926–39) and incorporates the dialectical relationship between life choices and life chances he proposed

L-style

Beh.

Choices

in his lifestyle concept. In a Weberian context, life choices represent agency and life chances are a proxy for structure. While health and other lifestyle choices are voluntary, life chances – which primarily represent class position – either empower or constrain choices as choices and chances work off each other to determine behavioral outcomes. The behaviors that are generated from these choices form an overall pattern of regular health-related practices – such as decisions about diet, exercise, smoking, alcohol and drug abuse, getting preventive checkups, and the like – that constitute a health lifestyle.

Chances

Weber associated lifestyles not with individuals but with status groups, thereby showing they are principally a collective social phenomenon. Status groups are aggregates of people with similar status and class backgrounds, and they originate through a sharing of similar lifestyles. People who wish to be part of a particular status group or social class adopt the appropriate lifestyle if they are to be accepted by people who already belong there. Status groups are stratified according to their patterns of consumption. These patterns not only establish differences between groups, but they also *express* differences that are already in place (Bourdieu 1984). Health lifestyles are a form of consumption in that the health that is produced is used for something, such as a longer life, work, or enhanced enjoyment of one's physical being (Cockerham 2000a; d'Houtaud and Field 1984). Moreover, health lifestyles are supported by an extensive health products industry of goods and services (e.g., running shoes, sports clothing, diet plans and vitamin supplements, health foods, health club and spa memberships) promoting consumption as an inherent component of participation.

Additionally, as David Gochman (1997) points out, positive health lifestyle behaviors are the opposite of risk behaviors. Good nutrition, for example, is the reverse of bad nutrition. The binary nature of health lifestyle practices means that the outcome generated from the interplay of choices and chances have either positive or negative effects on health. Gochman also observes that health lifestyles are intended to avoid risk in general and are oriented toward achieving or maintaining overall health and fitness.

However, while the term health lifestyle is meant to encompass a general way of healthy living, there has been discussion over whether or not there is an overall "health lifestyle." The best evidence suggests that for many people their health lifestyle can be characterized as either generally positive or negative. Research from Finland provides strong evidence that associations between health practices are related, with people who behave unhealthily in one respect doing so in others and vice versa (Laaksonen et al. 2002). Smoking had the

strongest and most consistent association with other unhealthy lifestyle practices in that people who smoked were also likely to drink,
have poor food habits, and not exercise. Multiple unhealthy practices
were most common among lower socioeconomic groups. A significant
body of research attaches the most positive health lifestyle practices to
higher social strata and women, the most negative to lower strata and
men (Abel et al. 1999; Annandale 2010; Antunes 2011; Blaxter 1990;
Cockerham 1997, 1999, 2000a, 2005, 2010a; Dolan 2011; Grzywacz
and Marks 2001; Link and Phelan 2000; Pampel 2009). It therefore
appears that health lifestyles are not the uncoordinated behaviors of
disconnected individuals, but are personal routines that merge into an
aggregate form representative of specific groups and classes.

Lifestyle: Health as an Achievement

There is no single all-purpose definition of health that fits every
circumstance, but there are many concepts that describe it such as
health as normality, the absence of disease, or the ability to function
(Blaxter 2010). Feeling well and being able to carry out one's daily
activities – namely, a state of functional fitness – are typically the
basis upon which people view themselves as healthy or not. In past
historical periods, people appear to have taken their health more or
less for granted (Crawford 1984). That is, they were either healthy or
unhealthy and that simply was the way life had turned out for them.
But this situation has changed dramatically. Most individuals begin
life in good health, but their social circumstances and lifestyle impact
on their prospects for staying healthy and personal efforts to maintain
it over time are typically required.

Consequently, health today has become viewed as an achievement –
something that people are supposed to work at to enhance their quality
of life or risk chronic illness and premature death if they do not (Clarke
et al. 2003). As Giddens (1991) and Bryan Turner (1992) conclude,
lifestyle options have now become integrated with bodily regimens
or routines, with people in advanced societies normatively assigned
greater personal responsibility for their health and even the design of
their own bodies. This circumstance originates from modifications in
(1) disease patterns, (2) modernity, and (3) social identities.

The first change is the twentieth-century epidemiological transition
from acute to chronic illnesses as the major source of human mortality
in most areas of the world. Much of this change is due to the success
of medicine in treating communicable diseases and improvements in

sanitation, water quality, and living conditions contributing to the longer life spans of people today that – in turn – increase their risk of a chronic ailment as they age. Chronic diseases – namely, heart disease, cancer, stroke, diabetes, and the like – cannot be cured by medical treatment and certain lifestyle practices, such as smoking, alcohol and drug abuse, eating high-fat foods, and unprotected sex in the case of sexually-transmitted diseases, can cause these afflictions and end life prematurely. The result has been greater public awareness that medicine is not the automatic answer to all health situations (Crawford 1984). The realization that this is a certainty carries with it the revelation that the responsibility for one's health ultimately falls on oneself through healthy living. Greater personal responsibility means that achieving and maintaining a healthy lifestyle has become more of a life or (time of) death option.

The second change is the current era of late modern social alterations creating a new form of modernity (Bauman 2000; Giddens 1991). While notions of an absolute break with the past modernity originating with the industrial age are unconvincing, it is nevertheless clear that society is in a transition to a new social form (Pescosolido and Rubin 2000). This is seen in changes stemming from the economic and cultural globalization of Western capitalism, deindustrialization trends in Western nations, the explosion of new forms of information technology, the increasing use of knowledge as a commodity, the collapse of state socialism in the former Soviet Union and Eastern Europe, the adoption of market capitalism in socialist China and its rise as the leading world center for many mass-produced goods, the expanding multiculturalization of Europe and North America, the upsurge of cultural and gender politics, the multiplicity of family forms, and changing patterns of social stratification. In health matters, we see the decline in the status and professional authority of physicians through lessened control over the medical marketplace and health care decisions requiring the approval of insurers in managed care systems in the United States. We also see greater movement toward the mutual participation model of the physician–patient relationship in which the patient shares in the decision-making about his or her medical care. This circumstance has accelerated with the advent of Internet medicine and the wide diffusion of medical knowledge in the public domain (Drentea and Moren-Cross 2005; N. Fox et al. 2005; Hardey 1999; Nettleton et al. 2005; M. Warren, Weitz, and Kulis 1998). In the still-emerging late modern society, where traditional industrial age centers of power and authority, such as medicine, are weakening, adopting a healthy lifestyle accords people more control over their health.

The third change is movement in late modernity toward an adjust-ment in the primary locus of social identity. Previously, work or occupation largely determined social class position and a person's way of life. Beginning in the second half of the twentieth century, lifestyle consumer habits have been increasingly experienced in advanced societies as a primary source of social identification (Bauman 1992; Chaney 1996; Crompton 2008; Giddens 1991; Stead et al. 2011). That is, what people consume reflects who they are. This situation was made possible by the rise in economic productivity promoting a general improvement in living standards and purchasing power after World War II. The easier acquisition of basic material needs allowed styles of consumption to supersede occupation for signaling social similarities and distinctions for many people (Crompton 2008).

John Scott (1996), for example, finds that the lifestyles of manual workers in Britain have been altered, with major implications for class identification. He observes that social distinctions within the working class are determined more by consumption patterns than relationships to the means of production. Affluent workers aspired to higher living standards and greater purchasing power, but they did not see this as a way of attaining middle-class status. "Their principal status con-cerns," states Scott (1996: 238), "were those of maintaining their posi-tion above 'rough' and relatively impoverished manual workers and of securing their own standing in what they saw as a social hierarchy defined in purely monetary, consumption terms."

Therefore, as Rosemary Crompton (2008) points out, the claim that lifestyles have become more significant in class formation and social identification needs to be taken seriously. This conclusion is consistent with Giddens's (1991) assertion that lifestyles not only fulfill utilitarian needs, but additionally express a person's self-identity. Giddens (1991: 81) explains it this way:

> The notion of lifestyle sounds somewhat trivial because it is so often thought of solely in terms of superficial consumerism: lifestyles as sug-gested by glossy magazines and advertising images. But there is some-thing much more fundamental going on than such a conception suggests: in conditions of high modernity, we all not only follow lifestyles, but in an important sense are forced to do so – we have no choice but to choose. A lifestyle can be defined as a more or less integrated set of practices which an individual embraces, not only because such practices fulfill utilitarian needs, but because they give material form to a particular nar-rative of self-identity.

An important lifestyle configuration and the accompanying social marker are those practices affecting health and the distinctions they also contribute to differences in social identities (Annandale 1998; Stead et al. 2011). Bourdieu (1984) furnishes us with an example in noting the distinctions between social classes in France with respect to differing tastes in foods (hearty versus tasty, light, and low in calories) and sports (wrestling and boxing versus sailing and tennis). The link between lifestyles and social identity therefore signals the growing importance of lifestyles in the analysis of social life. There have been suggestions that lifestyles are a better measure of social position than class as class boundaries become less distinct, but at this stage of history this is not the case as class remains a powerful variable. Nevertheless, as Giddens (1991: 5) concludes, the lifestyle concept has taken on a particular significance in understanding contemporary social life. It has also taken on particular significance with respect to health.

Sociologists, however, have been slow to recognize the impact of life-styles on behavior and ultimately on health. One reason may have been the influence of Thorstein Veblen's ([1899] 1994) classic, the *Theory of the Leisure Class*, which affixed the term "lifestyle" to modes of leisure adopted by the upper class. The term "lifestyle" became synonymous with upper-class styles of living. We now know, as Giddens (1991: 6) points out, that it would be a major error to suppose that lifestyles are confined to those in more privileged material circumstances as everybody has a lifestyle, even the poorest of the poor.

Methodological Individualism in Health Lifestyle Research

Much of what we know about lifestyles has its theoretical origins in the early twentieth-century work of Weber ([1922] 1978). However, Frohlich et al. (2001: 782) observe that "the term lifestyle, widely adopted by researchers in health promotion, social epidemiology, and other branches of public health, has taken on a very particular and different meaning from that intended by Weber." Although Weber's methodologies often reflected an individualist and agency-oriented "bottom-up" approach to the study of social structure, he did not view patterns of social action as the uncoordinated practices of discon-nected individuals (Kalberg 1994; Sibeon 2004). Instead, he saw social action in terms of regularities and uniformities repeated by numerous actors over time. His focus was on the way in which people act in concert, not individually.

The bridge from agency to structure for Weber was his use of the "ideal type," consisting of structural entities like his concept of bureaucracy or macro-level processes like the spread of formal rationality in Western society whose construction allowed him to make general statements about collective forms of social behavior (Kalberg 1994). For example, in *The Protestant Ethic and the Spirit of Capitalism* (1958), Weber emphasized macrostructure in an essentially "top-down" fashion by showing how social institutions (Calvinist religion) and widespread belief systems (the spirit of capitalism) were powerful forces in shaping the thoughts and behavior of individuals (Sibeon 2004). As Weber (1958: 55) states: "In order that a manner of life well adapted to the peculiarities of capitalism . . . could come to dominate others, it had to originate somewhere, and not in isolated individuals alone, but as a way of life common to whole groups of men."

Yet, as Frohlich et al. (2001: 782) point out: "When lifestyle is currently discussed within the socio-medical discourse, there is a decided tendency for it to be used in reference to individual behavioural patterns that affect disease status," thereby neglecting its collective (structural) characteristics. This approach is a another example of Archer's (1995) notion of "upwards conflation" in which individuals are seen as exercising power in a one-way, upwards fashion in society that seems incapable of acting back to influence them. There is research depicting health lifestyles as sets of individually constructed behaviors, with education serving as the most important determinant of agency and individuals themselves having the role of weaving various disparate practices into a coherent lifestyle designed to promote health (Mirowsky and Ross 2003a).

Although it is clear that education plays an especially powerful role in the selection of health lifestyle practices, income and occupational status join education as the major components of social class or socioeconomic status (SES). According to Nancy Adler and her associates (1994), the three variables are interrelated but not identical or fully overlapping. "The fact that associations between SES and health are found with each of the indicators," state Adler et al. (1994: 15), "suggests that a broader underlying dimension of social stratification or social ordering is the potent factor." Thus education can also be viewed in combination with the other components of class to constitute a structural variable that produces top-down distinctions in the quality and form of health lifestyles among individuals and determines the social context for the practice of such lifestyles. So while education, income, and occupational status are characteristics of individuals, collectively they constitute a structural variable whose influence is evident when people express the tastes, distinctions, outlooks, behaviors, and lifestyles common to their class as a whole.

Sociological concepts reflecting literally all theories of social life attest to the fact that *something* (namely structure) exists beyond the individual to give rise to customary patterns of behavior. These concepts range from Durkheim's ([1895] 1950: 13) notion of social facts as "every way of acting, fixed or not, capable of exercising on the individual an external constraint" to Mead's (1934: 155) view of the "generalized other" as the organized attitudes of the whole community and the social process through which "the community exercises control over the conduct of its individual members." To assign individuals complete freedom in their lifestyle choices overlooks the pervasive boundaries placed on those choices by the social structures in their lives.

Structural influences on health lifestyle practices are seen, for example, in the studies of Andrée Demers and her colleagues in Canada on alcohol consumption by married women (Demers, Bisson, and Palluy 1999) and university students (Demers et al. 2002). This research shows that the social relationships of the people drinking and the social context of the drinking situation have substantial effects on alcohol intake and drinking behavior. Married women, for example, were found to adopt the drinking patterns of their husbands, unless they were in an older age group or had children. The happier the couple were together, the greater the convergence in drinking. The alcohol intake of university students varied with the drinking situation. That is, why, where, when, and with whom students drank had an important effect on how much alcohol they consumed. The greatest amount of alcohol was consumed in the company of close friends in relaxed situations, while little or none was the norm in the presence of parents. Thus the drinking situation shaped their approach to drinking. "It is apparent from our findings," state Demers et al. (2002: 422), "that the individual cannot be conceptualized as an autonomous actor making self-governing decisions in a social vacuum."

Another example of structural influences on health lifestyles is the anti-smoking campaign in the United States. For over 20 years, massive efforts were made to reduce cigarette smoking through educational programs. "These individual approaches to the cessation of smoking encouraged many to stop," conclude Sweat and Denison (1995: S252), "however, not until smoking was banned in many public places did the prevalence of smoking significantly decline." This ban had the effect of labeling smokers as social outcasts, deviants, and threats to the health of others in their vicinity. Anti-smoking laws, social isolation, and stigma significantly increased smoking cessation "far beyond the results of purely individualistic approaches" (Sweat and Denison 1995: S252).

In a study in northeast England, Martine Stead and her colleagues (2011) found that the social and symbolic meanings associated with food prevented young teenagers from eating healthy lunches at school. High-status ("cool") teens ate quality chocolate bars and crisps (potato chips) for lunch and drank Coca Cola or Pepsi. Teens who ate healthy or inexpensive foods were ridiculed and categorized as "nerds" or "uncool." Bananas and yoghurt were especially taboo. Thus, social status dictated lunchtime food choices for teens who wanted to be popular and accepted by their peers. Stead et al. (2011: 1138) point out that it is not that healthy foods fail to appeal to young people, but rather that healthy eating symbolizes something undesirable and exposes them to social risks. While this may seem irrational to public health experts, Stead and her associates argue that unhealthy eating can be viewed by the teenagers as profoundly rational because of the risk of an impaired social identity and rejection by peers. They conclude that, in this circumstance, eating unhealthily can actually be positive for a teen's social and emotional well-being, even though nutritionally harmful.

Whereas these studies show structural influences have a significant effect on health lifestyles, there are situations in which structure can be so overwhelming that agency is rendered inert. Gareth Williams (2003) reports on the high mortality of a group of Welsh coal miners in the 1930s. These were men "unsung in any chronicle of existence" (cited in Williams 2003: 145). Their lives were severely curtailed by their punishing work and diet of beggars. However, the unremitting toll of childbirth and domestic labor impaired the health and shortened the lives of the women as much or more than that of the men. The weight of structural conditions was so heavy that individual capabilities and capacities were ineffective. This situation, comments Williams (2003: 146), "provides a salutary reminder of the way in which the balance between agency, context, and structure is itself highly determined by structural forces."

In research investigating contemporary social conditions in a working-class neighborhood in a city in northwest England, Williams observes that the influence of structure on agency in relation to health lifestyles is still heavy-handed. He finds that assuming people have the freedom to make healthy choices is out of line with what many people experience as real possibilities in their everyday lives. "The respondents," concludes Williams (2003: 147), "understood the behavioural risk factors that made ill-health more likely and for which they were in a limited sense, responsible, but they were also aware that the risks they faced were part of social conditions that they could do little to change." A theory of health lifestyles is needed to advance our understanding of these situations and the remainder of this chapter will consider the author's (Cockerham 2005, 2010a) concept of this social phenomenon. While agency is important, it will be argued that social structural conditions can act back on individuals and configure their lifestyle patterns in particular ways. Agency allows them to reject or modify these patterns, but structure limits the options that are available. This is not to say that considerations of agency should be minimized, but agency is not the whole story. In many situations it is not dominant and can even be passive. Structure invariably has a role in lifestyle outcomes and it is usually the interaction between agency and structure that is decisive. Yet when it comes to health, lifestyle is "predominantly understood as an individual rather than structural variable" (Korp 2008: 18). This needs to change because structure has a significant role in the production of health by individuals. We will begin with a brief comparison of agency and structure to set the stage for a presentation of a health lifestyles paradigm and the research literature that supports it.

The Agency–Structure Debate

The relative contributions of agency and structure in influencing social behavior have been *the* central sociological question since the beginning of the discipline. As Archer (1995: 1) explains: "the vexatious task of understanding the linkage between 'structure and agency' will always retain this centrality because it derives from what society intrinsically is." However, medical sociologists have paid little attention to the agency–structure debate, although it is clearly relevant to theoretical discussions of health and lifestyles (Pescosolido, McLeod, and Alegría 2000; S. Williams 1995). When applied to health lifestyles, the question becomes: Are the decisions people make with respect to food, exercise, smoking, and the like largely a matter of individual choice or are they principally molded by structural variables such as social class position and gender?

It is crucial to any scenario of *agency* that the actor could have acted otherwise in a particular situation if he or she had chosen to do so (Bhaskar 1998). Mustafa Emirbayer and Ann Mische (1998) suggest, accordingly, that human agency consists of three different elements: (1) *iteration* (the selective reactivation of past patterns of thought and action), (2) *projectivity* (the imaginative generation of possible future trajectories of action in which structures of thought and action may be creatively reconfigured), and (3) *practical evaluation* (the capacity to make practical and normative judgments among alternative possibilities). Agency can thus be considered a process in which individuals recall their past, imagine their future actions, critically evaluate their present circumstances, and choose their behavior based upon their assessment of the situation. When symbolic interactionist theorists like Blumer (1969) maintain that people construct their social behavior on the basis of their definition and interpretation of the situations they find themselves in, they are describing this very process.

William Sewell (1992: 19) provides a definition of *structures* as "sets of mutually sustaining schemas and resources that empower or constrain social action and tend to be reproduced by that social action." Schemas are transferable rules or procedures applied to the enactment of social life. Resources are of two types, either human (e.g., physical strength, dexterity, knowledge) or non-human (naturally occurring or manufactured) that can be used to enhance or maintain power. Sewell equates resources with the power to influence action consistent with Giddens's (1984) notion of the duality of structure as both constraining and enabling. This duality, while correct, nonetheless contains a contradiction. The enabling function suggests resources increase the range and style of options from which the actor can choose, but constraint means that resources invariably limit choices to what is possible.

Although agency theorists maintain that agency will never be completely determined by structure, it is also clear that "there is no hypothetical moment in which agency actually gets 'free' of structure; it is not, in other words, some pure Kantian transcendental free will" (Emirbayer and Mische 1998: 1004). This is because, as Zygmunt Bauman (1999) observes, individual choices in *all* circumstances are confined by two sets of constraints: (1) choosing from among what is available and (2) social roles or codes telling the individual the rank order and appropriateness of preferences. People do have the capability to act independently of the social structures in their lives, but the occasions on which they do so appear to be rare.

A Health Lifestyles Model

While definitions and a general concept of health lifestyles exist in the literature, it is only recently that a theoretical paradigm has been available. This paradigm is presented in figure 3.1. The arrows between boxes indicate hypothesized causal relationships.

Beginning with box 1, the uppermost box in figure 3.1, four categories of structural variables are listed that have the capacity to shape health lifestyles: (1) class circumstances, (2) age, gender, and race/ ethnicity, (3) collectivities, and (4) living conditions. Each of these categories is suggested by a review of the research literature.

Class circumstances

The first category of structural variables is class circumstances, which is the most powerful influence on lifestyle forms. The close connection between class and lifestyles has been observed since the nineteenth century. Veblen ([1899] 1994), as noted earlier, used a lifestyle concept as the basis for his theory of the leisure class. However, it remained for Weber ([1922] 1978) to produce the most insightful account of the link between lifestyles and socioeconomic status. Weber (1946) not only found that lifestyles expressed distinct differences between status groups and their adoption was a necessary feature of upward social mobility, but he also observed that powerful social strata were "social carriers" of particular ways of living. These carrier strata were important causal forces in their own right as they transmitted class-specific norms, values, religious ethics, and ways of life across generations (Kalberg 1994).

The seminal study detailing class as the most decisive variable in the determination of health lifestyles is Bourdieu's (1984) *Distinction*, which included a survey of differences in sports preferences and eating habits between French professionals (upper-middle class) and the working class. Bourdieu found the working class to be more attentive to maintaining the strength of the male body than its shape, and to favor food that is both cheap and nutritious; in contrast, the professional class prefers food that is tasty, healthy, light, and low in calories. As for leisure sports such as sailing, skiing, golf, tennis, and horseback riding, Bourdieu noted that the working class not only faces economic barriers, but also social barriers in the form of hidden entry requirements of family tradition, obligatory dress and behavior, and early socialization. Also these sports are usually practiced in exclusive locations with chosen partners and require investments of money, time, and training that the working class lacks. The working class, in contrast, opts for sports that are popular with the general public and equally accessible to all classes. These are sports like football, wrestling, and boxing that feature strength, endurance, and violence.

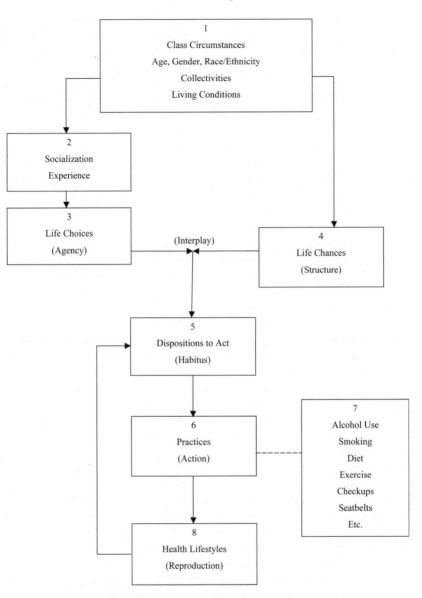

Figure 3.1 Health lifestyles paradigm

Thus, Bourdieu formulated the notion of "distance from necessity" that emerges as a key explanation of class differences in lifestyles. He points out that the more distant a person is from having to forage for economic necessity, the greater the freedom and time that person has to develop and refine personal tastes in line with a more privileged class status. Lower social strata, in turn, tend to adopt the tastes consistent with their class position, in which acquiring items of necessity is paramount. For example, Bourdieu (1984: 177) notes that as one rises in the social hierarchy, the proportion of income spent on food diminishes, or that within the food budget, the proportion spent on heavy, fattening foods, which are also cheap – pasta, potatoes, bacon, and pork – declines, whereas an increasing proportion is spent on leaner, lighter, non-fattening foods and especially fresh fruits and vegetables.

Bourdieu finds that social classes not dominated by the ordinary interests and urgencies of making a daily living claim superiority in social and cultural tastes over those who have only fundamental levels of material well-being. "As the objective distance from necessity grows," states Bourdieu (1984: 55), "life-style increasingly becomes the product of what Weber calls a 'stylization of life', a systematic commitment which orients and organizes the most diverse practices – the choice of a vintage or a cheese or the decoration of a holiday home in the country." The greater the social distance from struggling to obtain necessities, the greater the refinement of lifestyle practices. The relevance of the distance from necessity concept is seen in health lifestyles where classes higher on the social scale have the time and resources to adopt the healthiest practices.

In a similar fashion, research in France by Alphonse d'Houtaud and his American colleague Mark Field (1984) found that different classes also value health in different ways. Health was conceptualized as something to be cultivated for increased vitality and the enjoyment of life among the upper and middle classes, and for the capability to continue to work for the classes below them. For those closest to necessity, being unhealthy meant being unable to work and secure those necessities; however, for those whose resources placed them beyond the range of basic necessity, being unhealthy meant less enjoyment out of life. In sum, lower SES persons viewed health largely as a means to an end (to be able to work), while higher SES persons regarded health as an end in itself (vitality).

In Britain, Blaxter (1990) found important differences in health lifestyles persisted between the various social classes, with the upper and middle classes taking better care of their health than the working and lower classes. Of course, not everyone in the lower class has an unhealthy lifestyle, nor does everyone in the upper class live in a healthy manner. There are variations within classes. However, as Blaxter's data show, major distinctions *between* classes are readily apparent. Smoking was by far the most prevalent among male blue-collar workers in industrial areas, along with heavy alcohol consumption. More frequent drinking, but in lower quantities, was found among higher status males. Sports participation and good dietary habits were also significantly more common at the upper end of the social scale.

Blaxter concluded that socioeconomic circumstances and the living environment determined the extent to which health lifestyles were practiced effectively. This is an important finding in that it shows the structural conditions of people's lives make it probable or improbable that they can achieve a positive health lifestyle. As Blaxter (1990: 216) puts it: "If circumstances are good, 'healthy' behaviour appears to have a strong influence on health. If they are bad, then behaviours make rather little difference." Consequently, living a healthy lifestyle was not simply a matter of individual choice, but to a large extent depended upon a person's social and material environment for its success.

Other research in Britain has also identified major distinctions in health lifestyles between the various classes, with less positive lifestyles practiced the lower the rung a person occupies on the social ladder (Jones et al. 2011). A decline in smoking, for instance, was far greater among the affluent, but very little change was observed among the British poor (Jarvis and Wardle 1999). In the United States, the poor have likewise been found to be especially disadvantaged with respect to positive health lifestyles compared to other social classes. The lower class shows the highest levels of cigarette consumption, unhealthy eating and drinking, and less participation in exercise in adulthood (Grzywacz and Marks 2001; Jones et al. 2011; Narcisse et al. 2009; Pampel 2009; Snead and Cockerham 2002; Wickrama et al. 1999).

Elsewhere, in the former Soviet Union and Eastern Europe, negative health lifestyles – featuring heavy alcohol consumption and binge drinking, smoking, high-fat diets, and an absence of exercise – instigated a mortality crisis among middle-age, working-class men (Carlson and Hoffman 2011; Cockerham 1997, 1999, 2000b, 2006b, 2007a, 2009; Cockerham, Snead, and DeWaal 2002; Janečková 2005; Manning and Tikhonova 2009; Ostrowska 2005; Van Gundy et al. 2005). Whereas the health situation has significantly improved in many parts of the former Soviet bloc following the collapse of communism in 1989–91, the crisis continues in Russia, Belarus, Kazakhstan, and

Ukraine (Cockerham et al. 2006). Class plays a decisive role in this ongoing problem. Studies of social stratification in present-day Russia – the epicenter of the crisis – need to consider the legacy of the Soviet period and the current transition to a market economy. Theoretically, Soviet society was described as a classless society, without class oppression, private property, or inequalities in health (Dmitrieva 2005). Although the former Soviet Union was nonetheless socially stratified, the stratification system was neither as complex nor characterized as much by socioeconomic differentials – especially income – as in the West. The transition out of communism has changed the class structure as seen in the significant increase in the proportion of the population living in poverty and the emergence of a small, very wealthy elite.

However, a significant middle class associated with a market economy in a Western sense has yet to evolve (Cockerham 2006b, 2007a, 2009; Shankina 2004). Moreover, as Elena Avraamova (2002: 58) notes, a unified conceptual definition of exactly who makes up the middle class in Russia today has not been determined. This is significant because the middle class – especially the upper-middle class – has been identified as the social carrier of positive health lifestyles across class boundaries in Western countries (Cockerham 2006b, 2007a; Herzlich and Pierret 1987). The middle class typically serves as a social carrier of positive health lifestyles because its "distance from necessity" – to use Bourdieu's (1984) terminology – allows them the leisure time, access to sources of authoritative knowledge, and resources to learn about appropriate health behavior and adopt such behavior as a public model for other classes. The typical class serving as the carrier of negative health lifestyles is one who lacks these attributes but whose norms are nonetheless powerful because of their sheer numbers in the population and preferential position in the nation's culture. In Russia, this is the working class.

Overall, the lifestyles of the upper and upper-middle classes in Western countries are the healthiest. Virtually every study confirms this. These classes have the highest participation in leisure-time sports and exercise, healthier diets, moderate drinking, little smoking, more physical checkups by physicians, and greater opportunities for rest, relaxation, and coping successfully with stress (Antunes 2011; Blaxter 1990; Grzywacz and Marks 2001; Jarvis and Wardle 1999; Narcisse et al. 2009; Robert and House 2000; Snead and Cockerham 2002). The upper and upper-middle classes are also the first to have knowledge of new health risks and, because of greater resources, are most able to adopt new health strategies and practices (Link and Phelan 2000). The advantaged classes are able to move in a more fluid fashion to embrace

new health behaviors, such as adopting low cholesterol and low car-
bohydrate diets. Advantaged classes were able to reduce their risk of
heart disease in the United States (which at one time was high relative
to the lower class) so that lower-class individuals are now at greater
risk. While education is obviously a critical factor, it is, as noted, only
one feature of the broader dimension of class membership that enables
members of higher social strata to be healthier over the life course.
The other factors are income that provides them with the financial
resources to live a healthy life and occupational status that provides
them with high self-esteem and sense of responsibility.

Although capitalism is inherently a system of inequality, the paradox
is that it has clearly been compatible with major improvements in
overall standards of living and health. Today in most advanced
countries traditional health indicators such as life expectancy and
infant mortality have never been better. Communicable diseases that
used to take the lives of young and middle-aged people have been
severely diminished or curtailed as in the case of smallpox and polio.
Additional advances in medical care like organ transplants have saved
lives, progress in reproductive health has improved fertility, and
other measures like hip replacements and surgery for cataracts have
enhanced the quality of some people's lives. In the process, the health
and longevity of all socioeconomic groups have improved even though
the gap between the top and bottom of society not only persists, but
may even – as in Britain – increase. "General health improvement,"
states Michael Bury (2005: 24), "can therefore occur alongside persisting and even widening inequalities." When it comes to health lifestyles,
the advantage likewise accrues to higher social strata.

Age, gender, and race/ethnicity

Weber did not consider other stratification variables such as age,
gender, and race/ethnicity, yet contemporary empirical studies show
that these variables influence health lifestyles. Age affects health lifestyles because people tend to take better care of their health as they
grow older by being more careful about the food they eat, resting and
relaxing more, and either reducing or abstaining from alcohol use and
smoking (Backett and Davison 1995). Exercise, however, is one major
health lifestyle activity that declines and is often lost with advancing
age (Grzywacz and Marks 2001; Jones et al. 2011).

Yet we know that class can intersect with age to produce further
differences in lifestyle practices within age groups, as seen in teenage
smoking that appears significantly more among the lower strata than

the middle and upper (Jarvis and Wardle 1999; Narcisse et al. 2009). Ian Rees Jones and his colleagues (2011) found that class becomes less important as men age with respect to exercise, but other practices like smoking and alcohol use retain a strong class patterning. Jones et al. conclude that these health lifestyles become fixed or "locked in" and remain socially structured even in later life. The concept of a selective lifestyle "lock-in" along class lines illustrates the durability of class influences on health lifestyles over the life course.

Gender is a highly significant variable in that women eat more healthy foods, drink less alcohol, smoke less, visit doctors more often for preventive care, wear seatbelts more frequently when they drive, and, with the exception of exercise, have healthier lifestyles overall than men (Abel et al. 1999; Annandale 2010; Blaxter 1990; Cockerham 2000a, 2000b; Denton and Walters 1999; Grzywacz and Marks 2001; Roos et al. 1998; Ross and Bird 1994). Furthermore, in adolescence males tend to adopt the health lifestyles of their fathers and females those of their mothers, thereby setting the parameters for the transmission of gender-specific health practices into adulthood (Wickrama et al. 1999).

Whereas gender is a strong predictor of health lifestyle practices, its effects can also be moderated by class distinctions, as people higher on the social scale, regardless of gender, eat healthier diets, smoke less, and participate more in leisure-time exercise (Adonis and Pollard 1997; Blaxter 1990; Reid 1998). This is seen in research in Britain on the food preferences of middle-class and working-class women (Calnan 1987) and in the United States where lower-class women were exceedingly less likely to exercise (other than doing housework) than higher strata women and men (Ford et al. 1991).

Race and ethnicity are presumed to be important, but there is a paucity of research directly comparing the health lifestyles of different racial and ethnic groups. Black–white comparisons in the United States show that whites often drink alcohol, smoke, exercise, and practice weight control more than blacks (George and Johnson 2001; Grzywacz and Marks 2001; Hattery and Smith 2011; R. Johnson and Hoffman 2000; Lindquist, Cockerham, and Hwang 1999; Pampel 2008; Saint Onge and Krueger 2011), but the differences have not been fully documented. An effort to rectify this situation with respect to nutrition in the black population is found in the work of Angela Hattery and Earl Smith (2011). They link poor diets to diabetes, colon cancer, infant mortality, and premature deaths. Being disproportionally more likely to be poor, blacks were less likely to eat healthily and exercise. "And, just as the poor in other parts of the world are more vulnerable to diseases like malaria and cholera," state Hattery and Smith (2011: 55), "the poor, and increasingly African Americans, are more vulnerable to the diseases associated with an unhealthy lifestyle."

There is evidence that exercise declines more steeply for blacks than whites across the course of adulthood, yet this pattern may be caused by blacks having more functional health problems and living in less safe neighborhoods (Grzywacz and Marks 2001). The risk of victimization in an unsafe neighborhood can significantly undermine the motivation to engage in outdoor exercise. Other research by Jarron Saint Onge and Patrick Krueger (2011) finds that non-Hispanic whites and more educated individuals exercise more than non-Hispanic blacks, Hispanics, and less educated persons. Non-Hispanic whites and the educated also disproportionately participate in facility-based exercise (swimming, tennis, golf), while non-Hispanic blacks favor team sports (basketball) and fitness activities (running, walking) and Hispanics gravitate toward team sports (soccer). Recreational facilities are often absent in low-income areas and the ability to participate in team sports declines much earlier in life than facility-based exercise. This gives non-Hispanic whites and better educated persons an advantage in exercising longer as they age. Saint Onge and Krueger observe that the type and extent of leisure-time physical activity are shaped by the cultural identities and social circumstances of the participants.

Most studies on health and race, however, address levels of morbidity and mortality rather than specific health practices. These studies often suggest that racial disparities in health are largely but not exclusively determined by class position, with disadvantaged socioeconomic circumstances and the adverse life experiences associated with them promoting poor health (Bradby and Nazroo 2010; Robert and House 2000; Smaje 2000).

Research is also needed that investigates the relationship between health lifestyles and different ethnic groups, including how to best conceptualize and measure ethnicity. Existing studies of ethnicity, like those of race, have focused more on overall health profiles than health lifestyles. Nevertheless, some of these studies are instructive, as seen in research by Saffron Karlsen and James Nazroo (2002) on the respective influences of agency and structure on the health of ethnic minorities in Great Britain. The sample for this study consisted of people of Pakistani, Bangladeshi, Indian, and African Asian ethnic heritage. Ethnic identity was considered a consequence of agency, even though it is subject to external influences, because a person's identity is self-constructed and internally defined by the individual. "However, our findings suggest," state Karlsen and Nazroo (2002: 18), "that ethnicity as identity does not appear to influence health; rather ethnicity as structure – both in terms of racialisation [discrimination/harassment] and class experience – is strongly associated with health for ethnic minority people living in Britain." When it comes to health lifestyles, the effects of race and ethnicity may indeed reside more powerfully in structure than agency, as social discrimination and working/lower-class experiences had greater effects on health than personal identities.

Collectivities

Collectivities are collections of actors linked together through particular social relationships, such as kinship, work, religion, and politics. Their shared norms, values, ideals, and social perspectives constitute intersubjective "thought communities" beyond individual subjectivity that reflect a particular collective world view (Zerubavel 1997). The notion of thought communities is akin to Mead's (1934) concept of the generalized other in that both are abstractions of the perspectives of social collectivities or groups that enter into the thinking of the individual. While people may accept, reject, or ignore the normative guidance rendered, collective views are nevertheless likely to be taken into account when choosing a course of action (Berger and Luckmann 1967). Weber ([1922] 1978) notes that concepts of collective entities have meaning in the minds of individuals, partly as something actually existing and partly as something with normative authority. "Actors," states Weber ([1922] 1978: 14), "thus in part orient their action to them, and in this role such ideas have a powerful, often a decisive, causal influence on the course of action of real individuals."

Religion and ideology are examples of collective perspectives that have implications for health lifestyles. This is seen in the usual preference of highly religious persons and groups for positive health lifestyles since their beliefs invariably promote healthy living in the form of good nutrition, exercise, and personal hygiene, while discouraging alcohol use and smoking cigarettes (Brown et al. 2001; Hill et al. 2007; Idler 2010). However, the full extent of the relationship between religiosity and health lifestyles is not known because of a lack of relevant studies. This is an important area that needs further research.

Little is also known about ideology and health lifestyles. Research on the effects of the socialist heritage in contemporary Russia shows that pro-socialists (those who are in favor of a return to state socialism as it was before Gorbachev) have less healthy lifestyles than anti-socialists, even though neither group demonstrated exceptionally positive health practices (Cockerham et al. 2002). Pro-socialists had a particularly passive approach to health lifestyles that seemed left over from Soviet times. The choices of individuals in Soviet society were confined to a single social and political ideology (communism) and expected to conform to it. When a person got sick, the state was responsible for taking care of that person as a benefit of state socialism. Individual incentives in health matters were not encouraged. Thus it could be argued that communism was bad for one's health as it failed to promote healthy lifestyle practices. However, the extent to which ideology generally affects health lifestyles beyond this example has not been determined.

Surprisingly, there is also little research on family and kinship group influences concerning health lifestyles, although we know from K. A. S. Wickrama and his colleagues (1999) in the United States that such influence can be strong. The family typically influences how a particular person perceives his or her health situation (Cockerham 2012). Most individuals are born into a family of significant others – significant because they provide the child with a specific social identity and sense of self. This identity includes not only an appraisal of physical and intellectual characteristics, but knowledge about the family's social and medical history. In addition to learning the family's social status, perspective, and cultural orientation, the child learns about the health threats most common for the family and the measures needed to cope with them. As the child becomes older and takes as his or her own the values and attitudes of the immediate family, community, and wider society as presented through the mediating influence of the family, the child is considered properly socialized in that he or she behaves in accordance with group-approved rules.

While children can either accept or reject the social perspective put forth by their family as representative of their own social reality, the reality presented to them in the process of primary socialization is set by adults who determine what information is provided and make assessments of the validity of opposing viewpoints. Although children are not necessarily passive in the socialization experience, what is important is that they have no choice in the selection of their significant others so that identification with them is quasi-automatic (Berger and Luckmann 1967). This further means that children's internalization of their family's interpretation of social reality is quasi-inevitable. Although the initial social world presented to children by their significant others may be weakened by later social relationships and views, it can nonetheless be a lasting influence. Parental influence, for example, has been found to be the most important and persistent influence on the preventive health beliefs of their children (Lau, Quadrel, and Hartman 1990) and significant in shaping their health lifestyles (Wickrama et al. 1999).

Living conditions

Living conditions are a category of structural variables pertaining to differences in the quality of housing and access to basic utilities (e.g., electricity, gas, heating, sewers, indoor plumbing, safe piped water, hot water), neighborhood facilities (e.g., grocery stores, parks, recreation), and personal safety. To date there has been little research linking living conditions to health lifestyles, but the connection is important. As noted, Blaxter (1990) found in her nationwide British survey that the conditions within which a person lives have important implications for health-related behavior. Health lifestyles were most effective in positive circumstances and least effective under negative living conditions. In the United States, living in disadvantaged neighborhoods has been associated with a less positive health status (Browning and Cagney 2002, 2003) and growing up in affluent neighborhoods has been found to have positive long-term health effects (Vartanian and Houser 2010). Other research, as also previously noted, shows that living in less safe neighborhoods significantly contributes to the low participation of adult blacks in vigorous outdoor exercise (Grzywacz and Marks 2001). Consequently, living conditions can constrain or enhance health lifestyles.

Socialization and experience

Class circumstances and the other variables shown in box 1 in figure 3.1 provide the social context for socialization and experience as depicted by the arrow leading to box 2. This is consistent with Bourdieu's (1977) view that dispositions to act in particular ways are constructed through socialization and experience, with class position providing the social context for this process. The present model, however, adds the additional structural categories – age, gender, race/ethnicity, collectivities, and living conditions – depicted in box 1, since they may also influence the social environment within which socialization and experience occur.

Whereas primary socialization represents the imposition of society's norms and values on the individual by significant others and secondary socialization results from later training, experience is the learned outcome of day-to-day activities that comes about through social interaction and the practical exercise of agency. It is through both socialization and experience that the person or actor acquires reflexive awareness and the capacity to perform agency, but experience – with respect to life choices – provides the essential basis for agency's practical and evaluative dimensions to evolve over time. This is especially the case as people confront new social situations and conditions.

Life choices (agency)

Figure 3.1 shows that socialization and experience (box 2) provide the capacity for life choices (agency) depicted in box 3. As previously noted, the term "life choices" was introduced by Weber as one of the two major components of lifestyles (the other is life chances) and refers to the self-direction of one's behavior. It is an English language translation of *Lebensführung*, which in German literally means conducting or managing one's life. Life choices are a process of agency by which individuals critically evaluate and choose their course of action. Weber's notion of life choices differs from rational choice theory in that it accounts for both means-ends rationally as well as the interpretive process whereby the potential outcomes of choices are imagined, evaluated, and reconstructed in the mind (Emirbayer and Mische 1998). Weber (1949) maintained that individuals have the capacity to interpret their situation, make deliberate choices, and attach subjective meaning to their actions. All social action in his view takes place in contexts that imply both constraints and opportunities, with the actor's interpretive understanding (*Verstehen*) of the situation guiding behavioral choices (Kalberg 1994).

Life chances (structure)

Class circumstances and to a lesser degree the other variables in box 1 constitute life chances (structure) shown in box 4 of figure 3.1. Life chances are the other major component of lifestyles in Weber's model. Weber was ambiguous about what he meant by life chances, but the term is usually associated with the advantages and disadvantages of relative class situations. Dahrendorf (1979: 73) finds that the best meaning of life chances in Weber's work is the "crystallized probability of finding satisfaction for interests, wants and needs, thus the probability of the occurrence of events which bring about such satisfaction." Consequently, the higher a person's position in a class hierarchy, the better the person's life chances or probabilities for finding satisfaction and vice versa. Dahrendorf (1979: 65) adds the following clarification: "for Weber, the probability of sequences of action postulated in the

concept of chance is not merely an observed and thus calculable probability, but is a probability which is invariably anchored in structural
conditions." Thus a person's probabilities for satisfaction that constitute his or her life chances are based on the structural conditions in
their life, especially their class position. Weber's thesis is that chance is
socially determined and social structure is an arrangement of chances.
Therefore, life chances represent the influence of structure in Weber's
oeuvre and this paradigm.

Choice and chance interplay

The arrows in figure 3.1 indicate the dialectical interplay between life
choices (box 3) and life chances (box 4). This interaction is Weber's
most important contribution to conceptualizing lifestyle construction
(Cockerham, Abel, and Lüschen 1993; Cockerham, Rütten, and Abel
1997). Choices and chances operate in tandem to determine a distinctive lifestyle for individuals, groups, and classes. Life chances (structure) either constrain or enable choices (agency); agency is not passive
in this process, however. As Archer (2003) explains, whether or not
constraints and enablements are exercised as causal powers is based
on agency choosing the practices to be activated. "Constraints," says
Archer (2003: 4), "require something to constrain, and enablements
something to enable." Consequently, people have to consider a course
of action if their actions are to be either constrained or enabled. People
therefore align their goals, needs, and desires with their probabilities
for realizing them and choose a lifestyle according to their assessments
of their resources and class circumstances. Unrealistic choices are not
likely to succeed or be selected, while realistic choices are based upon
what is structurally possible.

   In this context, choices and chances are not only connected dialecti-
cally, but are analytically distinct. As Archer (1998: 369) points out:
"Because the emergent properties of structures and the actual experiences of agents are not synchronized (due to the very nature of society
as an open system), then there will always be the inescapable need for a
two-part account." Weber provides such a framework. He conceptualizes choice and chance as separate components in the activation and
conduct of a lifestyle and merges the different functions of agency and
structure without either losing their distinctiveness.

   Up to this point, the health lifestyles paradigm has been an example
of Archer's (1998) notion of downward conflation in which individual
behavior is molded by structure in the form of class circumstances,
gender, collectivities, etc. Even though structure is dominant initially

because people are socialized and have experiences within the context of the social structures that comprise their world, agency enters the model at the mid-point where choices and chances interact and outcomes are chosen from what is available.

Dispositions to act (habitus)

Figure 3.1 shows that the interaction of life choices and life chances produce individual dispositions to action (box 5). These dispositions constitute a habitus. The notion of habitus originates with Edmund Husserl ([1952] 1989: 266–93) who used the term to describe habitual action that is intuitively followed and anticipated. The concept has been expanded by Bourdieu (1977: 72–95) to serve as his core explanation for the agency–structure relationship in lifestyle dispositions (Bourdieu 1984: 169–225). Bourdieu (1990: 53) defines habitus as "systems of durable, transposable dispositions, structured structures predisposed to operate as structuring structures, that is, as principles which generate and organize practices and representations that can be objectively adapted to their outcomes without presupposing a conscious aiming at ends or an express mastery of the operations necessary in order to attain them." Put another way, the habitus serves as a cognitive map or set of perceptions in the mind that routinely guides and evaluates a person's choices and options. It provides enduring dispositions toward acting deemed appropriate by a person in particular social situations and settings. Included are dispositions that can be carried out even without giving them a great deal of thought in advance. They are simply habitual ways of acting when performing routine tasks.

The influence of exterior social structures and conditions is incorporated into the habitus, as well as the individual's own inclinations, preferences, and interpretations. The dispositions that result not only reflect established normative patterns of social behavior, but they also encompass action that is habitual and even intuitive. Through selective perception the habitus molds aspirations and expectations into "categories of the probable" that impose perceptual boundaries on dispositions and the potential for action. "As an acquired system of generative schemes," observes Bourdieu (1990: 55), "the *habitus* makes possible the free production of all the thoughts, perceptions, actions, inherent in the particular conditions of its production – and only those."

When Bourdieu speaks of the internalization of class conditions and their transformation into personal dispositions toward action, he is

describing conditions similar to Weber's concept of life chances that
determine materially, socially, and culturally what is probable, possible, or impossible for a member of a particular social class or group
(Swartz 1997: 104). Individuals who internalize similar life chances
share the same habitus because, as Bourdieu (1977: 85) explains, they
are more likely to have similar shared experiences: "Though it is impossible for *all* members of the same class (or even two of them) to have
the same experiences, in the same order, it is certain that each member
of the same class is more likely than any member of another class to
have been confronted with the situations most frequent for members
of that class." As a result, there is a high degree of affinity in health
lifestyle choices among members of the same class. Bourdieu maintains
that while they may depart from class standards, personal styles are
never more than a deviation from a style of a class that relates back to
the common style by its difference.

Even though Bourdieu allows agency some autonomy (e.g., agents
are determined only to the extent they determine themselves), his
emphasis on structure with respect to routine operations of the
habitus clearly delineates a lesser role for agency than the individualist
approach to health lifestyles. Some have argued that Bourdieu strips
agency of much of its critical reflexive character (Bohman 1999). Bryan
Turner and Stephen Wainwright (2003: 273), however, disagree and
find that Bourdieu gives "full recognition" to "agency through his
notions of strategy and practices," while illustrating the powerful role
of institutions and resources "in shaping, constraining, and producing human agency." Simon Williams (1995) also defends Bourdieu by
pointing out that choice is not precluded by the habitus, and he is able
to account for the relative durability of different forms of lifestyles
among the social classes. As the concept of the habitus is not original
to Bourdieu, even though he revitalized it, his lasting contribution may
in fact be his analysis of the importance of differential and durable
tastes and lifestyles that distinguish the social classes from one another.

It can also be argued that the *process* of experience rescues Bourdieu's
concept of habitus from the charge of downward conflation. Through
experience, agency acquires new information and rationales for
prompting creativity and change by way of the habitus. As Bourdieu
(Bourdieu and Wacquant 1992: 133) explains, even though experiences confirm habitus, since there is a high probability that most
people encounter circumstances that are consistent with those that
originally fashioned it, the habitus nevertheless "is an *open system of
dispositions* that is constantly subjected to experiences, and therefore
constantly affected by them in a way that reinforces or modifies its

structures." Thus the habitus can be creative and initiate changes in dispositions, although this potential is not stressed in Bourdieu's work.

Lifestyle practices originate in the habitus, but these and other practices are carried out in social settings that Bourdieu conceptualizes as "fields." Fields are networks or configurations of objective relations (domination, subordination, etc.) between social positions (Bourdieu and Wacquant 1992). A field is a social space or what Bourdieu describes as an "arena" in which people and institutions use their capital – economic, cultural, and social – to maneuver for advantage in a hierarchical structure of relationships. Amounts and types of capital determine positions in the hierarchy relative to others in the field. Some positions are clearly more powerful and so the power relations of a field typically shape the interaction that takes place within it. Peter Korp (2008) maintains that healthy lifestyles can be viewed as the habitual practices of groups that dominate social fields where healthy living is considered important. The opposite could be the case in fields with different power dynamics. The exercise of agency is therefore influenced from outside the individual by fields and capital, while habitus shapes it from the inside.

Bourdieu calls for the abandonment of theories that explicitly or implicitly treat people as mere bearers (*Trägers*) of structure. Yet he also maintains that the rejection of mechanistic theories of behavior does not imply that we should bestow on some creative free will the exclusive power to generally constitute the meanings of situations and determine the intentions of others. The dispositions generated by the habitus tend to be compatible with the behavioral parameters set by the wider society; therefore, usual and practical modes of behaving – not unpredictable novelty – typically prevail. Consequently, Bourdieu emphasizes structure more than agency even though he accords agency the capacity to direct behavior when motivated; otherwise, his perspective largely accounts for routine behaviors that people enact without having to analyze or even think much about unless deeper attention is required.

Completing the Model

Figure 3.1 shows that dispositions (box 5) produce practices (action) that are represented in box 6. The practices that result from the habitus can be based on deliberate calculations, habits, or intuition. Bourdieu (1984) helps us to realize that practices linked to health lifestyles can be so integrated into routine behavioral repertoires that they can be acted out more or less unthinkingly once established in the habitus. Bourdieu observes that people tend to adopt generalized strategies (a sense of the game) oriented toward practical ends in routine situations that they can habitually follow without stopping to analyze them. As a routine feature of everyday life, it is therefore appropriate to view health lifestyles as guided more by a practical than abstract logic (S. Williams 1995).

The four most common practices measured in studies of health life-styles are alcohol use, smoking, diet, and exercise. These are shown in box 7 along with other practices such as physical checkups by physi-cians and automobile seatbelt use that comprise other typical forms of action taken or not taken. The practices themselves may be positive or negative, but they nonetheless comprise a person's overall pattern of health lifestyles as represented in box 8. It is important to note that these practices sometimes have a complexity of their own. Smoking tobacco in any form is negative, but moderate alcohol use (preferably red wine) reduces the risk of heart disease more so than heavy drink-ing (which promotes it) and abstinence (Klatsky 1999). In the United States, moderate drinking is considered to be the equivalent of one to two glasses of wine a day, while in Britain low consumption of one to two glasses five days a week is recommended. Eating fresh fruits and vegetables is positive, but consuming meat can be either positive or negative depending on how it is cooked and its fat content. Relatively vigorous leisure-time exercise has more health benefits than physical activity at work because the latter is subject to stress from job demands and time schedules, while walking and other everyday forms of exer-cise have some value (Dunn et al. 1999). However, measures of leisure-time exercise may not fully represent the physical activities of women who take care of children and do housework (Ainsworth 2000). It is therefore necessary that researchers take the multifaceted features of health lifestyle practices into account when analyzing them.

Action (or inaction) with respect to a particular health practice leads to its reproduction, modification, or nullification by the habitus through a feedback process. This is seen in figure 3.1 by the arrow showing movement from box 8 back to box 5. This is consistent with Bourdieu's (1977, 1984) assertion that when dispositions are acted upon they tend to produce or modify the habitus from which they are derived. As conceptualized by Bourdieu, the habitus is the centerpiece of the health lifestyle model.

Conclusion

A central theme of this chapter is that the individualistic paradigm of health lifestyles is too narrow and unrealistic because it fails to consider structural influences on health lifestyle choices. In order to correct this course and formulate a theory where none previously existed, a health lifestyle model is presented here that accords structure a role that is consistent with its influence in the empirical world. There are times when structure outweighs but does not negate agency and other times when structure overwhelms agency, and these situations need to be included in concepts explaining health lifestyle practices. A macro-social orientation does not mean that action is structurally predetermined; rather, it recognizes that social structures influence the thoughts, decisions, and actions of individuals (Sibeon 2004).

The theoretical model presented here is strongly influenced by Weber and Bourdieu. Although Bourdieu, in particular, has his critics, his notion of habitus nevertheless represents a novel and logical conceptualization of the internalization of external structures in the mind and perceptual processes of the individual. The result is a registry of dispositions to act in ways that are practical and usually consistent with the socially approved behavioral pathways of the larger social order or some class or group therein.

This model of health lifestyles states that four categories of (1) structural variables, namely (a) class circumstances, (b) age, gender, and race/ethnicity, (c) collectivities, and (d) living conditions, provide the social context for (2) socialization and experience that influence (3) life choices (agency). These structural variables also collectively constitute (4) life chances (structure). Choices and chances interact and commission the formation of (5) dispositions to act (habitus), leading to (6) practices (action), involving (7) alcohol use, smoking, diets, and other health-related actions. Health practices constitute patterns of (8) health lifestyles whose re-enactment results in their reproduction (or modification) through feedback to the habitus. This theory is an initial representation of the health lifestyle phenomenon and is subject to verification, change, or rejection through future empirical application. It is a beginning for theoretical formulations concerning a major aspect of day-to-day social behavior for which no other theory now exists. Moreover, it moves beyond current theoretical trends reflecting methodological individualism to bring considerations of structure consistent with the reality of everyday life back into the conceptual focus of theory in medical sociology. Finally, it shows that structure has a direct causal effect on health through lifestyle practices.

Suggested Further Reading

Blaxter, Mildred. 1990. *Health and Lifestyles*. London: Tavistock.
This is the first major study of health lifestyles that took place in the UK. While the findings are not current, the methodology, analysis, and conclusions are still relevant.

Christakos, Nicholas A. and James H. Fowler. 2007. "The Spread of Obesity in a Large Social Network over 32 Years." *New England Journal of Medicine* 357:370–79.
Demonstrates the greater likelihood of obesity among members of obese social networks of friends and family.

Christakos, Nicholas A. and James H. Fowler. 2008. "The Collective Dynamics of Smoking in a Large Social Network." *New England Journal of Medicine* 358:2249–58.
Finds that while smoking spreads through social networks, such networks also inhibit smoking when smokers are increasingly marginalized by network members because of their use of cigarettes, and potential smokers are discouraged from trying it.

Quah, Stella. 2010. "Health and Culture." In *The New Blackwell Companion to Medical Sociology*, ed. William Cockerham, 27–46. Oxford, UK: Wiley-Blackwell.
Discusses cultural influences on health and health behavior.

4

The Power of Class

Social class or socioeconomic status (SES) is the strongest predictor of health, disease causation, and longevity in medical sociology. This is particularly evident when social gradients in mortality universally display a hierarchical gradient from low to high in death rates according to class position (Beckfield 2004; Evans, Barer, and Marmor 1994; Lahelma 2010; Marmot 2004; Marmot, Shipley, and Rose 1984). While it might be argued there are other health and mortality hierarchies with respect to social demographic variables like age, gender, and race, the explanatory power of class is demonstrated when it interacts with these other variables to produce differences beyond those already produced. That is, the advantages or disadvantages that accrue to differences in age, gender, and race are magnified one way or the other by class position.

We know, for example, that aged persons tend to adjust their food habits as they grow older; but lower strata elderly – who are more likely to have a negatively anticipated future – have been found to make negative changes in their diet or to disregard it altogether, while higher strata old people typically have more positive diets to begin with and make positive changes (Shifflet 1987; Shifflett and McIntosh 1986–7). Structural variables (class and age cohorts) are decisive in this outcome, with age (and the aged cohort's reduced requirements for high-energy foods) producing changes in eating habits and class producing further change. For most elderly, food habits and other health lifestyles have been "locked in" along class lines over the life course,

Aged

and are still reflected in modifications undertaken in late life (Jones et al. 2011).

In the example above, class position makes the greatest difference, although age clearly has explanatory power. An alternative view to the proposition that class or SES overrides age, gender, race, and similar variables is found in intersectionality theory. The theory challenges any prioritization because it holds that all social structures are subject to the negative effects of capitalism, patriarchy, racism, and other discriminatory influences. This approach originated in the work of African American feminist scholars such as Kimberlé Crenshaw (1989) and Patricia Hill Collins (2000, 2005). It was intended to take relevant forms of social inequality and oppression into account at the same time. The goal was to promote social justice for black women who felt oppressed not just because of their race but also their gender. Consequently, much of the work has been focused on the intersection of race, gender, and sexuality, and the ways in which these variables interact to disadvantage marginalized groups. Intersectionality theory takes the position that race and gender, as well as class, and similar sociodemographic variables are mutually constructing systems of power. Since these systems or structures pervade all social relationships, the theory maintains that individual and group characteristics cannot be reduced to single variables (such as class or gender) or fully understood by prioritizing one variable over others (Hankivsky 2012). All variables operate at the same time in the same context.

Researchers are therefore urged to move beyond single categories of analysis toward consideration of the simultaneous interactions between the different aspects of social identity. This approach, as Olena Hankivsky (2012) points out, is intended to provide the foundation for a new direction of inquiry in which no one category is rated the most important and is continuously highlighting some differences to the exclusion of others. Measures of the interaction or intersection of class with other variables is useful because the effects of class are not necessarily the same everywhere, and interactions may be informative. However, the intersectionality approach to date has tended to focus more on the intersection of gender, race, and sexuality, somewhat less so on class, and to the exclusion of disability, immigration status, and other variables (Collins 2005). Furthermore, it has proven difficult to separate the effects of all intersecting variables on those being studied. "Because these systems permeate all social relations," says Collins (2005: 11), "untangling their effects in any given situation or for any given population remains difficult." So rather than untangling them, intersectionality theory has turned to viewing them in terms of their relationships to each other.

Nevertheless, until strong evidence emerges showing otherwise, class remains the primary determinant of social stratification. As Reid (1998: 238) observed years ago in a statement that is true today, "being black, female or elderly and middle class is different from being black, female or elderly and working class." And this is especially the case in medical sociology where study after study invariably finds strong links between class position and health – both positive and negative. The social gradient in health and mortality appears to be a fact of life. As British epidemiologist Michael Marmot (2004: 2) asks: "why should educated people with good stable jobs have a higher risk of dropping dead than people with a bit more education or slightly higher status job?" Or why should people with a four-bedroom house live longer than those with a three-bedroom apartment? Or why is having a master's degree better for life expectancy than having a bachelor's degree and astronomically better than having less than a high school education? Marmot says the answer is that for people *above* a threshold of material well-being, another type of well-being is central to longevity – namely, that of autonomy. Autonomy in making decisions and the control it gives those that have it over their lives is essential, in his view, for a sense of well-being, social engagement, health, and longevity.

Class and Heart Attack Survival

Marmot (2004: 2) suggests that if you want to get a sense of how SES affects health, then take a ride on the metro system in Washington, DC from the deteriorated neighborhoods southeast of downtown to upscale Montgomery County in Maryland. For every mile traveled, life expectancy for the residents rises approximately one-and-a-half years. There is a 20-year gap in life expectancy between the low-income blacks at the beginning of the journey and the wealthy whites at the end.

However, differences in mortality are not the only class-based outcomes that fit into a social gradient, but also various diseases. Which ones? The answer, according to Michael Marmot (2004), is most of them. "In general," states Marmot (2004: 23), "the lower the social position, the higher the risk of heart disease, stroke, lung diseases, diseases of the digestive tract, kidney diseases, HIV-related diseases, tuberculosis, suicide, and other 'accidental' and violent deaths." An example of the significance of class is the experience of three persons who survived a heart attack in New York City: a 66-year-old white male upper-middle-class architect, a 53-year-old black male middle-class transportation coordinator for the city's electric power company, and a 59-year-old white working-class female Polish immigrant who was a hotel maid. Their stories were reported in the *New York Times* in a special investigative series in 2005 on social class in America (Scott 2005). Does class matter in recovering from a heart attack? Yes, it does . . .

The architect collapsed on a city street in Midtown Manhattan after lunch with two colleagues. His friends ignored his request for them to call him a taxi and instead called for an ambulance. He was given a choice of going to one of two nearby major medical centers equipped with the latest technology in emergency cardiac care; he picked an academic hospital frequented by relatively affluent patients instead of a very busy city-run hospital. Within minutes, he was on an operating table in the hospital's cardiac catheterization laboratory where a potentially serious ventricular fibrillation (abnormal heart rhythm) was quickly fixed, followed by angioplasty to unclog an artery. Less than two hours after his first symptom, his artery had been reopened by an experienced cardiac surgeon and a stent implanted to keep it open. His brother, chairman of the board at another hospital, called his counterpart at the hospital where the architect was a patient to personally request his brother's treatment be closely monitored as a "professional courtesy," while his brother-in-law, a surgeon, referred him to a top specialist for follow-up care. The architect subsequently took several months off from work, adjusted his diet, lost weight, joined an exercise club near his home, and his blood pressure and cholesterol levels improved. His family was very supportive. The only unpleasant outcome was that his firm asked him to retire because of his long absence, which he did on his terms and before he started working from home as a consultant.

In contrast, the middle-class transportation coordinator had his heart attack in his fiancée's apartment. It was his second. Nevertheless, he thought at first he had heartburn. But his girlfriend insisted on calling an ambulance and he was given the choice of two nearby hospitals, neither of which was licensed for angioplasty. He selected a hospital other than the one that served the city's poor. He was given a drug to break up the clot clogging an artery. The clot reformed, so the next day he was transferred to another hospital in the city for angioplasty. The doctor doing the operation observed that it would have been better if he had been brought directly to him, since the earlier the procedure is performed, the better the recovery.

After his prior heart attack, his attempts at exercising and changing his diet away from the fried chicken and pork chops he loved were half-hearted and he stopped seeing cardiologists when his doctor moved away and he found the new doctor's staff to be rude. This time, he tried to do better by improving his diet, although his fiancée noted that it was hard to find fresh vegetables and fish in their neighborhood and they weren't sure about the dietary benefits of some foods, like whole grains. He still ate fried shrimp on special occasions when he went to a favorite seafood chain restaurant, but took his medications regularly. He had to drive downtown to a cardiac rehabilitation exercise program, but stopped driving after parking problems and took the subway instead. He joined a health club and planned to retire in two years.

The maid had the most difficult experience of all. She suffered her heart attack at night at home and hesitated before letting her husband call an ambulance. She had to be talked into going to the hospital by the paramedics and was taken to one that served the poor without being asked. She was not seen by a physician in a busy emergency room for over two hours and when tests finally confirmed she was having a heart attack, she was given medication to remove a clot. She was transferred to another hospital the next day for an angiogram to assess the probability of a second heart attack. However, she came down with a fever that prevented her from being given the angiogram. Later it was found she had heart damage. She took public transportation to her doctor appointments and coped by herself with problems with her health insurance. This meant several phone calls, letters, and subway trips to the insurance company's office to resolve the situation. She went on a diet, but gave it up, as her husband refused to change his eating habits and she liked to indulge herself with sweets. She did stop smoking. She wanted to work part-time, but her employer refused and soon she was back on her old job schedule. Her husband was out of work for weeks because of pneumonia and the money from her job was important. She started gaining weight and her blood pressure and cholesterol reached dangerous levels, despite medication. Her doctor said she was becoming a full-time patient.

In each of these cases, class circumstances played a major role in either promoting or reducing risks to health. Prospects for the recovery of the three heart patients can be ranked from good to fair to poor in descending social order. However, promoting or reducing the prospects of survivability from a heart attack is not the same as causing it. The *New York Times* story focused on the aftermath of the heart attacks, rather than the prelude. Nevertheless, the article powerfully demonstrates the impact of class on recovery from a heart attack. It is obviously better for one's health outcomes to be situated in the upper-middle class than lodged in the lower-middle or the bottom of the working class.

As noted, the social behaviors and conditions that influenced the onset of the heart attack for the 66-year-old architect and the two other people who were younger but lower on the social scale was not part of the write-up. But there are social clues that have causal implications for the three people involved. The white architect was working full-time past the age of 65 and was perturbed when his firm asked him to retire after his heart attack, suggesting he may have been a self-motivated workaholic in addition to being overweight and not exercising. The 53-year-old black transportation coordinator did not exercise, indulged his appetite for fried foods, and stopped getting follow-up care after his first heart attack because he did not like the cardiologist's staff. The 59-year-old white immigrant maid was overweight, smoked, worked long hours dictated by her employer's schedule, loved sweets, and her husband did not support her efforts to have a healthy diet. Social factors, especially class as determined by education, income, and occupation, can be seen in this report to have a likely causal role through multiple pathways of risk for these individuals. However, before examining more direct evidence of the ways in which class differences can indeed be causal in this and the next chapter, we will first look at the general characteristics of class that make it so important for health.

Class Structure and its Components

A social class is a category or group of people who have approximately the same amount of wealth, status, and power in a society. The various classes are arranged in a hierarchical pattern from top to bottom and constitute a layered system of social stratification. The pattern is one of inequality in which classes at the top have superior living conditions and greater access to quality goods and services while those at the very bottom have none of these things. The relevance of social inequality in the daily lives of most individuals is that it determines their personal opportunities and life experiences in very powerful ways. To be poor by definition means having more of the bad things in life and fewer of the good things, including health. As Ralf Dahrendorf (1990: 25) explained several years ago: "Life chances are never distributed equally. We do not know a society in which all men, women, and children have the same entitlements and enjoy the same provisions. We do not know of one in which all have the same status. Probably there cannot be such a condition."

Much of the initial conceptualization of class in sociology originates in the work of Marx and Weber. Both observed how industrialization, urbanization, and the process of modernization produced a more complex pattern of social stratification than those previously existing. The mass movement of the peasant population into cities as an industrial labor force and the rise of a strong middle class had a dramatic effect upon Europe's class structure. This change was stimulated by the Industrial Revolution that began around 1780 in Great Britain and resulted in a social and economic transformation more profound than any other previous development in the history of the world. The substitution of machines for the muscles of animals and humans in work created a massive increase in productivity, which produced greater demand for more machines, more raw materials, improved means of transportation, more efficient forms of communication, better-educated workers, and a more specialized division of labor. New and better products were manufactured and distributed at reasonable prices, thereby making a wide variety of goods available to the public that was not possible prior to industrialization.

Europe's development also brought significant social problems. The cities and towns of the late eighteenth and early nineteenth centuries were not prepared to accommodate the large influx of people who left the countryside to seek work in urban centers. Large sections of many medieval cities were transformed into sprawling, chaotic slums. Squalor, poor sanitation, long working hours, low wages, and poor health became commonplace as a rural peasant population was transformed into an industrial working class. Alexis de Tocqueville ([1835] 1958: 107), the French historian and sociologist known for his commentaries on early nineteenth-century Europe and North America, described the newly industrialized city of Manchester, England, during this period: "From this foul drain the greatest stream of human industry flows out to fertilize the whole world. From this filthy sewer pure gold flows. Here humanity attains its most complete development and its most brutish, here civilization works its miracles and civilized man is turned almost into a savage."

No longer did the majority of people live in small, rural villages within an extended kinship system and produce for themselves most of what they needed to live. The rise of trade dissolved the subsistence economy of medieval society and generated towns which became the economic and cultural centers of the new society. Financial wealth replaced land ownership as the major basis for affluence, while some families in the middle class prospered through business and sought social advancement through their wealth and marriage into the upper class. Rich industrialists joined aristocrats at the top of society, the size of the middle class increased significantly, and a large working class emerged between the middle and lower classes. Western society was permanently changed.

Class schemes

Marx used a two-class scheme consisting of the bourgeoisie (owners and managers) and the proletariat (workers) in his analysis of class relations during industrialization, while Weber in *Economy and Society* ([1922] 1978) identified four: (1) the class of those privileged by great property or high education, (2) less propertied but highly educated intellectuals, technical specialists, white-collar employees, and civil servants, (3) the lower-middle class, and (4) the working class. Negatively privileged persons, who today would qualify as the lower class, were classified as lower-level workers of various sorts in the working class (Ringer 2004). Weber's placing of the highest educated persons on the top rung of the social hierarchy was a reflection of the stratification system prevalent in his native Germany in the late nineteenth and early twentieth centuries when differences in education were potent social barriers and university professors were accorded particularly high prestige. However, the rise of a powerful and wealthy industrially-based elite was beginning in Weber's time to take over the formerly dominant position of both the highly educated and those with high inherited status (Ringer 2004).

Many different class models, including the basic three-class scheme of upper, middle, and lower, are used in medical sociology. However, the scheme often followed today by medical sociologists in the United States who desire greater precision in their analysis is similar to Weber's format and consists of a five-class model: (1) the upper class (extremely wealthy top corporate executives and professionals), (2) the upper-middle class (affluent, well-educated professionals and high-level managers), (3) the lower-middle class (office and sales workers, small store owners, teachers, nurses, etc.), (4) the working class (skilled and semi-skilled workers, lower-level clerical workers), and (5) the lower class (semi-skilled and unskilled workers, the unemployed).

In recent years, downward social mobility increased when profit-maximizing strategies of major financial institutions failed and the disregard for risks led to the global sub-prime mortgage crisis of

2008–9. Some banks and businesses failed, massive government loans were needed for others, there were losses in investments, the economy weakened, unemployment increased, and there was a dispossession of assets, particularly homes, from vulnerable people. Only now are there signs of a recovery. British sociologist John Goldthorpe (2007: 94) describes the years after World War II as "boom" years for Western countries in which living standards generally improved and class inequalities began to decline. But from the mid-1970s onward, this optimistic view has been more difficult to sustain because of increased inequities in earnings and household incomes with a clear basis in class differences. The "Occupy Wall Street Movement" in several American cities in 2011 was a class-based protest against the lack of legal consequences for corruption in financial and real estate markets, the widening income gap between rich and poor, and growing social inequality.

The source of wealth for the richest segment of American society has shifted away from industry to finance, real estate, and information technology. This group has prospered so much that they have pulled far ahead of the rest of population (Johnston 2005). Those at the top in income, some 0.1 percent of the population whose personal income averaged more than $3 million a year in 2005, saw their wealth more than double since the 1980s. By way of comparison, the bottom 90 percent of the population in income in 2005 were persons and households earning between $0 and $117,000. For every extra *one dollar* in wages and salary increases brought in by the bottom 90 percent from 1990 to 2002, those in the top 0.1 percent in income brought in an extra *$18,000* (Johnston 2005: 17). A similar situation continues today. Money has come from opportunities in investments, the global marketplace, new technologies, and extraordinarily high salaries at the top of the corporate business ladder. Due to upward social mobility, the size of the upper and upper-middle classes has expanded somewhat in recent years and the size of the lower class has increased – but the working class has decreased with vast losses in manufacturing jobs. As Goldthorpe (2007: 94) observes, the main losers would appear to be skilled wage workers in manual occupations and employees with routine nonmanual jobs because of a decline of their real (after inflation and taxes) earnings and increased risk of unemployment.

Class distinctions have traditionally been much sharper in Britain than in the US and studying class became "something of an obsession in British social science" since it proved to be a powerful analytic tool for understanding inequality, social division, and political change (Abercrombie and Warde et al. 2000: 145). Britain was the first country to industrialize and its stratification along economic lines has been long-standing. Unlike the US, Britain has a royal family and an aristocracy whose lineage extends back to the Middle Ages. The aristocracy, whose traditional wealth was based on land ownership, suffered a decline in power and influence beginning in the late nineteenth century because of a general downturn in the economic advantages of agriculture (Cannadine 1999). Nevertheless, at the top of British society today is a small upper class of wealthy families, many of them members of the nobility, and a new elite of top professionals in financial and legal services and corporate managers that have emerged in particular strength since the 1960s. The upper strata is followed by a small upper-middle class of professionals and managers, a large lower-middle class of white-collar workers, and a very large working class. At the bottom is the lower class, many of whom live in poverty or on the edge of it.

The relevance of class in British life is summarized by Reid (1989: 365) who concludes:

> I think it's a pretty serious and important factor to the extent that we have a good deal of evidence to show that, right from the beginning of life, one's life chances, the chance of surviving birth, of suffering certain illnesses, the chances of living in certain types of accommodation, of receiving certain types of education, and indeed the likelihood of earning a given income, are very much related to divisions in our society we call social class. In fact, there seems to be very little of life in our society which isn't in some way characterized by differences between the social classes.

The most frequently used class model in Britain until recently has been the central government's Registrar-General's Social Class (RGSC) scheme. This model was initially formulated by T. H. C. Stevenson who held the post of Registrar-General in 1913 and used it to demonstrate the existence of a social class gradient in infant mortality (Chandola 2000; Crompton 2008; Lahelma 2010). This is a six-class model based on occupation and consists of: (I) professionals, (II) intermediate (managerial and technical) occupations, (III [N]) skilled nonmanual occupations, (III [M]) skilled manual occupations, (IV) semi-skilled manual occupations, and (V) unskilled manual occupations. Criticized for classifying social classes simply in terms of job skills, and although other models like that of Erickson–Goldthorpe and the Cambridge Scale were available, the Registrar-General's model stood the test of time for many years. Its strength was its correlation with a wide range of disparities in income, education, and health in Britain (Crompton 2008; Reid 1998).

In 2001, however, the government adopted a new scheme, the National Statistics Socio-Economic Classification (NS-SEC) model for its official measure of class position. This system is based on differences in employment relationships (like autonomy and job security) and work conditions (such as promotion opportunities and the planning of work). People are assigned to particular social classes according to their occupation and work responsibilities (Bartley 2004; Chandola 2000). Based upon the Erickson–Goldthorpe model, the NS-SEC does not take job skills into account or separate manual from nonmanual workers. The most commonly used version of the NS-SEC seems to be its seven-class model: (1) higher managerial and professional occupations, (2) lower managerial and professional occupations, and higher technical occupations, (3) intermediate occupations (clerical, administrative, sales), (4) small employers and self-employed workers, (5) lower technical occupations, (6) semi-routine occupations with moderate job security, few career prospects, and limited autonomy, and (7) routine occupations with low job security, no career prospects, and closely supervised routine work (Bartley 2004; Lahelma 2010).

A new development in 2008 was the appearance of the European Socioeconomic Classification or ESeC that was developed to measure class position and social inequality throughout the European Union (Rose and Harrison 2010). Based upon the UK's NS-SEC, the ESeC features nine class categories and allows more precise comparisons with past models, thereby preserving the integrity of time-series studies investigating long-term trends. The ESeC's first three categories are essentially the same as those in the NS-SEC: (1) higher managers and professionals, (2) lower managers and professionals, and (3) intermediate occupations. However, the small employer class is divided into two groups as (4) small employers excluding agriculture and (5) small employers in agriculture. Next, in descending order, are a merger of (6) lower supervisory and lower technicians, followed by separate classes for (7) lower services, sales, and clerical, (8) lower technical, and (9) routine. Eric Harrison and David Rose (2010: 41) point out that the "ESeC is rooted in the theory of employment relations which in turn are embedded in occupations. Thus while a fully accurate classification draws upon a number of labour market variables, operationally the primary driver of class is occupation."

Weber: status groups

Although occupational rank usually determines an individual's class position in European studies, American sociologists often use a broader definition advanced by Weber. Weber (1946, [1922] 1978) had agreed with Marx that a fundamental source of class differences was the unequal distribution of material goods. However, he pointed out that there was more to social stratification than wealth and advanced the idea, as noted earlier, of status groups to account for the other factors involved. Status groups were defined as communities of people linked together on the basis of similar wealth, status, and power.

Whereas wealth is an objective dimension of a person's social standing based upon how much money and property he or she possesses, status is a subjective dimension in that it consists largely of how much esteem the person is accorded by other people. Status indicates a person's level of social prestige, which may or may not correspond to wealth. In Weber's view, status is derived particularly from judgments about a person's lifestyle and also from that person's level of education and occupational rank. As Weber (1946: 187) explains, "status is normally expressed by the fact that above all else a specific *style of life* can be expected from all those who wish to belong to the circle." Lifestyles are based upon what people consume rather than what they produce. Thus, for Weber the difference between social classes did not lie in their relationship to the means of production as advocated by Marx, but in their relationship to the means of consumption. It is obvious to say that the affluent consume considerably more and higher quality resources than the poor.

To be part of a group or class and share its status means to live in the manner or style of that group or class. Even though a certain feature of a group's lifestyle, as Weber (1958) found in his analysis of the spread of the Protestant ethic of early Calvinists, may penetrate the boundaries of other groups and even become part of the general culture, different status groups tend to maintain distinct lifestyles. Therefore, people of a similar station in society generally share similar characteristics that are reflected in the way they live. As for power, Weber defined it as the ability to realize one's will even against the resistance of others. Weber was vague about what he meant by power in relation to status, but most sociologists agree that its contemporary meaning is the amount of political influence a person has or that person's authority to give other people orders. Power can be affected by wealth and status, status by wealth and power, and wealth by power and status, so all three variables are interrelated.

Weber's influence on modern studies of social stratification is seen in the widespread use of socioeconomic status (SES) in American sociology to determine a person's position in society. SES typically consists of measures of income, occupational prestige, and levels of education.

The advantage of using this scheme in quantitative studies is that the income, occupation (through the use of scales ranking occupational prestige), and years of education of an individual or head of household can all be assigned numbers with values that can be used statistically to analyze the effects of SES on dependent variables. Obviously, the higher the score, the higher the class position, and the lower the score, the lower the class position.

In studies of health and illness, income reflects spending power and quality of housing, diet, and medical care; occupation measures job status and level of responsibility at work, physical activity, and health risks associated with work; and education is indicative of a person's skills for acquiring positive social, psychological, and economic resources (Winkelby et al. 1992: 816).

While income and occupational rank are important, American studies often show that education is the strongest single SES predictor of good health (Mirowsky and Ross 2003a; Schnittker 2004). Education is such a strong variable in relation to health that Adriana Lleras-Muney (2005) investigated whether it has a casual effect on mortality. She found that between 1915 and 1939, some 30 states in the US changed their compulsory schooling and child labor laws to require children to stay in school longer. Some states had previously allowed children to drop out of school whenever they or their parents wanted in order to get a job, but the new compulsory laws required anywhere from four to ten years of schooling for everyone, depending on the state, and child labor laws that prevented employers from hiring them before this time. Lleras-Muney hypothesized that if education increases health, people living in states that required them to stay in school longer than other states should be relatively healthier and live longer.

Using US Census data from 1960, 1970, and 1980, she categorized persons who were 14 years of age between 1915 and 1939 into cohorts and calculated the mortality rates for each cohort. She then matched the cohorts with the compulsory school attendance and labor laws in force in their state of birth when they were 14 years old. "The results," state Lleras-Muney (2005: 191), "provide evidence that suggests there is a causal effect of education on mortality and that this effect is perhaps far larger than the previous literature suggests." In 1960, for instance, life expectancy at age 35 was extended by as much as 1.7 years by only one extra year of education. Lleras-Muney suggests that education provides individuals with critical thinking useful in producing health and that the more educated are more likely to adopt and use new medical technologies and drugs, and she calls for future research

to determine more precisely the pathways by which education influences health.

John Goldthorpe and Richard Breen (2000) observed that over
the last half of the twentieth century levels of education expanded in
all economically advanced societies. In the UK, for example, some 9
percent of the population had a university education in the 1960s compared to some 40 percent today. Thus younger persons in all classes
are likely to be better educated than in the past. Does this mean that
class differentials in health are disappearing? The answer is no, because
Goldthorpe and Breen find that class differences in educational attainment have tended to display a high degree of stability. That is, while
children of all classes have participated in the expansion of education,
the association between class origins and the relative probabilities of
attaining a higher education have been little altered in all societies
– with the exception of Sweden and perhaps the Netherlands and
Germany.

Therefore, the children of upper- and upper-middle-class parents
in almost all countries are still significantly more likely to acquire a
university-level education, while children from less advantaged classes
remain less likely to seek and obtain ambitious educational credentials.
However, one major change with respect to education is that from the
1970s onward Goldthorpe and Breen note that gender differentials in
educational attainment favoring males over females have either been
eliminated or even reversed in all advanced societies. So the expansion
of education has not meant the children from less advantaged families
are catching up with the children from more advantaged backgrounds
in their average levels of education, but rather that daughters in families across the class structure are rapidly catching up with sons.

The significance of persisting class differences in education signifies the continuation of class differentials in health. Highly educated
people typically have good health and poorly educated people do
not. Moreover, people who are well-educated, especially those with a
university education, are usually the best informed about the merits
of a healthy lifestyle consisting of exercise, not smoking, moderate
drinking, a healthy diet, and similar practices, along with knowing the
advantages of seeking preventive care and medical treatment for health
problems when they arise. They are also more likely to have well-paid
and more personally satisfying jobs, giving them better control over
their lives and the way they live.

John Mirowsky and Catherine Ross (2003a) determined that literally all the pathways from a good education to health are positive and
that higher-education and being healthy are virtually synonymous.

They found in every measure that American adults with a college education have better health than those with less education. Overall, Mirowsky and Ross (2003a: 49) conclude that: "The better-educated feel healthier, have less difficulty with common activities and tasks, more frequently feel vigorous and thriving, less often suffer aches, pains, malaise, less often feel worried or depressed, carry fewer diagnoses of threatening or debilitating disease, expect to live longer and probably will live longer."

In an earlier study in the United States, Ross and Chia-ling Wu (1995) compared people on the basis of their educational level and found that well-educated persons were the most likely to have subjectively rewarding jobs, high incomes, little economic hardship, and a greater sense of control over their lives and their health. They were also more likely to exercise, get periodic examinations from physicians, and drink alcohol moderately, while being less likely to smoke. The Ross and Wu study thus helped explain why the relationship between education and health is so strong. This relationship, in fact, gets stronger over the life course – producing a cumulative effect – as less educated persons have increasingly more sickness and die sooner than the well-educated (Lahelma 2010; Quesnel-Vallée and Jenkins 2010; Robert and House 2000). A recent nationwide study of coronary heart disease, for example, found that less educated persons had significantly greater odds of having a heart attack over their lifetime than the better educated (Kelly and Weitzen 2010).

A computation of age-adjusted mortality rates by years of educational attainment for the United States is shown in table 4.1 to demonstrate this point. Table 4.1 shows mortality from all causes for the years from 1994 to 2007. While not all states are included in the rates for 2003 and later, the pattern remains virtually unchanged. For both sexes, for each year, table 4.1 indicates that death rates were highest for persons with less than 12 years of education (less than a high school graduate), lower for those with 12 years (high school graduates), and lowest for persons with 13 or more years of education (some college and beyond). As seen in table 4.1 for 2007, mortality rates ranged from a high of 664.4 deaths per 100,000 persons in the population for those with less than 12 years of education to 477.0 for those with 12 years, followed by a steep drop-off to a low of 195.4 for persons with 13 years or more. Table 4.1 also shows the same pattern exists separately for both males and females and the results are even more striking. Males with less than 12 years of education have the highest death rates of all categories (799.3 per 100,000), with male high school graduates somewhat behind (606.3) and males with some college or more far behind

Table 4.1 Age-adjusted mortality by sex and years of education, all causes, United States, 1994–2007 (death per 100,000 population)

	Both sexes			Male			Female		
				Years of education					
	Less than 12	12	13 or more	Less than 12	12	13 or more	Less than 12	12	13 or more
1994	594.6	506.4	254.8	793.6	707.1	323.5	397.3	342.9	182.1
1995	604.7	512.5	251.9	801.1	713.2	316.8	408.6	348.1	183.5
1996	579.6	492.5	241.8	763.9	669.6	300.7	396.6	344.2	180.3
1997	554.1	473.4	232.7	719.7	634.4	283.4	387.2	337.5	180.2
1998	561.6	465.8	223.9	727.6	627.1	271.9	395.6	330.9	174.3
1999	585.3	474.5	219.1	763.7	636.7	264.2	409.9	337.3	172.6
2000	591.0	484.5	216.7	780.2	641.8	260.8	409.0	347.7	171.9
2001	576.6	480.9	214.6	745.8	631.2	257.3	407.1	348.6	171.5
2002	575.1	490.9	211.3	726.1	650.2	253.5	416.6	350.7	168.8
2003*	669.9	490.9	211.7	826.8	650.9	252.5	496.8	349.4	171.0
2004**	667.2	477.1	208.3	838.7	618.8	250.7	486.2	344.9	166.7
2005#	650.4	477.6	206.3	821.4	605.8	249.4	471.7	352.3	164.9
2006**	685.8	482.5	197.6	841.5	613.5	238.5	506.7	354.3	159.1
2007##	664.4	477.0	195.4	799.3	606.3	234.6	503.1	349.9	158.2

Note: This table reports figures from the National Center for Health Statistics (2010) using the 1989 version of the US Standard Certificate of Death with varying number of states adopting the new method in 2003. * 43 reporting states. ** 36 reporting states. # 31 reporting states. ## 22 reporting states.

(234.6). For females, the less educated have death rates of 503.1 per 100,000, followed by 349.9 for high school graduates, and a low of 158.2 for those with some college and beyond.

The widespread use of SES to determine a person's location in a social structure would seem to suggest that the term "status groups" would be preferred over that of "class" if a purely Weberian approach to analyzing social structures was followed. Weber ([1922] 1978) viewed "classes" as aggregates of people with similar life chances determined strictly by the possession of goods and opportunities for income that were distinct from considerations of status. However, Weber's notion of status groups did not take precedence over the use of the term "social class" in either sociological or lay discussions. The term "class" in its popular usage came to incorporate notions of status and power within it, even though Weber himself had not done so. Thus we see, for example, that Bourdieu (1984) links class and status in a complementary fashion in grounding the prestige associated with particular lifestyles with the material conditions that support it. Consequently, David Swartz (1997: 45) notes that: "Status groups and status distinctions are [actually] classes and class distinctions in disguise." In effect, the terms class and SES are popularly regarded as the same thing, although it can be argued by academics that this is not exactly what Weber meant.

The end of class?

There have been suggestions that class is an outmoded nineteenth-century concept becoming less relevant as society changes over time into a late modern form (Kingston 2000; Pakulski and Waters 1996). The spread of lifestyles across class boundaries, changes in occupational structures generated by the demise of mass-production industries, the entry of large numbers of females into the labor force, and increased individualization in daily life are all cited as reasons for the declining significance of class. However, despite these developments, the evidence is too strong to downgrade the effects of class position on people's lives in general and their health in particular. As Crompton (2008) concludes, there is simply insufficient evidence for the rejection of class as a dated concept. Study after study underscores the fact that class matters greatly (Adonis and Pollard 1997; Crompton 2008; Lareau and Conley 2008; Marmot 2004; Reid 1998).

Therefore, as will be discussed in this chapter, class not only remains an important force in causing good or bad health, susceptibility to or avoidance of disease, and early or late mortality, but it is in fact the most powerful social structural determinant of a long and healthy life.

The Social Gradient in Mortality

Some of the strongest evidence demonstrating the causal strength of social class in health situations comes from the research of Marmot and his colleagues (1984, 1991; Banks et al. 2006; Marmot 2004). Marmot et al. (1984, 1991) investigated the mortality of about 18,000 British male civil government employees that showed a distinct social gradient in longevity. Known as the Whitehall I study, the men were classified according to their occupational status, with senior administrators ranked at the top; followed by professionals (such as scientists, economists, and statisticians) and executives who implement policies; clerical workers (who handled the paperwork); and other (which consisted of jobs lowest in status, such as messengers, porters, and various other unskilled manual workers). The senior administrators were men that Marmot (2004: 40) describes as "high flyers" who became the permanent secretaries running the various government ministries and responsible for working with elected politicians and appointed cabinet ministers to help formulate policy. He says they likely had graduated from either Oxford or Cambridge universities, excelled on the entrance exams, and entered the civil service on a fast track. One such man was identified to Marmot (2004: 40) simply as: "That's R. Reached the top without touching the sides."

In the first Whitehall study, these men, whose ages at the time ranged from 40 to 64 were initially interviewed in the late 1960s with respect to their health practices and then reinvestigated ten years later in relation to mortality. Regardless of the cause of death, those with the highest occupational rank had the lowest percentage of deaths, and the percentages increased the lower the rank, with the lowest-ranked occupations having the highest percentage of deceased civil servants.

Marmot (1996) states that it seemed unlikely at the time that social class differences in mortality would be as large for the civil servants as they were in the country as a whole. It was thought that civil servants would live longer than the general population, regardless of rank, because all the jobs were stable, provided security, and were free of chemical and physical hazards. Yet Marmot (1996: 43) observes that he and his associates were surprised "to discover that the nearly three-fold difference in mortality between the top and bottom grades of the civil service was larger than the difference between the top and bottom social classes in national mortality data." As one observer (Epstein 1998: 27) put it:

> Perhaps the most surprising finding of the Whitehall study at the time was that everyone in the hierarchy seemed to be vulnerable to the effects of social status, not just those at the bottom. Even a small increment in social status could be reflected in statistics on life and death. For example, "administrators," those in the civil service who design policies and set the strategies for executing them, were half as likely to have a fatal heart attack as the "executives" who ran the various departments and carried out the policies dictated to them by the administrators. For the clerks, who worked for the executives, the risk of a fatal heart attack was three times as high as it was for the administrators.
>
> The risk of dying of a heart attack increased steadily, right down the chain of command. For the remaining support staff, such as assistant clerks and data processors, the risk was four times as high as for the administrators. These were middle-class people, and yet all of them seemed to be part of some mortality gradient. In his book *Unhealthy Societies* (1996), Wilkinson writes that if a virus or something was killing as many civil servants as the professional hierarchy itself seemed to be, the Whitehall buildings would be evacuated and shut down.

This pattern is seen in table 4.2, showing mortality percentages from the Whitehall I study. Most of the deaths had been from heart disease and table 4.2 shows, for example, that 2.16 percent of the senior administrators had died from this cause and the percentage of deaths increased across all job ranks with the lowest category of "other" showing the highest percentage of 6.59. The results were the same for all of the other causes of death, including various cancers, stroke and other cardiovascular ailments, bronchitis and other respiratory diseases, accidents/violence, suicide, and other health problems. The higher the occupational rank, the lower the percentage of deaths and, conversely, the lower the rank, the higher the percentage of deaths. When deaths from all causes were combined, table 4.2 shows that 4.73 percent of the senior administrators died compared to 8.00 percent of the professionals/executives in the second category, 11.67 percent of the third-rung clerical workers, and 15.64 percent of the other occupations at the bottom.

Marmot and his associates (1991) conducted a second study to check their results that included women and found the same pattern. As in the first study, each occupational category had higher mortality than the one above it in the social hierarchy. What Marmot and his associates had uncovered was striking evidence of a social gradient from low to high in mortality. "In the higher grades of the civil service," states

Table 4.2 Percentage of British civil government employees dying over a
ten-year period (1969–1979) by civil service grade and cause of death

Cause of death	Senior administrators	Professional/ Executive	Clerical	Other
Lung cancer	0.35	0.73	1.47	2.33
Other cancer	1.26	1.70	2.16	2.23
Heart disease	2.16	3.58	4.90	6.59
Stroke	0.13	0.49	0.64	0.58
Other cardiovascular	0.40	0.54	0.72	0.85
Chronic bronchitis	0.00	0.08	0.43	0.65
Other respiratory	0.21	0.22	0.52	0.87
Gastrointestinal	0.00	0.13	0.20	0.45
Genitourinary	0.09	0.09	0.07	0.24
Accidents/violence	0.00	0.13	0.17	0.20
Suicide	0.11	0.14	0.15	0.25
Other deaths	0.00	0.16	0.26	0.40
All causes	4.73	8.00	11.67	15.64

Source: Adapted from M. G. Marmot, M. J. Shipley, and Geoffrey Rose,
"Inequalities in Death – Specific Explanations of a General Pattern," *Lancet*
83 (1984): 1004.

Marmot (1996: 48), "there is no poverty, yet those who are near the top
have worse health than those at the top and the gradient continues all
the way down." An intriguing aspect of this research is the finding of
a social gradient linked to differences in hierarchy rather than deprivation. As noted, all of these persons had stable, secure, and hazard-free
jobs. They were all white-collar workers, most were Anglo-Saxon,
many wore the same dark suits and had similar haircuts, and almost
everyone was middle class. They all had access to free health care
provided by the British National Health Service. There were some differences, however, as those with the highest ranked job positions had
larger houses, all owned cars, and they smoked less and were slimmer
overall. And, of course, they lived longer.

When the social gradient in mortality is extended from the Whitehall
studies to society generally, the pattern is the same: the upper class has
the lowest mortality, the upper-middle class the next lowest, and so on
down the social scale until the lower class is reached (Banks et al. 2006;
Evans et al. 1994; Marmot 2004). So it is not only the case that people
at the top of society live longer on average than those at the bottom,
but also that the different classes live less longer than those above them
and have greater longevity than those below them. Whereas the

differences between the upper and lower classes are both extreme and obvious – what is particularly revealing about the strength of the social gradient is the fact that the upper class enjoys better health and longevity than the upper-middle class just below them, even though both are distinctly affluent.

Interestingly, the results of the Whitehall studies are not inconsistent with a study of physiological changes associated with social status among rhesus macaque monkeys by Jenny Tung and her associates (2012). Some 49 female rhesus monkeys were divided into groups of four to five each and their social status was controlled by the order in which they entered the group (newcomers tended to be subordinate to established group members). High- and low-status monkeys subsequently showed different levels of gene activity in responsiveness to glucocorticoids (a class of hormones) which regulate the immune system and responses to stress. Differences in blood samples also correlated with social rank with 80 percent certainty. When a few monkeys changed status within their groups over the course of the experiment, changes in gene activity appropriate to the new status soon emerged. "These results," state Tung et al. (2012: 1), "illuminate the importance of molecular response to social conditions, particularly in the immune system, and demonstrate a key role for gene regulation in linking the social environment to individual physiology."

The Whitehall studies are important because they show position in a social hierarchy does affect health either positively or negatively. This circumstance has persisted despite the transition from acute to chronic disease and improved access to medical care. The next step is to determine the social mechanisms behind the gradient. Marmot, in considering the epidemiological triad of agent, environment, and host, focuses on the environment. Marmot (2004: 33) states that the social gradient is caused by people in different social groups being exposed to different social and economic conditions and "it is these differences in the social environment that are responsible for the gradient." Group differences are depicted as outweighing individual differences in producing health outcomes, but such differences are not produced just by a person's material circumstances. Rather, a host of other factors are also identified as contributing to the gradient, such as self-esteem, status differences, self-direction in work, control over one's environment, social capital, and sense of social support – all variables which decline in strength as one descends the social ladder.

For example, one of the more interesting studies cited by Marmot is that of Canadian researchers Donald Redelmeier and Sheldon Singh (2001) who calculated that the actors and actresses who won Oscars for best acting in films over a 72-year period lived four years longer on average than other actors and actresses who either were in the same film with the Oscar winner or had been nominated but never won. It was not the case that people who lived longer were more likely to win Oscars (since young and middle-age persons often win), rather it was that winning seemed to prolong their lives. When the winners did die, they generally died from the same causes as the non-winners, only not as soon. This study supported the thesis that a person's position in a hierarchy relative to other people and their feelings about it is important for their health. Feeling good about who you are may help you live longer.

Another study is that of Canadian economist Robert Evans and his associates (1994) who suggest that stress helps shape the social gradient in mortality. After reviewing numerous studies of both humans and primates, Evans et al. determined that social rank could be correlated with the ability to handle stress. The higher one's position in a social hierarchy, the better a person can deal with stressful situations and the effects of stress on the body. This is because the level of stress experienced, the amount of resources available to cope with stress, and the degree of control over one's life situation all vary by social class position. Evans et al. suggest it is the quality of the "microenvironment" (defined as relations at home and work) that provides a buffer to stress or facilitates its transformation into a less harmful experience. It is the enhanced capability to deal with stress that may underlie the mortality differential between the upper class and the upper-middle class and especially between the upper class and the lower class in the social gradient.

Evans et al. likely overstep their analysis, however, when they highlight Japan as an important example of the social gradient thesis. They link Japan's rise in the late twentieth century to the top ranks of the economic hierarchy of nations to its dramatic rise to the top in life expectancy. Evans et al. maintain that Japan's rapid economic growth and striking success in world trade promoted a strong sense of self-esteem that yielded health benefits. Russia, on the other hand, descended in the same hierarchy after the collapse of the former Soviet Union and experienced a major decline in male longevity. While this comparison has a logical appeal in support of the social gradient concept, the present author and his Japanese colleagues (Cockerham, Hattori, and Yamori 2000) found that it did not apply to life expectancy and the rank order of Japan's prefectures (provinces). The highest life expectancy in Japan, especially females, has traditionally been in Okinawa Prefecture which was last in per capita income. Okinawa, however, has some special characteristics like close-knit families, healthy diets, and a lack of urban stress. Okinawa is also not poor and the fact that social gradient theory does not apply to intermediate state units like prefectures reflecting a diverse array of macro-level social, cultural, and economic variables in an affluent country like Japan, does not negate the social gradient with respect to class.

In other research in Britain, where the various classes tend to be spatially segregated by neighborhood, geographer Mary Shaw and her colleagues (Shaw, Dorling, and Brimblecombe 1998) found a social gradient in mortality reflected in housing patterns. In fact, Shaw et al. not only supported other studies showing deaths in disadvantaged neighborhoods were excessive in comparison to more affluent areas, but concluded that mortality rates by area have been polarizing in Britain. "Indeed," states Shaw et al. (1998: 705), "the extent of inequality in Britain is so strong that, if the Registrar General of 1951 were to repeat the study of mortality carried out then, he would no doubt be shocked by the extent, persistence and widening of the basic divide in British Society."

Other studies that explicitly investigate the social gradient in relation to various aspects of health include a comparison of the United States and England in which a steeper social gradient in health was found among Americans than the English (Banks et al. 2006). In Canada, a clear gradient in poor self-rated health was observed as well as higher exposure to stress with decreasing SES (Orpana and Lemyre 2004) and poorer health was found as income, levels of personal control, and social support decrease (Kosteniuk and Dickinson 2003). In Great Britain, other research identified a social gradient in psychological distress from low to high among women of different classes (Matthews and Power 2002), and in Sweden, an occupational gradient in coronary heart disease from low to high was found for women (Wamala et al. 2000). In Spain, research on deaths from all causes among males aged 35–64 years in 1996 found that mortality along occupational and especially educational lines matched the social gradient, with higher-level professionals having the lowest mortality (Regidor et al. 2005).

While the precise pathways through which social mechanisms trigger health and mortality patterns along socioeconomic lines need to be more fully ascertained, the existence of the social gradient and its effects on health are difficult to dispute. Virtually all studies confirm the health advantages and disadvantages supplied by class position. The lower class without exception has the worst health and shortest life spans as seen in studies conducted in the United States (Phelan et al. 2004; Robert 1998; Wray et al. 1998), Canada (Humphries and

Van Doorslaer 2000), Great Britain (Arber 1997; Borooah 1999; Chandola 2000; Marmot 2004), Britain and Finland (Lahelma et al. 2000; Rahkonen et al. 2002), Finland and Norway (Sihvonen et al. 1998), Sweden (Hemström 1999), Germany (Mielck et al. 2000), Spain (Antunes 2011; Regidor et al. 2005), Spain and France (Lostao et al. 2001), Russia and Eastern Europe (Bobak et al. 1998; Cockerham 1999; Shkolnikov et al. 1998), and throughout Western Europe (Kunst et al. 1998; Whitehead 1990). An even more extreme pattern of social disadvantages in health and longevity exists in Latin America, much of Asia, and especially Africa (Wermuth 2003). We will now examine some of the studies that assign class a causal role in health and disease.

Confirming the Relationship

Decades of study in medical sociology have linked social factors to health and disease (Cockerham 2012). As Link and Phelan (1995) point out, the most obvious and strongest relationship is that between health and socioeconomic status. They point out that medical soci- ologists and some epidemiologists have moved away from simply describing the social patterning of disease toward identifying social structural health risk factors that cannot have been caused by an indi- vidual's illness condition. Two American studies they cite are those of Lee Hamilton et al. (1990) and Rudy Fenwick and Mark Tausig (1994). Hamilton and his associates compared the health effects on auto workers of the closing of their plant to workers at other plants who were uncertain they might be laid off or knew for sure their plant was not closing. Among the workers who lost their jobs, those who were racial minorities and especially of low SES suffered the greatest adverse health consequences. The illness conditions of the workers did not cause the plant closing; rather, the plant closing had caused the illness conditions of the workers. Fenwick and Tausig also inves- tigated unemployment among workers and found unemployment was not caused by the workers' ill health, but the workers' ill health was brought on by being unemployed.

More recently, as discussed in chapter 1, Phelan et al. (2004) showed how people in higher social strata used their resources to be more successful in averting preventable causes of death than persons lower down the social scale who were more likely to die of such causes. Also, Lutfey and Freese (2005) were able to successfully demonstrate how high SES diabetic patients controlled their blood sugar levels sig- nificantly better and had better survival prospects than patients from socially disadvantaged backgrounds. Again, in each study, it was not a particular disease causing the different health outcomes, but class position.

Another relevant American study is that of physician researcher Mehdi Shishehbor and his colleagues published in *JAMA* (2006) who investigated the relationship of SES with functional capacity, heart rate recovery, and all cause mortality of nearly 25,000 patients from surrounding counties tested at the Cleveland Clinic in Ohio. Lower SES patients had significantly greater physical incapacity, lessened heart rate recovery following peak exercise, and much higher mortality from all causes, not just from cardiovascular disease. An interesting facet of this study is that the researchers were able to successfully match 3,579 patients in the lowest quartile of SES scores with 3,579 patients in the highest quartile with respect to age, male sex, race, and smoking status. They determined that being in the lowest quartile of SES scores was *independently* associated with greater impaired functional capacity and abnormal heart rate recovery, and was predictive of increased mortality. Shishehbor et al. (2006: 790) concluded that: "the current findings support strategies that extend targets for interventions beyond purely biological characteristics of individuals to those addressing social or economic factors that influence health."

How persistent is the relationship between health and class? A comparative study in Germany by health services researcher Andreas Mielck and his associates (2000) provides important evidence. They sought to determine whether health inequalities varied between eastern and western Germany and if they were caused by social inequalities. "It is particularly interesting to compare health inequalities between East and West Germany," state Mielck et al. (2000: 262), "as both shared a long period of common history and culture, then experienced very different [communist and capitalist] socioeconomic and health care systems for approximately 45 years, and are now merging into one system again, accompanied by severe social problems which are mainly in the Eastern part." In East Germany, after it became communist, the government firmly adopted a state socialist ideology oriented toward ending class differences. East Germany recognized itself as a "class-like" society; that is, it was not a "class" society because class antagonisms and exploitation had officially ended but the Marxist stage of being a "classless" society had not been fully realized because some class distinctions remained (Dennis 1985).

The study, taken in the aftermath of the collapse of the East German state in 1991, compared a population in which class distinctions were deliberately modified to a Western population in which no attempt had been made to alter the pattern of class stratification. The data, obtained from household surveys conducted throughout Germany, showed that while there were no significant differences in the extent of health inequalities between the former communist East Germany and capitalist West Germany, upper socioeconomic strata in both parts of the country were nevertheless healthier than their counterparts in the classes below them.

Medical Care as an Intervening Variable?

Since the social gradient in health and mortality is so enduring, it is a logical assumption that if quality medical care was available to people at the bottom of the social scale their disadvantaged health position would change. In 1948, socialized medicine was initiated in Great Britain intended to equalize care throughout the social structure. A national health service (NHS) was created by the central government as it took control of the nation's health care delivery system. The NHS made medical services more accessible to the general population and established one of the most egalitarian health systems in the world. The lower classes had access to the same medical services as the upper class, but their respective social circumstances remained the same.

The assumption that health care alone could eliminate or reduce class differences in health proved to be wrong. The publication of the Black Report in 1980 shattered this illusion. The Black Report found that although the health and life expectancy of the entire nation had improved, a very large gap between the upper and lower classes had not only persisted but widened. The lower class had the highest rates of illness, disability, and infant mortality and the lowest life expectancy. The lower class also used prenatal and preventive health services less frequently than members of the other classes. Although medical treatment was equalized and subsequently utilized more often by the poor, their use of services was directed largely toward treatment rather than prevention. The Black Report provided strong evidence that the lower a person is on the social scale, the less healthy that person is likely to be and the sooner he or she can expect to die.

As Mel Bartley and her colleagues David Blane and George Davey Smith (1998: 564) noted, this outcome "was shocking to some and to others simply unbelievable. How could this be happening in a Britain that had 'never had it so good,' in which the political complaints given greatest expression dealt with excessive equalization, too much public spending, and excessive generosity to the poor." The Black Report, along with two other national studies, showed that the health inequalities were not the result of statistical bias, but did in fact exist. One of these studies, the Office of National Statistics' Longitudinal Study in 1982, showed that health inequalities in Britain were continuing to widen (A. Fox and Goldblatt 1982). The other was a re-examination in the mid-1990s of respondents from the 1946 National Study of Health and Development and the 1958 National Child Development Study that determined unhealthy children were significantly less likely to be upwardly mobile in society and acquire a better social station in life (C. Power and Matthews 1997; C. Power, Matthews, and Manor 1996).

Sally Macintyre (1997) observed that the Black Report had a major impact on research concerning class differences in health in Britain. It was not, she points out, either the first or the last word on the subject. "It was preceded," Macintyre (1997: 723) says, "by some 140 years of concern with socio-economic differentials in death rates, and it was followed by an intense period of empirical and conceptual research on the subject." The Black Report laid the blame for the persistence of class differences in levels of health directly on the socioeconomic environment, citing such factors as smoking, work accidents, overcrowding, poor living conditions, overexposure to cold and dampness and the like as responsible for the gap. An update of the Black Report ten years later in 1990 showed that the same conditions persisted (Whitehead 1990). Even though the health of the British population in general and the lower class in particular continued to improve, serious class disparities remained. The conclusion was:

1 Whether social position is measured by occupational status, or by assets, such as house and car ownership, or by employment status, a similar picture emerges. Those at the bottom of the social scale have much higher death rates than those at the top. This applies at every stage of life from birth through to adulthood and well into old age.
2 Neither is it just a few specific conditions that account for these higher death rates. All the major killer diseases now affect the poor more than the rich (and so do most of the less common ones). The less-favored occupational classes also experience higher rates of chronic sickness and their children tend to have lower birth-weights, shorter stature and other indicators suggesting poorer health habits.
3 The unemployed and their families have considerably worse physical and mental health than those in work. Until recently, however, direct evidence that unemployment *caused* this poorer health was not available. Now there is substantial evidence of unemployment

causing a deterioration in mental health, with improvements on re-employment. (Whitehead 1990: 351–2)

Whereas improved access to quality medical care by the lower class has undoubtedly assisted many of the poor in having better health relative to people in the classes above them, the fact remains that medicine alone has not been able to reduce the disparity in health between the British social classes. This is because living conditions and negative health lifestyles could not be equalized as well. After the poor are treated by physicians for their ailments, they return to their usual social environments featuring dwellings that are damp, inadequately heated, and perhaps moldy and infested with lice and mites, in which colds, bronchitis, skin diseases, allergies, and other ailments are commonplace. They still consume the same less-healthy diets lacking fresh fruits and vegetables and featuring high-fat meats and fried cheap foods, lack exercise, and either smoke and heavily consume alcohol or live where exposure to the smoking of others or the adverse consequences of drunkenness like accidents and violence are likely. In circumstances such as these, the capability of medicine to intervene to produce good health is significantly undermined.

Conclusion

Social class position undoubtedly plays a causal role in the distribution of health and disease in human populations and likely has done so since the beginning of large stratified societies. To maintain that class is merely associated with or linked to health as a background variable is to overlook the power of class to sort people into social categories that enjoy health and longevity or reduce their potential to do so in a top-down stepwise fashion. This enduring outcome is aptly expressed by the social gradient in health and longevity. The next chapter will examine the various explanations of the relationship.

Suggested Further Reading

Lahelma, Eero. 2010. "Health and Social Stratification." In *The New Blackwell Companion to Medical Sociology*, ed. William Cockerham, 71–96. Oxford, UK: Wiley-Blackwell.
Provides an overview of the relationship between health and social class in an international context. Discusses both the pat-

terns of health by class and the causes and explanations for the differences.

Marmot, Michael. 2004. *The Status Syndrome: How Social Standing Affects Our Health and Longevity.* New York: Times Books.
Marmot discusses the evidence showing the importance of class and social status for health, well-being, and life expectancy. Explains that where you are located in a social hierarchy affects how long you will live.

5

Class and Health: Explaining the Relationship

For over 50 years, medical sociology has mapped out the social configurations of disease and the most obvious pattern is that initiated by social class. The enduring outcome of good health at the top of society and worse health in descending order at the bottom marks class as a "fundamental cause" of health, disease, and death in human populations. As previously stipulated by Link and Phelan (1995: 87), the requirements that a social variable must meet to qualify as a fundamental cause are fourfold: (1) influencing multiple diseases through (2) multiple pathways of risk that are (3) reproduced over time and (4) involve access to resources that can be used to avoid these risks or minimize the consequences if they should occur. Class or socioeconomic status clearly meets each of these requirements.

Req. of Social Variables

While health is a social problem throughout the world because it is spread unevenly in all human societies, the provision of health care – as the American situation illustrates – is also a problem when costs and availability act as obstructions to medical treatment. The health care systems in the United States and Great Britain will be contrasted in this chapter as one provides national health insurance and the other does not, but the focus is on examining various pathways of risk through which class causes the unequal distribution of health – since this circumstance precedes problems in obtaining care and promotes the differential need for such care. We will see that class acts similarly upon health in both countries, although the health care delivery systems vary.

This chapter will also explore some of the multiple pathways in which class exercises potency in determining health outcomes, such as through stress and culture, followed by an examination of the role of class in inducing health practices like smoking and conditions like obesity that cause death. While people can exercise agency and make their own choices about their health, class provides some individuals more options than others making it difficult if not impossible to avoid the structural constraints and enablements associated with social hierarchies. This chapter provides illustrations of this process.

Class, Health, and Medical Care in the United States

As elsewhere in the world, class is the strongest and most consistent social predictor of health and longevity in the United States. Traditionally the poor have had the worst health and shortest lives. For example, rates of coronary heart disease – the nation's leading killer – have declined for all Americans, but the decrease has been greatest for the upper and middle classes. Fifty-five years ago, coronary heart disease was associated with an affluent way of life (e.g., rich diets, smoking, well-paid but stressful jobs). However, as the affluent became more knowledgeable about heart disease, began to practice healthier lifestyles, and routinely sought preventive care in the form of medical checkups and drugs to reduce high blood pressure and harmful low-density lipoprotein cholesterol levels, heart disease was postponed until later in life or avoided altogether. Preventive health care has never been a trait of help-seeking among the lower classes, who typically wait to visit physicians until they feel bad, are less likely to have a regular physician familiar with their medical history and lifestyle, and are more likely to go to a hospital emergency room to see whatever doctor is on duty when sick (Cockerham 2012).

Other heart disease risk factors reflected by class position are seen in studies showing the lower class has the steepest decline in physical activity in adulthood (Grzywacz and Marks 2001), as well as greater stress, inadequate diets and housing, and more alcohol abuse and smoking (Link and Phelan 2000; Mirowsky, Ross, and Reynolds 2000; Ross and Mirowsky 2001; Ross and Wu 1995). The result is that coronary heart disease is now concentrated more among the poor.

The shift in the quantity of heart disease downward in American society lodges its prevalence solidly within the social pattern of the other chronic and communicable diseases that likewise reside more substantially in the lower class. The lower class is also disadvantaged with respect to mental health. The basic finding of most studies is that highest overall rates of mental disorder are found in the lower class – including schizophrenia – the most severely disabling form of mental affliction (Cockerham 2010b; Kessler et al. 1994). Anxiety and mood disorders, however, tend to be more prevalent among the upper and middle classes, yet the lower class suffers from these problems as well. Whether the disparities in mental health are due to genetics or greater stress in coping with the deprivations of lower class living or a combination, or another variable is not known. Nevertheless, for mental as well as physical difficulties, socioeconomic factors are major determinants of the types and extent of an individual's health problems.

Moreover, the lower class has historically not received the same quality of medical care available to the classes above it because they lacked the money or health insurance to pay for care in the American fee-for-service health care delivery system. The poor often relied on charity care or teaching hospitals to meet their needs. Much of the literature in American medical sociology in the 1950s and early 1960s documented the problems of the poor in obtaining quality medical care. This situation changed in 1965 with the passage of two federally sponsored health insurance programs: Medicare for persons over the age of 65 years and Medicaid for people with the lowest incomes. The passage of these two health insurance programs over the strong opposition of the American Medical Association, who wanted to keep government out of medicine, signaled a turning point in medical politics: the federal government emerged as a dominant actor in health care delivery for the first time.

Medicare and Medicaid not only set the precedent for the federal government's involvement in health care delivery, but the programs provided needed public health insurance coverage for the elderly and persons living in poverty that was previously unavailable. Prior to this time, the upper class made more visits to physicians for care than the other social classes, followed by the middle classes, with the lower class seeing doctors least often. This pattern changed temporarily in the late 1960s, with the upper class seeing doctors the least and the middle class seeing them the most. However, as the lower class increasingly took advantage of the new insurance programs, they replaced the middle class – in a pattern that continues today – as the strata utilizing physician services the most. This is appropriate because they have the worst health problems overall, but indications are that they should visit doctors even more often because they still tend to delay in seeking care until their health worsens (Cockerham 2012). Part of the delay stems from the lack of treatment facilities in poor neighborhoods (Robert and House 2000).

Even though health care has become more accessible for the lower class in the United States, equity has not been achieved. In a free market system lacking national health insurance covering the general population, those persons who are socially disadvantaged are also medically disadvantaged. The United States has a two-track system of medical care: public and private. The public track is a system of welfare medicine supported by Medicare and Medicaid. The urban poor have traditionally been dependent on public – state, county, or municipal – hospitals and clinics, and this situation has not changed. Often these facilities are underfinanced, understaffed, and overcrowded with patients. Few hospitals exist in inner-city areas or neighborhoods populated by the poor. The rural poor also have problems of access, as doctors and hospitals may not be readily available where they live.

The problems of access, high costs, and availability of quality care are compounded by the large percentages of Americans without health insurance. Table 5.1 shows that in 2009, some 17.7 percent of the population between the ages of 18 and 64 years did not have health insurance. This includes 34.3 percent of all Hispanics and 32.5 percent of Native Americans in this age group, followed by 19.5 percent of non-Hispanic blacks, 17.3 percent of non-Hispanic whites, and 15.7 percent of Asian Americans. Only some 36 percent of all Native Americans and 38.9 percent of Hispanics had private health insurance compared to 65.5 percent of non-Hispanic whites, 71.1 percent of Asians, and 47.7 percent of non-Hispanic blacks. When it comes to Medicaid that pays for treatment needed by the poor, 27.9 percent of non-Hispanic blacks had this coverage, followed by 24.4 percent of Native Americans and 24.1 percent of Hispanics.

People without health insurance are typically the near-poor who work in low-income jobs and whose employers do not provide such insurance. Their annual family income is often less than $25,000, which may be too much money to allow them to qualify for Medicaid and too little for them to afford health insurance for themselves and their families. And, particularly in the case of some Hispanics, they may be illegal immigrants ineligible for welfare benefits or reluctant to expose their presence to government agencies. The near or working poor who have jobs and "are playing by the rules" are employed, pay taxes, and are productive members of the economy, yet their employers may not provide health insurance which leaves them on their own financially in paying for health care (Seccombe and Amey 1995: 179).

An effort to remedy this situation took place in 2010 when Congress passed the Patient Protection and Affordable Care Act and President Barak Obama signed the measure into law. The full force of the

Table 5.1 Health insurance coverage for persons under 65 years of age, Hispanic origin, and race, United States, 2009

Insurance type	Total US %	White non-Hispanic %	Black non-Hispanic %	Hispanic %	Asian %	Native American %	Pacific Islander %
Private	63.0	65.5	47.7	38.9	71.1	36.0	51.5
Medicaid	15.8	13.8	27.9	24.1	10.3	24.4	10.6
Other public	3.4	3.2	4.9	2.7	2.9	4.1	10.3
Uninsured	17.7	17.3	19.5	34.3	15.7	32.5	27.6

Source: National Center for Health Statistics 2010.

legislation was not scheduled to take effect until 2014, although some measures began immediately. Among its major provisions were (1) the stipulation that pre-existing medical conditions could no longer be used to deny coverage; (2) all health insurance plans had to provide at least a minimum level of benefits set by the federal government; (3) state insurance exchanges were to be established to offer competitive health plans at affordable prices that could be purchased by anyone under age 65, including people without employer provided insurance; (4) employers with more than 50 workers were to be fined if they did not provide health insurance for their employees; (5) government subsidies would be available to help low-income persons purchase policies; (6) Medicaid was to be expanded to cover more of the poor; (7) children could remain on their parent's health plans until age 26; and, finally, in a particularly controversial measure, (8) most Americans *(repealed)* would be required by law to purchase health insurance or face tax penalties. It was estimated that with this legislation some 95 percent of the American population would be covered by health insurance by 2019.

There was intense opposition to the legislation – called "Obamacare" by its opponents – first in Congress and later after its passage. Weighed against providing health insurance coverage for more of the uninsured was the largest federal budget deficit in history, a major economic recession and high unemployment, higher taxes for Medicare, a rise in costs for Medicare beneficiaries, and the legal requirement to purchase health insurance. Some 26 states joined in a lawsuit to challenge the federal law requiring Americans to have health insurance by claiming it is unconstitutional to make people buy commercial goods or services as a condition of lawful residence in the United States. The federal government countered that it has the authority to regulate interstate commerce, including the health care market, and, moreover, has broad powers of taxation that allow it to assign an income tax penalty for noncompliance. The US Supreme Court made the final decision on the constitutionality of the health care reform act in mid-2012 by ruling in a 5–4 decision that the law was indeed constitutional because the penalty for noncompliance qualified as a tax.

Class, Health, and Medical Care in Great Britain

Class differences in mortality have been observed in Britain since the first Registrar-General's Occupational Analysis of 1851 that continues into the twenty-first century. The negative gradient in mortality by class has been evident from the beginning of statistical record-keeping and persisted even though life expectancy for the entire population continued to improve through the years. The social gradient in mortality exists for infants, as well as children and adults. The gradient not only reflects class differences in mortality, but also in injury and morbidity as injuries and sickness decrease the higher the social ladder is climbed (Marmot 2004; Reid 1998). Earlier in the twentieth century, heart disease was an exception to the general pattern in that the affluent were more prone to this ailment and other cardiovascular problems than manual workers. By the early 1970s, as in the United States, the situation was reversed, with heart disease now far more prevalent at the bottom of the class structure. Consequently, the epidemiological transition in Britain from acute to chronic diseases as the major cause of mortality did not alleviate the health circumstances of the poor. Heart disease shifted more strongly into their ranks than ever before.

The reasons for this development were social and due to differences in living conditions and class-based health lifestyles with respect to alcohol use, smoking, diet, and exercise – especially leisure-time exercise unaccompanied by the stress and strain of manual labor and deadlines, quotas, demands, and schedules for physical outputs mandated by others. More judicious use of physician services, particularly preventive care by the affluent, was also important. Britain is of special interest in studies of class and health because the country established equity in health care. Since 1948, as noted in the last chapter, Britain has had a national health service providing the lower class with medical care similar to people higher on the social scale. Services are essentially free at the point of contact between patient and provider and the care rendered is generally paid out of government tax revenues and deductions from salaries and wages for national health insurance.

A major assumption was that the provision of quality care to all classes would improve levels of health throughout society, as poverty would no longer prevent someone from obtaining professional medical treatment. Health did improve for all classes. But, again as discussed in the last chapter, the British public was surprised by the Black Report in 1980 that disclosed the *gap* in health between the classes still prevailed. Current studies show that despite the continued upward trend in life expectancy, the highest social strata not only live much longer than the lowest, but the gap is widening (Bury 2005; Nettleton 2006; Popay and Williams 2009).

That is, the upper class has even greater longevity in relation to the lower class than it did in the recent past, despite improvement for all classes. A government report showed, for example, that in a single decade (1977–81 to 1987–91), males in the two highest classes gained an additional year of life expectancy over men in the two lowest classes, while upper strata women added an additional 1.3 years – even though there was equitable health care for all (Drever and Whitehead 1997). In addition to less life expectancy, the lower classes still have higher infant mortality, more chronic disability, more absence from work due to illness, and higher ratios of risk behavior like obesity, lack of exercise, and smoking. While the United States is striving to gain greater class equality in health insurance coverage, the United Kingdom has had it for over 60 years and class differences in health and mortality remain strong. It was thought that free health services in the UK would improve levels of health throughout the class structure, as an inability to pay would no longer prevent people from obtaining professional medical treatment. All classes experienced an improvement in health, but class differences remained. The adverse effects of unhealthy living conditions and lifestyles could not be overcome by medical care alone.

Stress

Other evidence of the causal role of class position in poor health is found in stress studies. Stress is a heightened mind–body reaction to stimuli inducing fear and anxiety in the individual and originates in situations that people find threatening or burdensome. When a person perceives a stressor, the resulting stress reaction can produce a physiological or emotional arousal involving autonomic (e.g., heart rate, blood pressure, gastrointestinal functions) and neuroendocrine adaptations. These changes can literally wear down the body's defenses against disease over time and make the person more susceptible to becoming sick, or act directly on the body's organic systems to cause physiological damage. A number of studies have shown that the inability of the individual to manage the social, psychological, and emotional aspects of life and respond suitably to a social situation can lead to cardiovascular complications, hypertension, peptic ulcers, muscular pain, asthma, migraine headaches, and other physical ailments (House 2002; Siegrist 2010).

There are three major types of social stressors: life events, chronic strains, and daily hassles (Avison and Thomas 2010; Pearlin 1989; Thoits 1995). Life events research is based on the assumption that the accumulation of several events in a person's life (e.g., death of a spouse, divorce, weddings, loss of job, change in financial status, change in residence, taking a vacation) within a relatively short period of time can build up to a stressful impact. Any life event can be stressful, but whether the event is negative or positive, the speed with which

it occurs, and the extent to which it affects a person's life are all important variables. Chronic strains are persistent demands that require
readjustments over a prolonged period like coping with poverty, while
daily hassles are mini-events (e.g., traffic jams, long lines or queues
at check-out counters) that require small behavioral adjustments.
Negative life events and chronic strains occur throughout the class
structure, but the preponderance of both is greatest at the bottom of
society (Lantz et al. 2005; Thoits 2010). The unequal distribution of
stress in the general population promotes inequality in physical and
psychological well-being with low SES persons being penalized the
most (Thoits 2010).

Recent research has confirmed the significant impact of stressful life
events on the lower class. R. Jay Turner and William Avison (2003)
used a life events checklist to determine that such events produced
significant levels of stress on lower SES youth in a study of high school
students in Miami, Florida. "The findings presented," state Turner and
Avison (2003: 501), "thus represent one of the clearest demonstrations
so far available that the social context implied by lower socioeconomic
status puts young people at risk for the potent risk factor of high stress
exposure." Paula Lantz and her colleagues (2005) subsequently found
significant socioeconomic disparities in both life events and chronic
strains in a nationwide study, and determined that some of these variables were predictive of higher mortality and poorer health over time
for the lower class. Lantz et al. (2005: 285) concluded: "First, there is
indeed differential exposure by socioeconomic position to negative life
events and other types of stressors. Second, some types of stress and
life events are predictive of general physical health outcomes, with the
more proximate measures of stress generally more powerful in terms of
producing subsequent health status outcomes."

In addition to being subjected to a preponderance of negative life
events and chronic strains, other research shows that people in the
lower social strata are stressed by their living environment (Browning
and Cagney 2003; Downey and Van Willigen 2005; Hill et al. 2005)
and that financial adversity over their life course is a powerful stressor
(Angel et al. 2003; Kahn and Pearlin 2006). Poverty that is unbroken,
for example, has a greater effect on health than poverty that is intermit-
tent (McLeod and Shanahan 1996). Among the stressors closely linked
to social status are those that continue or are repeated across the life
course, such as persistent financial strain and victimization by discriminatory practices. In Britain, Alan Dolan (2007) found that men
with the lowest incomes and poorest living conditions also experienced
stress and anxiety as a result of their treatment by other people. Their

low social position blocked job opportunities and exposed them to disdainful treatment from welfare agencies, social workers, and people in higher social stations. The men in this study endured both the direct consequences of their poverty and social rejection from others. Dolan (2007: 726) concludes that "not only do they feel undervalued and excluded, but they *are* undervalued and excluded." Their poor material circumstances hampered their ability to live in a healthy manner and subjected them to stress because of it.

According to Leonard Pearlin and his colleagues (Pearlin et al. 2005), people with the least privileged statuses have the highest probabilities of exposure to health-related stressors. Pearlin et al. note the importance of the life course in analyzing stress as they and others (McLeod and Almazan 2003; Wickrama et al. 2003) find uninterrupted stressful circumstances and hardships of early life are linked to health problems that emerge in later life. Pearlin et al. (2005: 208–9) find that:

> The consequences of chronic or recurring stressors may be particularly severe when they surface within major social domains, such as breadwinning, job, and family. . . . Their potency stems from the fact that roles within these institutional domains are of vital importance to both the larger society and their individual incumbents, and consequently adversities that arise within them typically exert a heavy impact. . . . Continuous and repeated stressors, moreover, are likely to have a cumulative effort on the *allostatic load*, which refers to the burden placed on the organism and its biological functions in responding to hardship and demand.

Mirowsky and Ross (2003a) came to a similar conclusion when they used the term "structural amplification" to refer to situations where well-educated individuals accumulate advantages and poorly educated persons amass disadvantages that are bundled over time into "cascading sequences" impacting either positively or negatively on health. They describe how structural amplification concentrates poor health in those persons with multiple disadvantages. This happens when the factors that make a situation less damaging are less common among the people in that situation. Cascading sequences of negative factors make harmful situations worse at each step by the conditions that gave birth to those situations.

A particularly crucial variable in coping with stress is the amount of personal resources, social or economic, a person has available – a situation that clearly goes against the poor. This is because whatever resources lower-class persons possess are likely to be outweighed by their much greater exposure to stress. Moreover, a lack of resources can promote feelings of fatalism or powerlessness. Fatalism is a term used to describe beliefs that the outcomes of situations are determined by forces external to the individual. These outside forces are thought to be fate, luck, chance, or perhaps other, more powerful and distant people. There is research showing that many people in the lower class tend to be more fatalistic than people in the classes above them and that this sense of fatalism is associated with higher levels of psychological distress (Mirowsky and Ross 1989). Lower-class persons apparently learn through recurrent experiences that they have limited opportunities, no matter how hard they try they cannot get ahead, and more powerful people and unpredictable forces control their lives. By continually experiencing failure, low-status people in adverse situations learn their actions are not generally associated with successful outcomes. This assumption is not only depressing and demoralizing, but it can also degrade the will and ability to cope with life's problems that ultimately leads to greater susceptibility to poor mental and physical health.

Moving higher in the class structure, we find that the working and lower-middle classes have stresses of their own that lead to health problems. Economic recessions and factory closings in the United States have been found, for example, to adversely affect the health of workers both physically and mentally (Fenwick and Tausig 1994; Tausig and Fenwick 1999). Other research on workers who lost their jobs as they neared retirement shows that such an event takes an extremely heavy toll on their health. William Gallo and his colleagues (2006) examined the health outcomes of 582 persons in a larger nationwide sample for a decade who had experienced involuntary job loss after the age of 50. Gallo et al. found that persons in this group – even after taking smoking, problem drinking, depression, obesity, physical functioning, and overall health into account – had twice the risk of stroke and heart disease compared to others in their sample without this negative experience. They suggest physicians treating individuals who lose their jobs as they near retirement should consider loss of employment as a major risk factor for adverse changes in cardiovascular health.

Elsewhere, German medical sociologist Johannes Siegrist (2010) investigated the effects of stress on heart disease among male blue-collar workers in relation to quality of life, work load, job security, coping styles, emotional distress, and sleep disturbances. He found that the failure to cope with job-related stressors promotes heart problems. Siegrist also determined that high personal effort (competitiveness, work-related over-commitment, and hostility) and low gain (poor promotion prospects and a blocked career) – what he calls the effort–reward imbalance model – is linked to higher risk of heart disease. The adverse psychological effects of such "dead-end" jobs were aptly described by Lillian Breslow Rubin many years ago in her interviews of working-class families. Rubin (1976: 158) states:

> The men who hold these jobs often get through the day by doing their work and numbing themselves to the painful feelings of discontent – trying hard to avoid the question, "Is this what life is all about?" Unsuccessful in that struggle, one twenty-nine-year-old warehouseman burst out bitterly: "A lot of times I hate to go down there. I'm cooped up and hemmed in. I feel like I'm enclosed in a building forty hours a week, sometimes more. It seems all there is to life is go down there and work, collect your paycheck, pay your bills, and get further in debt. It doesn't seem like the circle ever ends. Every day it's the same thing; every week it's the same thing; every month it's the same thing."

As previously discussed, Evans and his colleagues (1994) believe the close link between stress and social class is behind the social gradient in health. They found that social rank correlates inversely with stress and the ability to cope with stress. The higher the rank, the less the stress and the greater the ability to contain its effects on health, while the lower the rank, the greater the stress and the worse the ability to cope with it. People at or near the top of society are also subject to stress and strain and some may feel their stresses are greater because their burden of responsibilities is greater. Yet Evans et al. note that such persons also feel better about themselves, have greater control over their lives, more and better resources to cope with problems, including stress, and usually live in supportive microenvironments – all of which promotes their capability to handle stress. Evans et al. feel, however, that it is not stress per se that is bad, since people differ in their stress reactions and some stress can be challenging and its resolution satisfying; rather, trouble arises when the strain is too great. People in the lower ranks are hit harder because they are less able to cope with stress and the stresses they face are typically more proximate for their survival, and their environments at home and work are not as likely to help them to satisfactorily resolve the strain.

These studies support a *social causation* explanation of poor health by showing that people in the lower class are in poorer health because they are subjected to greater stress and adversity by way of a deprived life situation. Although much of the social causation thesis in the stress literature is found in studies of mental health, there is strong evidence showing it can also be applied to physical health (Angel et al. 2003; Evans et al. 1994; Kahn and Pearlin 2006; Lantz et al. 2005; J. Warren 2009). An excellent summary of the class/stress/health relationship is provided by Pearlin et al. (2005: 206):

Salient among the circumstances linking status and health, we submit, is the differential exposure to serious stressors, both those built into the warp and woof of social and economic life and those that are eventful. We refer to the dogged hardships, demands, conflicts, and frustrations that may be instrumental in structuring people's experiences across time and to events that may disrupt the continuities of their lives. It can be seen that the notions of risk avoidance and health behaviors are not congenial with many stressors known to undermine well-being, such as having to endure economic strain, being in an exploitive job that is lost because of a plant closing, being drawn into a demanding caregiving role, or being the target of unfair treatment because of race. Exigencies such as these have neither the specificity of risk *nor the quality of being preventable through purposive behaviors* [italics added].

That is, some stresses cannot be changed by an individual simply changing his or her behavior, such as a lower-class diabetic deciding to eat a healthier diet, since that person's stresses resulting from class situations are beyond that individual's control. Life events and strains embedded in class hierarchies can create stressful circumstances in which people are forced to respond to conditions not of their own choosing and these circumstances can have adverse effects on physical and mental health.

Income Inequality

Another class-based but controversial explanation of health differences emerging from research in Britain is Wilkinson's (1992, 1996; Wilkinson and Pickett 2006) income inequality or relative income thesis. Wilkinson focuses on the health of whole societies, rather than individuals. He suggests that a person's position relative to other people in a social hierarchy can be determined by their relative incomes, and that the psychosocial effects of the different social positions have health consequences. In his view, stress, poor social support networks, low self-esteem, depression, anxiety, insecurity, and loss of a sense of control are reduced and social cohesion is enhanced when income levels are more equal.

While it is an established fact that people with low incomes have worse health and shorter lives than those with high incomes, Wilkinson claims that relative levels of income *within* a society have greater effects on health and mortality than the society's absolute level of wealth. That is, what matters the most in determining health and mortality is not how wealthy a society is overall, but how evenly wealth is distributed within it. Countries with the most wealth may not have the longest life expectancy; instead, the best health and longevity is to be found in those nations with the smallest differences in income levels and smallest proportion of the total population living in poverty. This is seen in countries like the United States, for example, that have wide disparities in income and lower life expectancy than countries like Sweden, where income is more evenly distributed and life expectancy is higher.

But the most recent research does not confirm Wilkinson's results. One problem is that data from developing countries do not show the same pattern. This is particularly the case in nations with subsistence agricultural economies where cash income may bear little relation to material and psychosocial well-being, while many goods and services are obtained directly from the environment and barter is common (Ellison 2002). This situation limits the utility of relative income theory to developed countries. But new studies conducted in countries with high per capita income likewise failed to find a significant association between income inequality and health (Beckfield 2004; Coburn 2004; Eberstadt and Satel 2004; McLeod, Nonnemaker, and Call 2004). The evidence is now mounting against the relative income thesis as increasing numbers of studies find it does not apply to either a broad spectrum of countries (Beckfield 2004; Judge, Mulligan, and Benzeval 1998) or the US (McLeod et al. 2004).

The popularity of the relative income thesis appears to be based less on empirical research and more on its logic that suggests health and longevity can be improved by restructuring society and redistributing its wealth – thus making it more of "a doctrine in search of data" than an accurate scientific hypothesis (Eberstadt and Satel 2004: 36). Few, if any, medical sociologists would deny that income is an important variable in health outcomes and that relative differences in income are typically reflected in relative differences in health. However, it cannot be proven that reducing income differences will reduce health differences and the likelihood of wealth being redistributed in capitalist countries to test this outcome is virtually nil. Even in Sweden, where social equality in income and living conditions is perhaps the best in the world, the lower class has the poorest health and shortest life spans (Hemström 1999; Sundquist and Johansson 1997). This situation has led Finnish medical sociologist Eero Lahelma (2010: 90) to note that it remains a puzzle why class inequalities in health "in the relatively egalitarian Nordic welfare states are not smaller than elsewhere." A central problem in treating income inequality as the primary cause of poor health is that income is only part of the overall capability of social class to affect health (Coburn 2004, 2009). As a fundamental cause of health, we know that class operates through a variety of pathways and income inequality qualifies as only one of these paths.

Culture

Another way in which social class influences health is through culture. Cultures are ways of living that have been passed on from one genera- tion to the next in the form of abstract ideas, norms, habits, customs, and in the creation of material objects, such as food, dress, housing, art, music, automobiles, and various other items. Culture thus refers to a body of common understandings that represent what groups of people and societies think, feel, and act upon. The knowledge, beliefs, values, customs, and behaviors shared by people in a particular society reflect the culture of that society. Although people can be influenced by other cultures, they tend to be most comfortable with their own culture since it is the culture handed down to them by their family and society – so they usually live in a manner that is consistent with it. As Bourdieu (1984: 12) puts it: "There is no way out of the game of culture."

Obviously, culture plays an important role in how health and disease are viewed by a population. Primitive societies, for example, tend to have different ideas about disease causation (e.g., evil spirits) and cures (e.g., potions, spells) than modern ones whose ideas are based on scientific investigation (Cockerham 2012). While the class/culture/ health relationship might imply that culture rather than class has the most direct link to health, Bourdieu (1984) points out that class and culture are correlated. Class distinctions underlie cultural practices, as particular classes reflect their own particular cultures. Whereas members of the upper and lower classes in American or British society share their respective national popular cultures, the class-based dis- tinctions in cultural practices between the top and bottom of society are so extreme as to be almost totally dissimilar. Cultural tastes or preferences, states Bourdieu (1984: 36), are the practical affirmation of inevitable differences.

Singapore medical sociologist Stella Quah (2010) finds that culture is most important in relation to health through its influence on health- related behavior, with Parsons' (1951) concept of the sick role serving as a prime example of a middle-class orientation (the class-based normative mandate to seek technically competent help) toward health care in the United States. However, there are few studies in medical sociology that explicitly focus on culture as that is an area typically studied by anthropologists, or on the culture/class interface. One exception is a study of the male mortality crisis in Russia by the author (Cockerham 2006a, 2007a, 2009) that included consideration of the cultural origins of the country's drinking pattern. The objective of the study was to determine causes of the downturn in male longevity. In 2009, life expectancy for Russian males had actually improved to 62.9 years – but it was still some 1.1 years less than in 1965. For females, life expectancy was 75 years in 2009 compared to 72.2 years in 1965. Thus, in 2009, Russian females outlived their male counterparts an average of 12.1 years; in the United States, in contrast, the gender gap in life expectancy that year was 5.0 years. The gender gap in longevity in Russia is the largest in the world and more than double that of Western countries. Obviously something is ending the lives of Russian men before they reach old age, while the longevity of the women has stagnated.

The author suggests that the principal determinant of the mortality crisis is unhealthy lifestyles, especially on the part of men. This research identified the origin of the dominant male lifestyle in peasant and working-class culture. Historically, Russian male agricultural workers engaged in binge drinking that often resulted in drunkenness – but usually only on Sundays, especially if there were weddings, parties, or fairs, or on Russian Orthodox Church holidays (Shkolnikov and Nemstov 1997). This pattern accompanied men to the cities when they migrated to urban areas to become industrial workers and spread there as well. The drink of preference was vodka. Men did not drink frequently, but when they did drink, they traditionally drank heavily. Steady moderate drinking was unusual.

However, during the Soviet period religion was suppressed and heavy consumption became common any day of the week in both urban and rural areas. The dominant drinking pattern that emerged consisted of rapid group consumption of large doses of vodka (Shkolnikov and Nemstov 1997). Participants are expected to drink as long as they are able or until the supply of alcohol is consumed. Little or no social stigma is attached to being drunk. The author (Cockerham 1999, 2000b, 2007a, 2009) found that the excessive alcohol consumption – the highest per capita for males in the world – stems from the normative demands of this particular lifestyle practice. Males are expected by their fellows to drink vodka and drink heavily. This practice has evolved through socialization and experience to become an established disposition toward drinking reflected in the habitual outlook of many Russian men. It is reproduced over time and in subsequent generations by its continual practice and has become a cultural norm. Moreover, the integration of massive numbers of peasants into an urban working class under communism reinforced this drinking style as a working-class cultural trait that spread throughout society.

The well-established association between alcohol and cigarettes, along with reports that almost 80 percent of males in some industrial areas smoke, links smoking to this pattern as well (Hurt 1995). One major study (McKee et al. 1998) found smoking is common among males of all ages and in all areas of the country, with 65 percent of those aged 18–24 years smoking and 73 percent of those aged 25–34 years. Some 27 percent of younger women aged 18–34 years smoke, but only some 5 percent smoke in older age groups. Smoking among women is largely confined to large cities. In both sexes, heavy drinking was related to smoking.

This study acknowledged that the primary level cause of the mortality crisis was premature male deaths from heart attacks, followed by deaths from alcohol-related poisonings and accidents. In order to uncover the ultimate cause of the crisis, however, it is necessary to drop down to a secondary level to determine what caused the increase in cardiovascular and alcohol-related deaths. Although stress factors are likely of some importance, this study found that these problems were largely due to negative male health lifestyles featuring heavy drinking and smoking, high-fat diets, and a lack of exercise. Female drinking and smoking practices are consistent with working-class norms that approve of such behavior for males and not females.

Thus, a tertiary level explanation of the mortality crisis is the generating of dominant health lifestyle practices by the behavioral dispositions of the male working class – what Bourdieu (1984) would call a habitus. The working class was officially favored in Soviet society, as was the upward social mobility of people whose families originated in this stratum. The prevailing social carrier of health lifestyles, as noted in chapter 3, has been the working class which has historically favored binge drinking as a normative practice and other habits harmful to health. The resulting causal chain is one that runs from working-class dispositions (tertiary cause) to health lifestyles (secondary cause) to heart disease and alcohol-related causes of premature mortality (primary cause). The ultimate cause, however, is the working-class dispositions that cause the lifestyle that causes the high mortality. Remove the tertiary factor and the secondary factor would be significantly altered leaving the primary factor diminished. Just because a tertiary factor is tertiary does not mean it is neither causal nor ineligible to be a direct cause since it triggers the practices that end in early mortality from heart disease.

While the middle class – primarily the upper-middle class – has been responsible for the expansion of positive health lifestyles in Western society, a similar process has not occurred in Russia. Why? The best answer is that a middle class similar to that of Western countries does not yet exist (Beliaeva 2000; Shankina 2004; Sitnikov 2000). As Russian sociologist Liudmila Beliaeva (2000) observes, market reforms have conferred benefits and improved the social status of only a very narrow segment of the population. "In these years," Beliaeva (2000: 43) concludes, "it has not yet been possible to establish a full-fledged modern middle class such as constitutes the nucleus of society in the developed countries." Consequently, a middle class has yet to emerge that can serve as a social carrier of more positive health lifestyles into the general culture (Cockerham 2006a, 2007a, 2009). Again, however, we see the relevance of social class as a determining factor for health.

An example of a binge drinking culture that exists on a more limited scale than in Russia, but is nonetheless harmful to health is found in Britain. This culture emerged in the last 20 years as an urban age-based phenomenon featuring mass hedonistic drinking in pubs by young adults (Hadfield 2006). Binge drinkers and those who drink expressly to become drunk in the UK are most likely to be under the age of 25, and involve males more than females. The drink of choice is typically beer, although wine or whiskey is preferred by some. Britain has the most developed pub culture among advanced societies, as pubs ("public houses") have become a center for socializing for many people (Hadfield 2006). In order to promote a more relaxed drinking culture common on the European continent and avoid the binging that typically takes place just before closing time, the British government in 2005 extended the period that pubs can stay open to as long as 24 hours for some establishments.

With the exception of persons at the lowest level of subsistence, Reid (1998) finds that the upper-middle class visits pubs less frequently than the lower-middle and skilled, semi-skilled, and unskilled working classes. About 90 percent of the British population drinks alcohol and self-reported daily drinking is more frequent in the upper-middle class who prefer wine. The lower class, in turn, has the greatest proportion of abstainers as the socializing function of alcohol is more representative of the drinking culture of the classes above them. Those at the top of society, however, including the upper class, are more likely to drink in private compared to those lower on the social ladder. And it is youth in strata below the upper and upper-middle classes who likely comprise the greatest proportion of binge drinkers in public settings. British male football (soccer) fans have become particularly known in Europe for public drunkenness and rowdiness.

The increase in per capita alcohol consumption has led to a higher prevalence of heavy drinking, cirrhosis of the liver, and alcohol-related violence (Hall 2005). Rates of alcohol dependence in Britain are now among the highest in Europe (Hall 2005; Leon and McCambridge 2006). About one in every eight deaths of young British men is caused by alcohol abuse that stems from a drinking culture that promotes it. Some 8.5 liters of pure alcohol per capita are consumed in the UK which is less than half that of Russia, but higher than most countries in Western Europe. In both Russia and Britain, a binge drinking culture has caused national harm through premature male mortality, but the harm has been substantially greater in one country (Russia) where it is almost universal than the other (Britain) where it is not so widespread.

Smoking

One of the major multiple pathways by which class impacts on health is through smoking. It is common knowledge that smoking tobacco is bad for your health. There is strong evidence linking smoking to the risk of heart disease, atherosclerosis, stroke, lung and other cancers, emphysema and other respiratory diseases, liver disease, and various other health problems, thereby making it the lifestyle practice with the largest number of negative consequences for health (Jarvis and Wardle 1999; Ross and Wu 1995). As noted earlier, in the United States, smoking causes a man to lose more than 13 years of life on average and a woman 14.5 years. Some 440,000 people die each year from smoking-related causes.

Although the proportion of smokers in Western countries has substantially decreased as awareness of the effects of smoking on the body become generally known, some people nevertheless choose to smoke – with the decision to smoke or not smoke an exercise of agency. That is, the decision to smoke is a choice. But is that choice independent of structure? The answer is that it is not. Structure intervenes in this decision as distinct differences persist between classes, suggesting that decisions about smoking are not entirely an individual matter. In the United States, for instance, the Center for Health Statistics reported in 2010 that adults with a high school education are twice as likely to smoke as those with a bachelor's degree and nearly five times more likely to smoke as those with a graduate degree. In England, the General Household Survey showed in 2009 that 28 percent of men and 24 percent of women in routine and manual occupations smoke compared to 16 percent of men and 14 percent of women in managerial and professional jobs.

As Jarvis and Wardle (1999) observe, smoking, along with drinking and drug use, are individual risk factors that involve an element of personal choice and have therefore been characterized by some researchers as simply a matter of individual responsibility. The reasoning is that if people choose to smoke, what happens to them physiologically is no one else's fault but their own. This approach (blaming the victim), state Jarvis and Wardle (1999: 241), is not helpful, since it fails to account for the underlying reasons why socially disadvantaged people are attracted to smoking and the nature of the social conditions that reinforce this behavior.

The social factors identified by Jarvis and Wardle that induce people to smoke are adverse socioeconomic conditions, deprivation, and stressful circumstances. "This illustrates what might be proposed as a general law of Western society," conclude Jarvis and Wardle (1999: 242), "namely, that any marker of disadvantage that can be envisaged, whether personal, material or cultural, is likely to have an independent association with cigarette smoking." Growing up in a household where one or both parents smoke, having a smoking spouse, and socializing with smokers regularly are other reasons that invoke smoking in a social context. These situations are also more likely toward the bottom of the social scale. Of course, some affluent people likewise smoke and the reasons for doing so may be different than those listed above – although stress is a likely culprit for everybody. Smoking among the affluent does not change the fact that this behavior is rare at the higher levels of society and the smoking habit is concentrated among lower strata groups, especially the lower class. In fact, corroboration of the powerful relationship between lower class position and persistent smoking has become routine in research on smoking (Narcisse et al. 2009). As Fred Pampel and Richard Rogers (2004) found in a nationwide study of smoking in the US, smoking inflicts greater harm among disadvantaged groups than advantaged ones, as smoking joins with alcohol abuse, poor diet, limited resources, and other factors to produce cumulative effects worsening the health of the poor.

Obesity

The lower an individual's income, the more likely they are to be obese and this is especially true for blacks and to a lesser extent for Hispanics in the United States (Boardman et al. 2005; Carr and Friedman 2005;

Robert and Reither 2004). Being obese is not only unhealthy, but also socially stigmatizing for individuals of any race who are severely over-weight (Carr and Friedman 2005). That is, in addition to health prob-lems, the very fat may also find themselves socially devalued, isolated, and discriminated against with respect to employment and personal relationships. While the causes of obesity are complex, involving a variety of factors, including genetics, we find that once again class position from high to low inversely matches the distribution of a nega-tive health condition from much less (at the top) to much more (at the bottom). As Canadian researcher Treena Delormier and her colleagues (Delormier, Frohlich, and Potvin 2009) suggest, research focusing on the eating behavior of individuals overlooks the fact that eating pat-terns characteristic of particular groups are best understood as being distinctively shaped by the groups themselves.

British geographer Steve Cummins and medical sociologist Sally Macintyre (2006) find obesity linked to poor diets among the lower class in several Western countries. The highest rates of obesity are located among persons with the lowest incomes and the least educa-tion, particularly among women and ethnic minority groups. They note that some observers have viewed this association as a paradox in that hunger and obesity exist side-by-side in the same social strata. Cummins and Macintyre explain this paradox, however, by noting the relatively low cost of energy-dense foods, the tastiness of sweets and fats associated with higher-energy foods, and the association of low incomes with lower intakes of fruit and vegetables – all of which are characteristic of lower-class food consumption. Other research in Scotland shows a similar eating pattern in that lower-class children consumed fewer essential micronutrients and more fat and sugar com-pared to children in other classes (Gallagher 2000).

Barry Glassner (2007) suggests that poor Americans are dispropor-tionately overweight because during the decades their rates of obesity increased, so did their economic hardships and financial insecurity. He suggests that higher stress levels resulting from this situation cause the body to produce less of a growth hormone that reduces fat and increases the body's metabolism that provokes cravings for soothing comfort foods like glazed doughnuts and chocolate fudge ice cream. Glassner further suggests that poverty promotes binge eating, in that when low-income persons have enough money they indulge in calorie-rich foods. Over time, the body adapts to this situation by storing more fat. Other factors like the decline in the family meal, fast-foods, drink-ing sodas as snacks in schools, and a lack of exercise also contribute to obesity among poor children and adults.

The preponderance of fast-food outlets in low-income urban areas in the United States has also been blamed for the high levels of obesity among the poor, but Cummins and Macintyre (2006) find research on this issue to be inconclusive since not all studies are able to link obesity with proximity to fast-food establishments. Some American studies claim that in low-income areas access to healthy foods is uncommon and food prices are high, but this is not the case in Britain and yet the poor still tend to have unhealthy diets. Consequently, food preferences and eating habits along class lines appear to be powerful influences on food selection. As Bourdieu (1984) found in France, the working class preferred meals that were hearty, nutritious, and cheap as strength was valued more highly than body shape among males, while the professional class favored foods that were healthy, light, and low in calories. In Britain, Michael Calnan (1987) found that women in both the middle and working classes recognized the importance of fresh foods in the diets of their families, but diets high in fiber and low in fats and carbohydrates were popular among middle-class women and less so among women in the working class. The working-class women emphasized having "good" food on a regular basis which meant serving cooked meat and vegetables regularly, including potatoes or chips ("French fries"). Middle-class women avoided serving a lot of processed or packaged foods that were fatty or had too much sugar. As one middle-class woman (Calnan 1987: 79) explained health and dietary differences between the classes:

> The unskilled worker is, I think, more likely to suffer from aches and pains and minor illnesses. He is bored with his work, he doesn't eat a good meal in the middle of the day; he probably takes something like jam sandwiches. I mean, the office worker is more likely to spend his money on proper food and that sort of thing. The factory worker is more likely to spend his money on booze and [cigarettes] – it's the economics of priorities.

The consistent association of socioeconomic status with dietary practices throughout the world highlights the powerful role of class position in relation to eating habits. In Canada, for example, the available evidence shows that income affects food intake directly through cost and indirectly through eating patterns associated with particular social classes, thereby suggesting the existence of a social gradient with respect to healthy eating (E. Power 2005). Since the early 1980s, several studies have produced convincing results linking high cholesterol levels to heart disease and encouraging the consumption of heart-healthy foods (Greenland et al. 2003; Khot et al. 2003). Virtually all major health organizations now urge people to decrease their consumption of sugars and saturated fats, lower their cholesterol, and lose excess weight. Higher strata persons have more readily adopted these measures than those at the bottom of society and once again class position shows itself to be a determining factor in health outcomes.

Conclusion: Social Causation or Social Selection?

As a concluding comment in this chapter on the class/health relationship, the social causation/social selection debate needs to be noted. The social causation argument maintains that the lower class is subjected to greater socioeconomic adversity as a result of a deprived life situation and has to cope with this deprivation with fewer resources. Thus, adversity and the stresses associated with it affect the lower class more severely than it does the other classes, and their health is more impaired as a result. The social selection explanation holds that there is more illness in the lower class because chronically sick persons tend to "drift" downward in the social hierarchy (the "drift" hypothesis), or conversely, healthy individuals in the lower class tend to be upwardly mobile and leave behind a "residue" of ill persons to populate the bottom of the social scale (the "residue" hypothesis).

Poor health can limit the upward social mobility of people if they lack the health to improve their station in life and dwell in a more or less permanent sick role, or poor health can cause them to drift downward in the social structure as their illness makes it difficult to maintain their position in society. However, most ill persons are not likely to be especially mobile in society, either up or down. Essentially, they stay where they are. When the question is whether class position determines health (social causation) or health causes class position (social selection), the strongest argument is on the side of social causation (Marmot 2004; Marmot et al. 1991). This evidence suggests that class position contributes considerably more to the onset of poor health than poor health causes class position (J. Warren 2009). But the two explanations are not mutually exclusive in which one explanation is totally wrong and the other totally correct (Lahelma 2010). There are undoubtedly situations where sickness locks a person into the lower class or causes downward movement in society. Nevertheless, class position and the various factors associated with it are the most powerful social determinant of health.

Suggested Further Reading

Avison, William R. and Stephanie S. Thomas. 2010. "Stress." In *The New Blackwell Companion to Medical Sociology*, ed. William Cockerham, 242–67. Oxford, UK: Wiley-Blackwell.

Provides a thorough review of the stress process model, differential exposure to stress, stress over the life course, major developments in contemporary stress research, and future challenges.

Carpiano, Richard M., Bruce G. Link, and Jo C. Phelan. 2008. "Social Inequality and Health: Future Directions for the Fundamental Cause Explanation." In *Social Class*, ed. Annette Lareau and Dalton Conley, 232–63. New York: Russell Sage.

Discusses the importance of class position for health, reviews the evidence for fundamental cause theory, and assesses the emerging future directions in research on this topic.

Lutfey, Karen and Jeremy Freese. 2005. "Towards Some Fundamentals of Fundamental Causality: Socioeconomic Status and Health in the Routine Clinic Visit for Diabetes." *American Journal of Sociology* 110:1326–72.

Utilizing ethnographic data from two diabetes clinics in a large Midwestern American city, this study provides strong support for fundamental cause theory and demonstrates the potent role of SES in determining the health outcomes of the patients.

6

Age, Gender, and Race/ Ethnicity as Structural Variables

Age, gender, and race/ethnicity are characteristics of individuals, but they are also characteristics of particular populations that have consequences for health and disease. As we saw in chapter 3 on health lifestyles, each of these population categories are structural entities that help mold health practices into particular configurations. Elderly persons, for example, usually adjust their diets as they age, women generally live healthier lifestyles than men, and different races and ethnic groups vary in their drinking, food habits, and use of preventive health care services. These are not acts of a few isolated individuals, but the practices of aggregates. The challenge is to demonstrate how these aggregate actions reflect structural qualities in determining health-related behavior and outcomes.

An example of this situation can be seen in gender patterns of smoking in American society. Prior to the twentieth century, smoking tobacco was almost exclusively a male practice. Norms regarding gender and smoking at the time were clear: it was socially acceptable for men, but not women, to smoke. Gentlemen were not even supposed to smoke when in the company of ladies. As Diana Chapman Walsh and her colleagues (Walsh, Sorensen, and Leonard 1995) conclude: "gender was the decisive axis dividing smokers and nonsmokers." The few women who smoked were typically considered to be rebellious, or of low morals and easy virtue. Smoking by a woman signaled her sexual availability to men, whether true or not. If a woman even allowed a man to smoke in her presence, she was not considered "proper" by the norms of the wider society.

Walsh and her colleagues identify the widespread condemnation of female smoking as a part of a male-dominated system of social control enforced by strict rules and norms concerning gender-appropriate behavior. "Respectable" women did not smoke, because to do so was socially unacceptable in polite society and condemned when it occurred. So cigarettes were generally smoked only by a few upper-class women who were independent enough to ignore any social sanctions or by much larger numbers of lower-class women who had no social reputations to protect. Even though the social prohibition of female smoking could be considered an example of male repression, Walsh et al. observed that the health outcome was nevertheless beneficial because tobacco-induced diseases like lung cancer were uncommon for women.

This situation changed during World War II when women entered the civilian labor force in large numbers as replacements for men serving in the military. Empowered by the greater equality and independence that resulted from employment outside the home, women smokers dramatically increased in number. However, the feminine embrace of smoking was limited to cigarettes, as social norms against women smoking cigars and pipes, and chewing tobacco remained and women themselves vetoed such practices as unsavory and personally objectionable. While the proportion of women cigarette smokers was never as large as that of men, their pattern of use was similar with respect to the age at which they began smoking (adolescence) and the number and type of cigarettes consumed. Female rates of lung cancer rose accordingly from 5.8 deaths per 100,000 in 1950 to 54.5 in 2007. Lung cancer ranked eighth among cancer deaths for women in 1961, but moved up to become the leading cause of female cancer mortality by 1986 where it remains today. Deaths from lung cancer now account for 25 percent of all cancer deaths among women. This rise is attributed to an aging of female cohorts with a higher prevalence of cigarette smoking than ever before.

The purpose of this chapter is to examine the ways in which age, gender, and race/ethnicity function as structural determinants of health and disease. Although the essential characteristics of these variables are biological in origin, it is their transformation into social variables by society at large that gives them their explanatory power in social situations. The definitions applied to them have resulted in each being a form of stratification that sorts people into different social categories according to their biological characteristics. Their role as causal factors in health matters will be reviewed in the sections that follow.

Age

Age is a relatively simple variable to understand as everyone goes through the process of biological aging and their health is affected along the way. What lifts age above the level of the individual and places it in position to serve as a social structural variable is that people belong to age cohorts that pass in an orderly and predictable fashion through the life course. The influence exerted by these cohorts as a whole on individuals and their families qualifies them as structural entities.

Age stratification theory

The basic features of age cohorts have been identified by Matilda White Riley (1987) who formulated age stratification theory. Riley maintains that each age cohort has both a life course and historical dimension. The life course dimension refers to stages of the life cycle. People belong to a particular age group depending on how long they have lived, and, as a result, they share similar social roles and experiences with others their age. At approximately the same point in their lives, they have all been children, students, workers, perhaps parents and grandparents, were retired, and so forth. Thus they have all had similar social roles in their respective pasts, are occupying similar roles in the present, and are likely to have similar roles in the future as members of the same age cohort moving through the life cycle. As they grow older, everyone else grows older as well, and younger people fill their former roles, while they move on with others of their age to assume roles consistent with their age cohort. Sharing similar roles at similar times in the life cycle is held to foster common attitudes, interests, and views. Consequently, belonging to a particular age cohort is not only a characteristic of a person beginning at birth, but also has social consequences for that person at every age.

The historical dimension pertains to the fact that people experience distinct periods of history together and share particular events on the basis of age. For example, the fall of the Berlin Wall in 1989, subsequently signaling the end of the Cold War between the West and the Soviet bloc, is likely to have had a different meaning for people who were children at the time, or who were older and had experienced the

Korean War, the Cuban Missile Crisis, the Vietnam War, or other conflicts involving the former Soviet Union or its allies. Each person shared an event but brought a perspective to it that was influenced by age. Today's generation of younger adults who experienced none of these things have a different outlook influenced by more recent events that occurred in their lives.

Riley also argues that different age cohorts age differently as the societies they live in change; that is, both similarities and differences can be found between age cohorts. Similarities stem from younger people replacing older people in the same roles, whereas differences emerge not only because of historical events but because society itself changes over time. Riley explains that people who were young earlier in the twentieth century learned from the age norms and patterns of behavior prevalent in that period and from their parents that only a few years of schooling suffice for most jobs, and from their grandparents that old age can be bleak. But now they themselves have grown old, the world for which they were initially prepared is gone. "Similarly," states Riley (1987: 5) "cohorts of people who are young today are perceiving the entire occupational ladder as it is now – before it has time to be further transformed by fast-breaking technological innovations and accompanying changes in the age structure of the future." Therefore, these young people will not be old in the same society in which they were born.

Age stratification theory finds that not only are new patterns of aging caused by social change, these patterns also contribute to the change that is taking place. At every level of the social system, society and the process of aging influence each other sequentially. The link between the aging of individuals and the larger society is the flow of age cohorts. Cohort flow affects the numbers and kinds of people in a particular age strata, as well as the capacities, attitudes, and activities of people in that strata. Riley (1987: 4) points out that, as society moves through time, the age structure and people within that structure are altered. Nor are people in a particular age strata contained indefinitely within that strata, as they are replaced by younger people as they themselves replaced the older people before them.

Consequently, age stratification theory provides a view that emphasizes a continuing interplay – generated by cohort flow – between social change and individuals as they age. Though interdependent, the process of aging and social change are not synchronized. People follow a sequential life cycle, but social change moves along its own axis of historical time and according to its own rhythm. Some periods of history witness greater social change than other periods, but people follow the same life course. As a result, the degree of difference between age cohorts due to social change can vary from great to small.

In sum, Riley finds that society is composed of successive cohorts of individuals who are aging and continually following older cohorts into and out of the next stage of life. "This flow of cohorts," states Riley (1987: 5), "forms the channel that connects the two dynamisms of aging and social change: it ties them both to the forces of history, creates the asynchrony between them, and presses for still further alterations." The larger society, institutions, groups, social networks, and strata, and individuals, are all affected by the aging process of particular cohorts, as these cohorts are, in turn, affected by them. Through such a dialectical sequence, Riley says the members of each cohort exert a collective force for further change as they move through the age-stratified society.

Cohort effects of age

An example of the cohort effects of age is found in a study of smoking among male British doctors spanning 50 years from 1951 to 2001 (Doll et al. 2004). Excess mortality associated with cigarette smoking was less for men born in the nineteenth century and greatest for men born in the 1920s. This was because tobacco was primarily smoked in pipes or as cigars in the nineteenth century and little was smoked as cigarettes. However, during the first few decades of the twentieth century, cigarette smoking dramatically increased as smoking became common among young men in Britain during World War I (1914–18) and remained so for half a century. Men who were born in the first three decades of the twentieth century and still smoking after age 60 had smoked substantial numbers of cigarettes throughout their adult life. Lung cancer and chronic obstructive lung disease were closely related to continued smoking. In comparing doctors in the 1900–30 birth cohort, it was determined that smokers lost an average of ten years of life expectancy compared to non-smokers. Overall, about half of the smokers were killed by their habit and some of them may have lost decades of life – since a quarter died between the ages of 35 and 69 years.

Furthermore, as the cohorts moved through the twentieth century, longevity improved for the non-smokers but not for the smokers as the gain in years lived in the general population during this period was wiped out by smoking. A large proportion of doctors stopped smoking during the study as it became generally accepted by the British medical profession after 1951 that cigarette smoking caused most of the country's mortality from lung cancer. Doctors who stopped smoking at age 30 avoided almost all smoking-related health problems, while those who stopped at age 50 halved the hazard. Stopping smoking at age 60 produced only a three-year gain in longevity. In this research, we see smoking patterns change on the part of age cohorts over their life course during different historical periods in which cigarette smoking was either modest (1851–99), heavy (1900–50), or deviant (1951–2001). The decisive factor was the attitude of the age cohort toward smoking.

The influence of age cohorts on health policy is another age-based area of research. In the United States, elderly persons have collectively influenced health policy. They accomplished this by becoming an important voting bloc and forming organizations to represent their interests with lawmakers. The American Association of Retired Persons (AARP), for example, has a successful record in lobbying Congress to support programs benefiting the elderly, such as the Medicare Catastrophic Act and Medicare Part D Supplement Plan. This influence is likely to grow as the number of aged persons is significantly expanding, making it impossible for politicians and policymakers to ignore their needs. Almost 13 percent of the American population is currently age 65 and over and this proportion is expected to increase to 20 percent of the population or one in five of all Americans by 2050. The proportion of elderly in Great Britain is even higher, with some 33.5 percent or one-third of the population expected to be age 60 and over by 2041.

The oncoming cohort of aged persons is from the "Baby Boomer Generation" that comprised the population explosion of people born between 1946 and 1964. It is the most affluent, best-educated, and healthy in history. Because of their large numbers and experience with the political process, they have the capacity and resources (voting power) to influence legislation to meet their needs. Thus demands for health and other services for the aged are likely to increase in accordance with their proportion of the population.

So there is a paradox in that the aged are likely to be healthier overall than previous generations, but they will place greater cohort demands on the health care system to help keep them that way as there will be so many more of them.

Change in the health of age cohorts over time has indeed been profound. A comparison of randomly selected medical records of some 50,000 white male veterans of the Union Army in the American Civil War – the first generation to reach age 65 in the twentieth century – with those of males born in the twentieth century show striking differences (Kolata 2006). Most of the Union veterans suffered from chronic diseases by early middle age and 80 percent had heart disease by age 60 compared to less than 50 percent of men this age today. Among men age 50–64, some 44 percent had difficulty bending over in the 1860s compared to 8 percent in 1994, while 39 percent had back problems in comparison to 32 percent in the mid-1990s, 29 percent had trouble walking compared to 10 percent, 45 percent had problems with their joints versus 20 percent, and 28 percent had heart murmurs compared to 2 percent. Not only are current cohorts healthier, but they are also bigger. Men living in the 1860s had an average height of 5 feet and 7.4 inches and weighed 146 pounds; in 2000, men had an average height of 5 feet, 9.5 inches and weighed 191 pounds – an average gain of over 2 inches in height and 45 pounds in weight.

Another major factor in improved life expectancy is a reduction in infant mortality. High rates of infant mortality at the beginning of the twentieth century were important in keeping overall rates of life expectancy below the age of 50 years in the US. Low infant mortality rates obviously signal longer lives on average in countries that have such rates. In 1900, there were 140 infant deaths per 1,000 live births in Britain and 162.4 per 1,000 in the US; however, in 2007, the most recent year data were available, Britain went on to have an infant mortality rate of 5.01 and the US rate was 6.75. Most people in these two countries and other advanced societies can expect to live to old age if they survive the first year of life and do not succumb prematurely to disease or injury.

People today thus have bigger bodies and longer lives. In 1900, both American men and women age 50 could expect to live 21 more years, while in 2008 men could expect to live another 29 years and women 32.7 years. However, far fewer people reached age 50 in 1900 as overall life expectancy in the United States was just 47.3 years compared to 78.0 years in 2008. Longevity is similar in Britain with men living 45.5 years on average in 1901 compared to 78.2 years in 2010 and life expectancy rising for women from 49.0 years to 82.3 years, respectively, over the same period. The source of the change is not just better nutrition and medical care, but also improved living and social conditions. For example, the majority of workers no longer hold jobs until their death. The average age of retirement in the US is now 62 years compared to 1890 when people retired at 85 years if retirement came at all. Most men worked at that time until they died or were too disabled or infirm to continue. In the UK, compulsory retirement at 65 years was abolished in 2011, thereby allowing the aged population to continue to work. The average age of retirement had been 63 years for men and 60 years for women.

Consequently, as age cohorts themselves change, these changes impact on individuals in many different ways. These changes can be physical and medical as well as social and cultural, but they combine to produce multiple cohort effects on people in those cohorts. Age stratification theory shows how age acts as a social force in health matters through cohort effects on individuals. Although this discussion has focused on the elderly, younger age cohorts are also capable of generating cohort effects that impact on health. In the 1940s, for instance, adolescents and young adult cohorts, both men and women, smoked in large numbers as smoking became popular for many in their generation. This promoted higher mortality rates from lung cancer for both sexes over time among those who did not stop using cigarettes. While the strength of age as an independent variable can be undercut by variables like class and gender, there are situations in which age cohort effects can be powerful causal factors as well and these circumstances need to be recognized by researchers. As Bridget Gorman and Jen'nan Read (2006: 97) point out: "It is surprising that age is often glossed over, because we know that age is central to our understanding of gender [and other] differences in health."

Gender

Women have the greatest longevity in Japan, most of Europe, North America, and Australia where approximately 80 years of life expectancy or more is the norm and they typically outlive men by five to seven years. In some former socialist countries, however, there are even more extreme differences, such as that noted in the last chapter for Russia where females outlived their male counterparts 12.1 years on average in 2009. The paradox in this situation, however, is that females are sick more often than males but usually live longer (Cockerham 2010b). Not all medical sociologists fully agree with this statement as there are exceptions to this pattern, such as the potential for changing social conditions to modify sex differences in life expectancy and the example of longevity in South Asian countries like Afghanistan, Bangladesh, India, Nepal, and Pakistan where women do not have a large advantage in life expectancy compared to men (Arber and Thomas 2005; Nettleton 2006). In war-torn Afghanistan, for example, men and women both average about 43 years of life expectancy, while in Bangladesh men slightly outlived women for years until recently when longevity for women caught up to men at 63 years (Annandale 2010). Nutritional deficiencies, disadvantages associated with a devalued social status, and lessened access to medical care are among the leading factors undermining the usual female superiority in life expectancy in South Asia. "These cross-country differentials," states British medical sociologist Ellen Annandale (2010: 100), "also signal that, while women may enjoy some biological advantages in relation to longevity, this can easily be overridden by the circumstances of their lives."

Gender differences in physical and mental health

Female advantages in health and longevity are seen in the types of health problems that are more common among women as opposed to men. Females have higher rates of acute illnesses, namely, infectious, parasitic, digestive, and respiratory ailments. The rate for acute conditions not related to pregnancy in the US is 11 times greater for females than males. The only category of acute health problems in which males have a higher incidence is injuries. As for chronic conditions, females have higher rates of hypertension, thyroid, anemia, and gallbladder problems, as well as chronic enteritis and colitis, migraine headaches, arthritis, diabetes, diseases of the urinary system, and some skin conditions. Males have higher rates of heart disease, AIDS, gout, emphysema, and losses of limbs. Males also have higher rates of cancer at the youngest and oldest ages and females have the highest incidence between the ages of 20 and 55. Males, however, are more likely to die from cancer. The overall pattern that emerges from these disease outcomes is that females have a higher prevalence of ailments that are not a leading cause of death (except for diabetes), while men have more health problems that result in death.

Women ultimately die from the same causes as men (e.g., heart disease, cancer, stroke), but usually do so later in the life course.

There are also distinct differences between the sexes in mental health. A review of studies of the true prevalence of mental disorder by sex show that (1) there are no consistent differences by sex in regard to rates of schizophrenia, (2) rates of depressive and anxiety disorders are consistently higher for women, and (3) rates of personality disorders are consistently higher for men (Cockerham 2010b; Kessler et al. 1994; Rosenfield 1999). Additionally, substance-related disorders are more common among men and dementia is slightly greater among women. According to Sarah Rosenfield (1989: 77), these differences exist "across cultures, over time, in different age groups, in rural as well as urban areas, and in treated as well as untreated populations."

Researchers once thought that there were no differences between men and women in overall rates of mental disorders, but more recent nationwide research in the US suggests that females are more vulnerable to mental disorder than males (Kessler et al. 1994; Taylor and Turner 2001). The National Comorbidity Survey found, for example, that women had a higher prevalence of more mental disorders than men on both a lifetime and 12-month basis. A strong body of evidence is now developing that holds the number of females in the general population with mental disorders exceeds the number of males at any given period (Rosenfield 1999). The differences between the sexes have been found to be real and not due to underreporting by men (Rosenfield 1999; Taylor and Turner 2001).

One explanation for the differences is biological in that physiological and genetic variations are held responsible. While biological distinctions are clearly important, Sara Arber and Hilary Thomas (2005) find in Britain that biology is not the whole story since it cannot explain shifts in the mortality gap between men and women. The gap can narrow or widen in a particular society and biology may have little or nothing to do with it. Arber and Thomas maintain that the gendered nature of social roles and relationships, risk behaviors, work, and especially social structural variables can be more important than biology in explaining changes in longevity. In the United States, Gorman and Read (2006: 96) similarly point out that medical sociologists have long argued that biomedical research focusing on physiological differences between men and women "ignores the manner in which gender as a social construct affects the physical health of men and women." While in Canada, Barbara Murphy examined the longevity gap in her book *Why Women Bury Men* (2004) and found that the impact of biological factors was small when compared to lifestyle practices that men pursue involving smoking, heavy alcohol use, poor diets, little exercise, and reckless driving.

Gender differences in health practices

The consistent differences between men and women in physical and mental health show that gender is obviously important. But can it be shown that gender has a collective causal influence on health and disease? One strategy to answer this question is to examine health lifestyles. We know that females typically have healthier lifestyles than males. Males are more likely than females to smoke, drink large quantities of alcohol, and abuse drugs, but are more likely to exercise. Males also have less healthy food habits as females tend to eat less meat and more fresh fruits and vegetables. Additionally, females consult with physicians more often for preventive and routine physical checkups.

While there are exceptions in that not every female lives healthily, the overall pattern of health lifestyles by gender is clear: women collectively have more positive day-to-day health practices than men.

Drawing on the work of Bourdieu (1984), the author (Cockerham 2005) finds that class circumstances and other structural variables, including gender, provide the social context for the emergence of health lifestyles through socialization and experience. Beginning in childhood, females visit physicians more often than males and are socialized to take care of their bodies as seen in the continuing requirements for breast exams and pap smears that males do not have. Consequently, the number of females in a household largely determines the frequency of physician visits for that household. That is, the larger the number of females in a particular household, the greater the demand for physician services – all of which reflects a normative pattern of gendered health behavior based on norms common to females generally, rather than random acts on the part of individual women.

The childbearing role for women is also important in that women typically adopt and maintain healthy practices during pregnancy and usually continue to do so after giving birth – again something that men do not experience. Another variable is that women are the traditional caregivers in their families and they strive to be healthy so they can care for their children or other family members – like elderly parents – who need their attention. Smoking cigarettes, being drunk, eating or serving unhealthy foods, abusing drugs, and the like jeopardize the health and safety of their children and themselves, and are therefore unlikely behaviors for responsible mothers.

Patricia Drentea and Jennifer Moren-Cross (2005) observe that life today is more adult-centered and with greater female employment outside the home and a falling birth rate, there are fewer children and young mothers in neighborhoods to form the child-friendly social networks of support and advice that existed in the past. "As such," state Drentea and Moren-Cross (2005: 921), "women are even less familiar with child-bearing and rearing than they would have been in previous generations." Their source of advice in childrearing has been taken over by physicians and other "experts," as neighborhood groups of women serving as a resource for support are becoming rare. To counter the greater social isolation of young mothers with children, these researchers found that Internet sites for mothers were becoming popular for sharing information about childrearing. The sites were also creating female communities in cyberspace offering emotional and instrumental support in mothering as a form of social capital. Drentea and Moren-Cross (2005: 938) argue that the websites "created a source of feminine thinking, thus creating a circle of women who were empowered by taking some of the power away from the masculine medical establishment and back into the realm of women."

The tendency of women to form like-minded communities to cope with health-related situations – even on the Internet – underscores a fundamental difference between men and women. Women take better care of their own health and oversee the health of others in their family, including the men. Men are not usually as vigilant about their health and typically their wives will assume responsibility for seeing they take care of themselves and seek medical attention when they are sick or in need of a checkup. Except for sports injuries, baldness, impotence, and unexplained pain, men are often reluctant to schedule appointments with doctors.

Males also engage in more risky behavior than females (Cockerham 2006b). As Australian medical sociologist Deborah Lupton (1999) observes, risk taking is a gendered performance. What she means by this is that males are significantly more likely to take risks than females, especially males in their teens and twenties. Getting drunk, taking drugs, having sex at an early age, speeding in automobiles, engaging in petty theft, committing vandalism, standing up in roller coasters at amusement parks, and similar behaviors are all characteristic of young males. Young males do such things, Lupton suggests, because it adds thrills to their life, tests their courage, and they also believe it confirms their masculinity and prowess. Lupton bases her assessment on an extensive review of the research literature showing girls are much more likely than boys to avoid taking risks that cause accidents, as well as better at ensuring the safety of others, accepting adult authority, not courting danger, or proving bravery to others. Consequently, males are much more likely to be injured or have fatal accidents than females. Driving at high speeds and participating in violent sports are activities of males, not females. Higher mortality rates among males may likewise be attributed to increased exposure to dangerous activities like those of infantrymen and other combat soldiers, commercial fishermen, loggers, structural metal-workers on tall buildings, police officers, and firemen. Even though overt danger may not be present in other jobs, males are often more aggressive than females at their work and still more likely to have jobs where there is pressure to meet demands and competition from others, thereby rendering them more likely to encounter stressful work situations.

Women, however, experience stress raising small children and their experience in the workplace may be changing as they move into high-risk occupations and ambitious female executives and professionals experience career pressures similar to those once characteristic of men. Women are also moving into professional fields in large numbers that once largely excluded them – like medicine, law, finance, and higher education – and filling other jobs (e.g., construction workers, truck drivers, police officers) that once went largely to men as well. In the meantime, jobs that traditionally go to women in health care, teaching, and retailing are expanding. By 2010, some 70.2 percent of all working-age women (15–64 years old) in the US were employed compared to 59.5 percent in 1980. In the UK, some 58.2 percent of all women worked outside the home in 1980 compared to 70.4 percent in 2009. It is clear that the old traditional gender roles in which women stayed home and men supported their wife financially by earning the entire paycheck are disappearing.

Increased participation in the labor force and adverse changes in health lifestyles on the part of some women, such as increased smoking and drinking alcohol, seem to be leading to greater equality in mortality rates as men edge closer to women in health and longevity. There is some evidence to support this possibility as sex differences in mortality rates from some diseases in the US, such as lung cancer, have decreased, stabilized, or only slowly widened (Cockerham 2012). Moreover, in 2008, a national study of mortality at the county level in the US found that life expectancy for about 19 percent of the nation's women in 963 counties had actually *declined* 1.3 years or more between 1983 and 1999 (Ezzati et al. 2008). The counties with the longevity decrease were located in the Deep South, Appalachia, Texas, and the lower Midwest. The female populations most affected were rural and low-income whites and blacks. So gender, not race, was a major determinant. Some 4 percent of men were similarly affected, but their mortality figures were much less dramatic than those of women. This outcome is even more noteworthy when it is realized that between 1961 and 1983, *none* of the nation's counties showed a decline in life expectancy. A major factor in this development is the long-term effects of smoking on women, although high-fat diets and a lack of exercise were important as well. The transition from no decline in 1961–83 to a worsening of life expectancy in a large number of low-income counties is particularly troublesome because of what it signifies for the health of disadvantaged people – especially women (Ezzati et al. 2008: 8).

Another study of mortality that speaks to gender differences at the upper end of the social scale is research in Canada on the longevity of medical school class presidents over the course of a century at the University of Toronto (Redelmeier and Kwong 2004). This study found that the class presidents had significantly more professional accomplishments than their classmates during their careers. They also lived 2.4 years less on average. About a third of the class presidents were women and a third were non-white, so women and racial minority presidents had similar outcomes as men and whites holding the same office. Medical care was not a factor since they all had access to high-quality services. Rather, the crucial difference appeared to be that the presidents who took on added professional responsibilities throughout their career appeared to be workaholics who neglected their own health.

The trend for men and women in the US is seen in table 6.1, which shows life expectancy at birth for both sexes and the gender gap in longevity from 1930 to 2009. Table 6.1 shows the female advantage in life expectancy increased from 3.5 years in 1930 to a high of 7.6 years in 1970. At this point, however, the gap begins to shrink as it falls to a modern low of 4.6 years in 2011. Annandale (2010) finds the same pattern occurring in Canada, Europe, and Australia. Furthermore, she suggests that the extra years women have are not necessarily spent in good health. Even though "biological factors need to be taken into account," says Annandale (2010: 106), "they do not negate the likelihood that changes in life expectancy and in particular causes of death are significantly related to changes in gender expectations at the societal level." Arber and Thomas (2005) agree that the gap in life expectancy between men and women is closing because of changes in gender roles, risky health behavior on the part of women, and women's participation in the paid workforce. The primary causal factor in this development is not a changing biology, but changing gender roles.

Another look at smoking

Smoking stands out as an example of gender equality. The Walsh et al. (1995) study discussed in the introduction to this chapter found gender to be decisive in changing the configuration of smoking in the United States. Change came when women entered the labor force in large numbers during World War II and many started smoking. In the US, smoking had traditionally been a masculine activity, as it has world-wide. In response to the mounting scientific evidence that smoking is harmful to health, the proportion of men who smoke in the US declined from 51.2 percent in 1965 to 22.3 percent in 2007 and the pro-portion of women smokers decreased from 33.7 percent in 1965 to 17.9 percent during the same period. Whereas in 1965 half of all men and a third of all women smoked, the more rapidly declining rates for males suggests a future convergence of genders in smoking percentages.

Table 6.1 Life expectancy at birth by sex, United States, 1930–2009

	Life expectancy at birth					
Year	All	Male	Male gain over previous decade	Female	Female gain over previous decade	Male–female gap
1930	59.7	58.1	–	61.6	–	3.5
1940	62.9	60.8	2.7	65.2	3.6	4.4
1950	68.2	65.6	4.8	71.1	5.9	5.5
1960	69.7	66.6	1.0	73.1	2.0	6.5
1970	70.8	67.1	0.5	74.7	1.6	7.6
1980	73.7	70.0	2.9	77.4	2.7	7.4
1985	74.7	71.1	–	78.2	–	7.1
1990	75.4	71.8	1.8	78.8	1.4	7.0
1995	75.8	72.5	–	78.9	–	6.4
2000	76.8	74.1	2.3	79.3	0.5	5.2
2001	76.9	74.2	–	79.4	–	5.2
2002	76.9	74.3	–	79.5	–	5.2
2003	77.1	74.5	–	79.6	–	5.1
2004	77.5	74.9	–	79.9	–	5.0
2005	77.4	74.9	–	79.9	–	5.0
2006	77.7	75.1	–	80.2	–	5.1
2007	77.9	75.4	–	80.4	–	5.0
2008	77.8	75.3	–	80.3	–	5.0
2009	78.2	75.7	–	80.6	–	4.6

Note: Life expectancies for 2000–9 were calculated using a revised methodology.
Source: National Center for Health Statistics 2010.

Smoking by males began falling in the 1970s, but the percentage of female smokers did not seriously decline until the late 1980s and the rate of decrease has been much slower than that of males. The reduction in smoking among women is impeded by younger women taking up cigarettes as older women quit or die. Young female smokers are now the segment of the population most resistant to stopping cigarette use. Among today's high school students – the current generation of young smokers – the percentage of regular cigarette users is virtually the same (approximately 21 percent of each gender). While males are significantly more likely to quit smoking than females, females are less likely to do so and the proportion of smokers by sex is becoming more similar.

In Britain, men were also more likely than women to smoke in the

1970s, but today there is little overall difference – given the more rapid decline in smoking among British men (Nettleton 2006). The 2005 General Household Survey shows, for example, that 25 percent of men smoke in Great Britain compared to 23 percent of the women. However, a major exception is younger smokers in which females are now *over-represented*. According to Nettleton (2006: 51), young people's smoking is "gendered" in that 29 percent of young women smoke in comparison to 22 percent of young men. This is seen in the General Household Survey in 2005 where 15-year-old girls vastly outnumber boys the same age in smoking. Consequently, gender – either male or female – makes a difference in forming smoking patterns.

One reason for smoking that is more applicable to females than males is the use of cigarettes to maintain a slim body. In many societies, a slim figure symbolizes attractiveness, youth, and beauty. This image is imposed by society through the mass media and the preferences of males for slim teenage and adult females. Some females, in response, turn to cigarettes when they feel hungry to curb their appetite or take their mind off eating. They may skip meals and smoke instead, or eat only a few bites of food and then light up. Either way, the goal is to reduce caloric intake and the potential for weight gain and thus appear trim and sexually attractive.

Whether the reasons for smoking are assertiveness or attractiveness, gender is the decisive structural variable in the smoking pattern that emerged. The first instance is one of assertive independence first expressed by large numbers of women in the 1940s in contradiction of male norms regarding female cigarette smoking and the second is an example of women smoking in accordance with male norms favoring slimness as a standard for attractiveness. In both cases, gender-specific behavior produced the smoking pattern.

Race and Ethnicity

Race refers to a person's observed physical characteristics, with skin color the single most important determinant of an individual's racial status. Hair, eye color, and facial features are also major racial variables. Social opinions concerning these superficial external differences in appearance have resulted in racism – the belief that one or more races have innate superiority over other races. An ethnic group is identified largely on a cultural rather than a racial basis. Ethnic groups may belong to the same race or a different race than the ethnic majority in a society, but their culture, language, religion, geographical origin, and customs set them apart. Some people tend to rank ethnic groups, as well as races, in terms of superiority and inferiority that causes those ranked lower to be treated unfairly in ways that affect their quality of life, including their health and longevity.

Therefore, as Chris Smaje (2000: 115) points out, from a sociological standpoint, race and ethnicity describe the way that distinctive and often hierarchically ranked human collectivities are defined and invested with social significance. "It should be noted," states Smaje (2000: 115), ". . . that race as much as ethnicity is a *social* and not a *natural* or biological fact, a point that has now been so well established that no further justification is necessary." The concept of race has been linked historically with slavery and the colonial relationships between Europe, Africa, and the Americas that were accompanied by a racial ideology used to justify the unequal treatment of people defined as inferior by individuals and social institutions (Oliver and Muntaner 2005). The term "ethnic group" is more recent and its utility in sociological studies of health less developed in the United States than that of race. Hispanics might be thought to confound racial classifications in the US because they can be of any race, but they typically comprise a single racial minority category of "Hispanic" on the basis of their common culture and language. The categories of "black" and "white" both consist of non-Hispanics. In the United Kingdom, however, the emphasis is on ethnic groups and the term "race" is used sparingly in sociological research.

Ethnicity

Since ethnic groups have different national origins, cultural and linguistic heritages, and perhaps religious beliefs, the sociological study of such groups can be complicated – especially in multi-ethnic societies like the United States and Canada, or in European societies like Britain, France, Germany, and elsewhere that are becoming more multi-ethnic. Almost all countries are multi-ethnic to some degree. A particular problem is accurately conceptualizing and measuring ethnicity as definitions of ethnic groups vary, both over time and between countries (Aspinall 2001). In the UK, for example, ethnic identification has at times varied between England and Wales, Scotland, and Northern Ireland. Consequently, the aggregate contribution of ethnicity to health has yet to be determined.

Nevertheless, there are classic studies of ethnic groups in American medical sociology, such as Irving Zola's (1966) comparison of the way patients of Irish, Italian, and Anglo-Saxon descent differentially expressed their symptoms at two hospitals in Boston and Mark Zborowski's (1952) responses to pain among Jewish, Italian, and "old American" patients in a New York City hospital. However, there are few contemporary comparative studies of ethnic groups in the US that distinctly concentrate on health practices, disease, and mortality from the standpoint of ethnicity. They focus more on providing overall health profiles. Additionally, as Peter Aspinall (2001: 852) points out, "most studies on ethnic inequalities in health have either ignored socio-economic status altogether or regarded it as a confounding factor, frequently using measures that are imprecise or unsatisfactory."

An important exception is the study of Karlsen and Nazroo (2002) of Asian Africans, Bangladeshis, Indians, and Pakistanis in Great Britain where they found the structural variables of class experience and racial discrimination to be significantly related to health outcomes. The ethnic minority persons experiencing lower-class membership, racially motivated harassment, and discrimination by employers reported worse health than minority persons without these experiences. Another study by Helen Cooper (2002) of Pakistanis and Bangladeshis in Britain found distinct socioeconomic differences on the basis of gender and class and likewise determined that the highest morbidity was among those most socioeconomically disadvantaged. The failure to link ethnicity with class robs ethnicity of much of its explanatory power.

Race

Race might seem to be an especially powerful causal factor for health in countries like the United States and Britain, given the less healthy profiles of racial minority groups in their populations. However, Thisted (2003) argues that race is not a social determinant of health because of its lack of independent explanatory power. He observes that there are notable differences in mortality between blacks and whites in the US, yet is reluctant to say that race per se causes poor health and early death. This is because race differences in health are closely correlated with other factors like socioeconomic status and living conditions. "The problem," states Thisted (2003: S66), "with calling race itself a (social) determinant of health is precisely that we have only the correlation: we have no knowledge of how or even whether race by itself predisposes to poor health outcomes."

Since the concept of a determinant, as noted in chapter 1, requires a mechanism for action, finding a social mechanism at the aggregate level that affects the health of individuals is necessary to prove that social factors are causal. Thus far in this chapter, we have seen that age and gender produce health outcomes by way of cohort effects and socialization and experience, but race by itself does not appear to have its own independent social mechanism for doing likewise unless it is discrimination. David Williams, Harold Neighbors, and James Jackson (2003) examined 53 population-based empirical studies that investigated the association between perceptions of racial/ethnic discrimination and health indicators. They determined that despite methodological limitations in virtually all of the studies, discrimination nevertheless may have long-term consequences for health. The strongest effects were found in studies of mental health. However, their review shows that while studies of the relationship between discrimination and health may have potential for explaining health differences, past research has yet to be conclusive.

This situation is complicated by the curtailment of overt public racial discrimination in the United States making it more difficult to assess its effects on people. According to William Julius Wilson (1987), the civil rights movement of the 1960s generally ended overt discrimination on the basis of race. Wilson's basic thesis is that the social conditions facing low-income urban blacks have worsened to the extent that rates of unemployment, out-of-wedlock births, households headed by females, dependency on welfare, and violent crimes have significantly increased. He blames this development not so much on racism as on the increasing isolation of lower-class blacks in a changing economy. Wilson notes that both middle-class black professionals and working-class blacks have moved out of ghetto neighborhoods in the inner city in search of safer neighborhoods and better schools for their children. Left behind is a high concentration of the most disadvantaged segments of the black urban population whose social and economic isolation is more pronounced than ever before. At the same time, the American economy has changed from one based on manufacturing to one based on service and information. This situation has produced extraordinary rates of joblessness for those persons, many of them low-income blacks, lacking the education and skills to adapt to the broader economic changes in society. "Race relations in America," concludes Wilson (1987: 1), "have undergone fundamental changes in recent years, so much so that now the life chances of individual blacks have more to do with their economic class position rather than their day-to-day interactions with whites."

Ultimately, what makes race important in a causal sense for health is its close association with class circumstances. Subtract affluence or lack thereof from considerations of race and the causal strength of race in health and disease is severely minimized. This does not mean that race lacks any significance for health. Race continues to matter to some degree, for example, in studies of low-birth-weight babies as class is unable to completely explain racial differences (Conley et al. 2003). Conley et al. (2003: 34) go so far as to suggest that "almost all studies that factor out socioeconomic status are plagued with some level of unexplained racial variance" and that "race does not seem to be entirely reducible to class with regard to health." In another study of low-birth-weight babies, Cynthia Colen and her colleagues (2006) found that upward movement in the class structure by white mothers who were poor as children improved their possibility of avoiding having an underweight newborn by odds of nearly 50 percent. However, this was not the case for similarly upwardly mobile black mothers who had improved their class standing. Higher class standing did not significantly improve weights of black newborns. While some unexplained variance by race may occur in birth-weight studies, it does not mean differences are due to race per se; rather, other factors may be operative such as postponing childbearing that Colen et al. say upwardly mobile black women tend to do or adverse social experiences such as discrimination. Despite limited exceptions, it is the rule rather than the exception that almost every study shows class has a significantly more powerful effect on health generally than race (Issacs and Schroeder 2004; D. Williams and Sternthal 2010).

The author conducted an extensive review of the relevant research literature to determine if race alone acts independently of class to have a significant effect on health and mortality. Study after study was reviewed. Biologically race denotes differences in physical appearances (e.g., skin, hair, eye color), but there is a lack of viable evidence except for a few genetic afflictions (e.g., sickle cell anemia) that it has a singularly important role in health. Rather, it is the convergence of social, economic, cultural, and political variables impacting on health along racial lines that makes race important. When these nonbiological variables are applied in a discriminatory fashion to less powerful racial minorities, the disadvantages include reduced opportunities for good health and this is seen repeatedly in research outcomes. Does society cause sickness? Yes, it does.

The fact that non-Hispanic blacks in the US have the highest mortality rates for all causes and for most diseases is directly linked to levels of income and education in this population (Cockerham 2004, 2012). For example, as noted in chapter 1, the shift of AIDS cases and mortality away from non-Hispanic whites especially to non-Hispanic blacks and also to Hispanic males since the 1980s points to a pattern that is grounded in socioeconomic rather than biological factors. Each of these two racial minority groups has the highest rates of AIDS and the greatest proportion of poor in American society. Whereas a little more than 20 percent of all non-Hispanic whites in the United States are poor or near poor, slightly more than half of all Hispanics and slightly less than half of all non-Hispanic blacks are in this category (National Center for Health Statistics 2002). When it comes to health, disadvantaged social and economic circumstances are the driving force behind health adversities for racial minorities, not the direct effects of their skin color or other racial characteristics.

Race and physical health

There are, in fact, few diseases that can be identified with particular races. Sickle cell anemia is most common among people of African origin, as is a gene variation not found among Hispanics or non-Hispanic whites that increases the risk of developing a rare type of abnormal cardiac rhythm or heartbeat that can be fatal (Splawski et al. 2002). Swedes are prone to develop an iron metabolism disorder (hemochromatosis) that is absent in Chinese and Indians. Except for a few such anomalies, people of all races die from the same afflictions; it is the length of life and level of morbidity that varies.

Blacks live for fewer years than any other American racial/ethnic group and have more chronic health problems as well as higher mortality rates (Farmer and Ferraro 2005; Hayward et al. 2000; Issacs and Schroeder 2004; Lemelle, Reed, and Taylor 2011). This pattern, as noted, is primarily due to socioeconomic factors, not race or biology (Farmer and Ferraro 2005; Hattery and Smith 2011; Hayward et al. 2000; Oliver and Muntaner 2005; Robert and House 2000; D. Williams 1999; D. Williams and Collins 1995; D. Williams and Sternthal 2010). According to Williams (1999), socioeconomic status is not just a confounder of racial differences in health but a major component of the causal pathway by which race affects health. For most scholars, an understanding of the health status of African Americans requires an integration of racial stratification with class (Oliver and Muntaner 2005). That is, race and class are closely intertwined, so the effects of race cannot be assessed without considering the effects of class. "In sum," state Stephanie Robert and James House (2000: 84), "race and socioeconomic position are inextricably linked to each other and to health, and hence one cannot be considered without the other."

However, many African Americans have taken advantage of the increased opportunities in education and employment stimulated by the civil rights movement and significantly improved their life circumstances by acquiring the incomes, schooling, and quality of life of affluent whites. Blanket explanations about black health generally overlook the fact that many black families have experienced upward social mobility. In doing so, they have left behind socially and economically disadvantaged and less healthy segments of the African American population. The question thus arises as to whether or not their class advantage has promoted an advantage in health and longevity closer to that of affluent whites. There has been little research on this question and the answer is not fully known, but the best evidence suggests the gap remains.

One study, that of Melissa Farmer and Kenneth Farraro (2005), investigated this situation using data on self-reported health from the US National Health and Nutrition Examination Survey I and subsequent follow-up interviews covering a 20-year period. They found that black adults overall had more serious illnesses and poorer self-rated health than white adults over the 20 years. However, the racial disparity in health was highest at the higher levels of SES, showing that the health of blacks in higher social strata did not have the same gain in self-rated health as that of whites. "As education increased," states Farmer and Ferraro (2005: 201), "there was substantial improvement in self-rated health for white adults but there was no improvement for black adults." Why? Farmer and Ferraro note that it is unclear why black Americans do not show the same health benefit from education and speculate that increased awareness of racial oppression and discrimination may be a factor. They suggest that social awareness of hardships faced in everyday life could be internalized and expressed in self-rated health. Although self-reports of health tend to match physician evaluations (Ferraro and Farmer 1999), additional evidence, as discussed earlier, is needed to fully resolve this question.

Medical treatment may also be an important factor. There is evidence in recent years that the gap between blacks and whites in obtaining basic health care has narrowed, but this is not the case for more complex forms of treatment like heart by-pass surgery, appendectomies, and other surgical care; we also see blacks having fewer mammograms and tests and drugs for heart disease and diabetes than whites (Trivedi et al. 2005). The availability of physicians and hospitals in predominately black neighborhoods and communities may also be a reason for the differences in care. For example, the few cardiac surgeons in areas where blacks concentrate helps explain why blacks receive fewer coronary by-pass surgeries than whites. It is difficult to say with accuracy how much of the disparity in black mortality is due to unequal access to the full range of health care services and how much is due to adverse social conditions beyond the reach of health care systems (Kunitz with Pesis-Katz 2005). But, as stated, it is likely that disparities in access to quality health care are significant.

In future years, greater attention is undoubtedly going to be given to the health of Hispanics because they are now the largest racial minority in the United States. Because of immigration and high birth rates, Hispanics constituted 16.3 percent of the population in 2010 compared to 12.6 percent for blacks. While the black population is projected to remain stable, one in four Americans (24.5 percent) will be Hispanic by 2050. Health data on Hispanics are limited because, until 1976, federal, state, and local reporting agencies included Hispanics with whites and Hispanics were not listed as a separate category on death certificates until 1988. Despite the fact that many are poor or near poor, their overall level of health is better than that of blacks and on some measures it is better than non-Hispanic whites as they have lower rates of heart disease and cancer. Hispanic immigrants are also generally in good health when they arrive in the United States (Angel and Angel 2009; Lopez-Gonzalez, Aravena, and Hummer 2005). However, while Hispanics have mortality rates similar to non-Hispanic whites after age 45, they have much higher rates before 45 due to significantly greater mortality at younger ages from homicide, diabetes, HIV/AIDS, and liver disease (Wong et al. 2005).

Data on racial and ethnic differences in health are relatively recent in Great Britain where the national census did not include ethnic identity as a question until 1991. As Bartley (2004: 156) points out, the US government collects more extensive statistics on racial differences in health than governments of many nations, but not on class disparities in health. She notes that this is opposite from the UK where official government reports on class differences in health date back to 1921. Consequently, data on the health of minorities are much harder to come by. Further confusing attempts to analyze racial differences in the UK is that prior to 1991, mortality rates in census data were based on a resident's country of origin which meant children of Pakistani parents born in Scotland or England were classified as Scottish or English.

About 14 percent of the population in the UK belongs to an ethnic minority group or is a person of mixed race. The largest minority population is black, either African or Caribbean, followed by persons of Indian and Pakistani descent. Various other minorities like Bangladeshis and Chinese constitute the remainder. The health profile of Indians is not dissimilar to whites, but other minority groups have substantially poorer health compared to the UK average – especially

Pakistanis and Bangladeshis (Cooper 2002; Nazroo 1997). When it comes to medical care, there is evidence that Britons of all races tend to visit general practitioners more or less equally, but minorities are less likely to receive secondary (consultants or specialists) or tertiary (hospital) care (Adamson et al. 2003; Bradby and Nazroo 2010; Morris, Sutton, and Gravelle 2005). Overall, in Britain, as it is in the United States, racial differences in health are strongly related to class position (Bartley 2004; Bradby and Nazroo 2010).

Race and mental health

Research on racial differences in mental health is difficult to obtain as well in Britain, although this situation is changing (Pilgrim and Rogers 1999). One recent study shows that people of black Caribbean origin report twice as many psychotic symptoms as whites in England (King et al. 2005). However, South Asian populations have also been found to have high rates of schizophrenia and other nonaffective psychoses (Aesop 2002), so considerably more research is needed on the extent of racial disparities and the role of class in mental health outcomes by race.

The situation is far different in the United States where there is extensive research on racial differences in mental disorder. Claims that members of racial minority groups have higher rates of mental disorder than non-Hispanic whites are not supported by past studies – although debate continues (Cockerham 2010b). In fact, there is evidence that when it comes to mental problems, similarities between the races far outweigh any differences (R. Turner, Taylor, and Van Gundy 2004). Some claim that blacks have poorer mental health on average because of their increased exposure to race-related and generic stress (Tony Brown 2003). So even though there is some evidence of greater psychological distress among blacks than whites, especially in the lower class, there are other studies that say otherwise. Two studies in disadvantaged neighborhoods in Detroit found greater psychological distress among low-status whites than low-status blacks (Boardman et al. 2001; Schulz et al. 2000). Being a minority in a predominately black neighborhood, less effective coping resources with poverty, and movement of more mentally healthy whites out of largely black neighborhoods were suggested reasons for the greater mental distress among the disadvantaged whites. In other research, a nationwide study of four- to nine-year-olds by Jane McLeod and James Nonnemaker (2000) found that poverty had a greater effect on the emotional and behavioral problems of whites than blacks. The relatively high self-esteem of black mothers was observed to be an important buffer against the effects of poverty on black children.

However, studies showing differences within special population groups, like the poor, do not contradict the general position in the research literature that there is no difference *overall* between blacks and whites with respect to mental health. The National Comorbidity Survey, for example, provided strong evidence that there are no mental disorders for which either lifetime or active prevalence is significantly higher among blacks than among whites (Kessler et al. 1994). Other studies show Hispanics do not have high rates of mental disorder relative to whites and that Asian Americans have relatively low rates (Cockerham 2010b). It should not be concluded racial minorities are free of mental health problems associated with prejudice and discrimination, as they may live in distressing situations. But to date, race alone does appear to produce high rates of mental disorder. Such disorders appear to be largely due to also being poor, a condition that racial discrimination may have fostered (Bratter and Gorman 2011). The primary reason that race is associated with mental health is that many racial minority persons are found in the lower class, and class position is a much stronger predictor of mental health than race.

Conclusion

This chapter has examined the role of age, gender, and race/ethnicity as fundamental causes of health and disease. Age, through the influence of cohort effects, and gender, by way of socialization and experience, were found to be fundamental causes. Race/ethnicity, however, fails to be such a cause because its effects are so clearly undercut by the power of class position. Race and ethnicity are concepts that are socially constructed. That is, their significance is determined socially, not biologically. Critics of the fundamental cause thesis often use the weakness of race to rationalize that the entire thesis is deficient. This is an error because other social factors do operate as fundamental causes and race is not a proxy for all such variables.

Suggested Further Reading

Annandale, Ellen. 2010. "Health Status and Gender." In *The New Blackwell Companion to Medical Sociology*, ed. William Cockerham, 97–112. Oxford, UK: Wiley-Blackwell.

Examines the complexity of gender-related social change and its relationship to health and illness. Also discusses changing patterns of mortality and sickness between men and women in selected countries.

Bradby, Hannah and James Y. Nazroo. 2010. "Health, Ethnicity, and Race." In *The New Blackwell Companion to Medical Sociology*, ed. William Cockerham, 113–30. Oxford, UK: Wiley-Blackwell.
Examines the factors that cause racism and produce racial inequalities in health with a focus on the US and UK. Discussion includes the use of health services by racial minorities and the role of migration.

Payne, Sarah. 2006. *The Health of Men and Women*. Cambridge, UK: Polity.
Payne's book focuses on the health patterns of men and women in the US and UK as well as in developing countries. A wide range of gender-based health behavior is discussed, including diet, smoking, alcohol use, exercise, and drug use.

Williams, David R. and Michelle Sternthal. 2010. "Understanding Racial-Ethnic Disparities in Health: Sociological Contributions." *Journal of Health and Social Behavior* 51(Extra Issue):S15–S27.
Provides an overview of racial and ethnic inequalities in health in the US, noting how sociologists have challenged biological understanding of race, identified the role of social structure as a determinant of racial differences in health, shown how racism affects health, and discusses the effects of migration on health.

7

Living Conditions and Neighborhood Disadvantage

Living conditions are a category of structural variables pertaining to differences in the environments in which people live and work. It refers to the quality of housing, air, and water, as well as access to basic utilities (electricity, gas, heating, sewers, indoor plumbing, safe piped water, and hot water), neighborhood facilities (grocery stores, markets, restaurants, parks, libraries, recreation sites, and banks), and personal safety. These represent environmental conditions external to the individual that are generally determined by his or her social circumstances. The obvious importance of living conditions for health is the capability to affect a person's physical and mental health. Living conditions qualify as a fundamental cause of health and disease through social mechanisms like class position that impose health advantages or disadvantages on people.

A relatively new area of emerging research in medical sociology is "neighborhood disadvantage" which focuses on unhealthy urban living situations. Poor people are priced out of safe, well-located, and well-serviced housing and land; they have greater exposure to chemical pollutants and physical hazards like accidents, fires, and floods; they also experience overcrowding, poor building material, and greater noise and stress; and are least able to deal with the injuries and illnesses that result from their environment (Satterthwaite 1993). These environmental factors are further exacerbated by significantly more crime, drug abuse, alcohol-related problems, violence, and danger. Cities contain the best that human society has to offer in terms of jobs, arts and entertainment, and amenities, but also pockets of the worst social environments.

Examples of neighborhood characteristics that can be either health-promoting or health-damaging are found in the work of Sally Macintyre and her associates (2002) in the west of Scotland. They determined that five features of local areas can influence health: (1) the physical environment shared by all residents; (2) the availability of healthy environments at home, work, and play; (3) the services provided, publicly or privately, to support people in their daily lives like education, street cleaning and garbage pickup, hospitals, police, and health and welfare services; (4) the sociocultural aspects of a neighborhood like its norms and values, political, economic, ethnic, and religious features, level of civility and public safety, and networks of community support; and (5) the reputation of an area which signifies its esteem and quality of material infrastructure, level of morale, and how it is perceived by its residents and nonresidents.

Ross (2000) observed years ago that neighborhoods can be rated on a continuum in terms of order and disorder that are visible to its residents. Orderly neighborhoods are clean and safe, houses, apartments, and buildings are well-maintained, and residents are respectful of each other and each other's property. Disorderly neighborhoods present their residents with observable signs of a breakdown in social order; there is noise, litter, poorly maintained houses and buildings, vandalism, graffiti, crime, and fear. "Even if residents are not directly victimized," states Ross (2000: 178), "these signs of disorder indicate a potential for harm." Such signs signify that the people in the neighborhood are not concerned with social order and are, in fact, powerless or unwilling to enact positive change. These types of neighborhoods are increasingly being identified as causal factors in health and disease.

For example, Eric Klinenberg (2002) studied the unequal distribution of heat-related deaths in a heat wave in Chicago in the summer of 1995. Between July 14 and July 20, Chicago was unusually hot, registering temperatures of over 100 degrees Fahrenheit at times. Some 465 people died due to the heat during this one week and 739 people in total died from heat during the month of July, but Klinenberg finds the deaths were not random. Rather, some 73 percent of these deaths were people over 65 years of age. However, it was not just their advanced age that made them susceptible to succumbing to the heat; many were poor and lived alone without air-conditioning in socially isolated surroundings. Males were twice as likely to have died as females and African Americans died in much greater numbers than non-Hispanic whites. Few Hispanics were casualties. Rather, the primary causal factors were variables attached to this particular elderly age cohort – namely, the commonality of the composition of their households (a single person), living quarters (small, not air-conditioned), and limited social contacts with others in their neighborhood.

To illustrate the importance of neighborhood characteristics in this disaster, Klinenberg compared an area of Chicago that had a high proportion of heat deaths (North Lawndale) to an adjacent one that had a low number of such fatalities (South Lawndale). North Lawndale had once been largely white, but most residents moved away when local electrical manufacturing companies closed in the 1970s and jobs were lost. Since then the area had become 91 percent black and evolved into a high-crime and drug-infested locale, lacking commercial business, social organization, and public spaces. Klinenberg (2002: 91) described North Lawndale as a place where "the dangerous ecology of abandoned buildings, open spaces, commercial depletion, violent crime, degraded infrastructure, low population density, and family dispersion undermines the viability of public life and the strength of local support systems, rendering the older residents particularly vulnerable to isolation."

He illustrates this situation with interviews from residents who were afraid to leave their homes because of the potential for violence or robbery, or simply the lack of something to do outside. One person lamented: "There's no grocery store, no Walgreens [drug store], no pharmacy, nothing for us here. . . . All of the places here are deserted" (Klinenberg 2002: 94). Another said: "It's hard leaving your house, especially in this neighborhood. People are looking to see who's out. They'll come and rob you" (Klinenberg 2002: 102). Klinenberg (2002: 127) argued:

> There is little evidence that during the heat wave the most isolated and vulnerable residents of places like [North Lawndale] suffered because members of their community did not care about them. Yet there is good reason to believe that residents of the most impoverished, abandoned, and dangerous places in Chicago died alone because they lived in social environments that discouraged departures from the safe houses where they had burrowed and created obstacles to social protection that are absent from more tranquil and prosperous areas.

This circumstance contrasted to South Lawndale whose population increased through an influx of Mexican Americans who promoted a vibrant community life and developed businesses. In South Lawndale, "busy streets, heavy commercial activity, residential concentrations, and relatively low crime promotes social contact, collective life, and public engagement in general and provides particular benefits for the elderly, who are more likely to leave home when they are drawn out by nearby amenities" (Klinenberg 2002: 91). The social ecology of the neighborhood thus helped older people in South Lawndale survive as they had more social contact and opportunities for assistance in coping with the extreme heat.

In a subsequent study, Christopher Browning and his colleagues (2006) replicated Klinenberg's research in Chicago and supported his findings by showing that neighborhoods where commercial activity had declined were positively associated with heat wave mortality. Commercial decline in neighborhoods was determined by the presence of commercial buildings in fair or poor condition or burned-out, abandoned, or boarded up, and liquor stores, bars, pool halls, video game parlors, and signs advertising beer and whiskey. Conversely, neighborhoods with low commercial decline were largely protected from heat-related mortality. Browning et al. (2006: 661) concluded that the "unequal distribution of community-based resources had important implications for geographic differences in survival rates during the Chicago heat wave, and may be relevant for other disasters." This is because when one's own neighborhood is perceived with certainty to be dangerous by its residents, the more an uncertain risk posed by a potential disaster may be discounted as less relevant to their daily lives.

Analysis of the data from the Chicago heat wave study has led Klinenberg (2006) to point out the relevance of structural conditions for determining outcomes in disasters. Studies designed to make rapid assessments with individual-level data overlook the structural conditions that make people and places more vulnerable to the disasters that unfold. The effects of Hurricane Katrina on New Orleans and the Mississippi Gulf Coast in 2005 attest to the powerful role of social structure on the immediate survivability of the population and their degree of well-being in the aftermath.

Macintyre and her colleagues (2002: 125) in Britain express the same conclusion when they argue that the effects of "place" (residence) on health in industrial countries often appear "to have the status of a residual category, an unspecified black box of somewhat mystical influences on health which remain after investigators have controlled for a range of individual and place characteristics." Macintyre et al. argue that features of both the material infrastructure and collective social phenomena affect health. They suggest that future studies test hypotheses about specific chains of causation that link places of residence with health outcomes.

Unhealthy Places

Since the 1990s, the structural context in which people live their lives has become a significant area of study that goes well beyond simply linking bad housing with poor health. Frohlich and her colleagues Corin and Potvin (2001: 782) point out that the overall context of a person's living arrangements – both social and material – is a central factor in the health of that person. They explain that contextual effects not only operate where individuals depend on their personal characteristics for their level of health, but also on the attributes of the area where they live. For example, an upper-class person living in an upper-class area would have much better health than an upper-class person living in a lower-class area. Simply residing in a neighborhood that is a pocket of poverty is a risk factor for early mortality that goes beyond the characteristics of an individual. Blaxter (1990) took the same position when she points out that healthy lifestyles are most effective for people living in positive social circumstances and least effective in negative living conditions, like poverty. She suggests that the social conditions within which a person lives may be more important for health than health-related behavior.

Kevin Fitzpatrick and Mark LaGory (2000: 4) observe in the United States that "for certain segments of the population, being in the wrong place is not a matter of timing or accident, *but rather a function of the social structure.*" The place-bound risks of socially and economically disadvantaged urban areas like the inner city include homicide rates that are twice as high as elsewhere and show 25 percent greater infant mortality. The health of inner-city residents is worse than any other place in the US. For it is here, state Fitzpatrick and LaGory (2000: 8), that "the circumstances of poverty and minority status are exacerbated by segregation; the spatial concentration of these two characteristics apparently intensifies the disadvantages of low income and minority status." These disadvantages include more diabetes, heart disease, cancer, homicide, AIDS, mental disorder, and other health problems, as well as homelessness, much greater crime, and a host of other urban ills. Elsewhere, in affluent suburbs, with healthy living conditions and the ready availability of quality medical care, such risks are minimized or nonexistent. The places we live, work, and perhaps play fundamentally affect our health and well-being. This is particularly the case for the homeless who have no place of their own and live in public spaces or community shelters (Wasserman and Clair 2010). According to Fitzpatrick and LaGory (2011: 41):

Perhaps the worst-case scenario of the ecologically vulnerable is that of the homeless – a spatially dispossessed class in a variety of political and economic systems. What does it mean for humans to be placeless like the homeless are? A gathering body of evidence suggests grave consequences for the health and mental well-being of this group, with levels of criminal victimization, infectious disease, depression, and chronic health conditions many times higher than those of other low-income groups.

A person's living conditions obviously have profound consequences for his or her health and well-being. This is seen in research in Canada, where cardiovascular and stroke mortality was related to measures of neighborhood deprivation, including greater exposure to heavy auto traffic and air pollution that characterized these neighborhoods (Finkelstein, Jerrett, and Sears 2004). In Australia, chronic exposure to a low-income environment was a causal factor in the development of persistent asthma (Kozyrskyj et al. 2010). Elsewhere, research in Oslo, Norway found exposure to neighborhood deprivation early in life had a negative effect on mortality over the life course (Naess et al. 2006). Neighborhood characteristics and class position are obviously related, since people of similar class standing typically live in the same neighborhoods because the types of homes are consistent with the social standing of the residents since they are mutually affordable. However, socioeconomic status and neighborhood characteristics are not the same thing. Neighborhoods are objective physical structures and living conditions with discernible forms of social organization, while SES is a subjective social ranking based on objective measures of income, education, and occupational status. They both affect the health of individuals and often do so in concert.

The question thus arises whether health is worse in poor neighborhoods because poor people live there or do neighborhoods have characteristics beyond those of the residents which exercise independent effects on health and disease? The findings of Ana Diez-Roux and her colleagues (1997) indicate that both assertions are correct. They analyzed data from four different locales in Maryland (Washington County), Minnesota (Minneapolis), Mississippi (Jackson), and North Carolina (Forsyth County) and found that individual socioeconomic variables, especially income, were related to coronary heart disease. Persons in the lower class had the highest incidence of heart disease in comparison to people in the other classes. Diez-Roux et al. also categorized neighborhoods on the basis of median household income, level of education, median value of houses, and percent of persons in occupations II–VI (excluding category I of executives, top managers, and professionals) separately for blacks and whites. They found the more disadvantaged the neighborhood, the worse the health of the residents and this was the case for both blacks and whites. Consequently, health was worse in poor neighborhoods because poor people lived there and also because the neighborhoods themselves had characteristics promoting poor health. As Diez-Roux et al. (1997: 61) conclude: "Both neighborhood and individual-level social class indicators appear to be important in shaping cardio-vascular risk."

A subsequent study by Ross and Mirowsky (2001) likewise found that residents of disadvantaged neighborhoods in Illinois have worse health than people living in more advantaged neighborhoods. This study also tested the proposition that neighborhoods have characteristics of their own that impact on health and found that the daily stress associated with living in a neighborhood where danger, crime, trouble, and a lack of civility are commonplace apparently damages health. The conclusion was that neighborhood disadvantages negatively affect the health of its residents over and above the effects of personal disadvantages. As Ross and Mirowsky (2001: 272) put it:

> Living in a disadvantaged neighborhood is associated with worse health, net of the health consequences of individual disadvantage. Residents of disadvantaged neighborhoods tend to feel less healthy and have more physical impairments and chronic health problems such as high blood pressure, asthma, and arthritis. The impact of living in a disadvantaged neighborhood on physical well-being is mediated entirely by disorder in the neighborhood, which influences health both directly and indirectly, by way of fear. These neighborhoods present residents with observable signs that social control has broken down: the streets are dirty and dangerous; buildings are rundown and abandoned; graffiti and vandalism are common; and people hang out on the streets, drinking, using drugs, and creating a sense of danger.

In another analysis of their data, Mirowsky and Ross (2003b) correlated measures of neighborhood disadvantage with individual psychological distress to examine the possibility that disadvantaged neighborhoods only *seem* distressing because individuals distressed by their own personal disadvantages live there. They also considered the possibility that disadvantaged individuals are attracted to disadvantaged neighborhoods since it reduces the stress they might feel living in more advantaged neighborhoods. They used multilevel data with neighborhood measures parallel to those of the individuals and households in their sample. These consisted of the percentage of high school and college graduates, mean household income, unemployment rate, the percentage black, the percentage minority, and the percentages of residences owner occupied, headed by females, and headed by females with dependent children – all correlated with measures of depression.

They found that neighborhood disadvantage produces distress beyond that from individual disadvantages – with the prevalence of poverty and percentage of single-mother households the strongest predictors of depression. About 60 percent of the distressing contextual effects of neighborhoods were due to the characteristics of individuals who lived there, but elevated levels of depression also emanated from the distinctive and distressing quality of life in disadvantaged neighborhoods. Additionally, it was found that disadvantaged persons do not live in disadvantaged neighborhoods because they feel less disadvantaged there; rather, they live there because they have little or no choice. This sense of powerlessness appears to make the emotional consequences of living in a bad neighborhood even worse. Mirowsky and Ross (2003b: 155) conclude:

> People find life depressing in disadvantaged neighborhoods, characterized by high rates of poverty and mother-only households, because of the neighborhood disorder. They do not find urban residence depressing in itself. People living in the more orderly neighborhoods of Chicago are no more depressed than others similar to themselves in equally orderly suburbs, small cities, towns, and rural areas of Illinois. The distress resulting from life in the big city comes from high levels of neighborhood disorder produced by concentrated disadvantage. The residents of those neighborhoods are the ones who suffer the emotional burden.

Health and Neighborhood Disadvantage in Great Britain

The close association between neighborhoods and class is also seen in Britain where Shaw and her colleagues (1998) demonstrated the existence of a distinct social gradient in mortality ranging from low to high reflected in housing patterns. People in lower-quality housing had significantly higher mortality rates than people in other housing areas, especially when compared to those living in areas with high-quality housing. Shaw et al. provided support for earlier British studies showing mortality in disadvantaged neighborhoods to be more excessive in comparison to affluent areas and argued this situation was worsening. Several studies in recent years have likewise linked health in Britain specifically to housing conditions in which the quality of housing has been particularly associated with respiratory symptoms and infections resulting from dampness, overcrowding, and heating, ventilation, and insulation problems (Blaxter 1990; Stafford et al. 2005). Although the health of both men and women can be affected in such environments, Blaxter (1990) found that the health of men is most affected by poor housing in middle age, while among women the association is evident from the youngest years. More recent research finds that women seem to suffer the most as they perhaps spend more time in poor quality residences than the men (Stafford et al. 2005).

Home ownership is also an important factor in that it signals greater resources and motivation to maintain the quality of the property. Accordingly, owners are more likely to be healthier than renters. As Blaxter (1990: 93) observes: "Owner occupiers are always shown to have lower mortality than . . . tenants: indeed, there is more variation between owners and tenants within social classes than between social classes within [housing] tenure categories." In fact, Blaxter states there was little point in controlling for social class in housing data in her nationwide study of health lifestyles since there was so little variation by class *within* housing categories. She found that virtually no families with high incomes lived in low-quality housing and it was extremely rare for nonmanual workers with an employed breadwinner to do so either. Rather, persons in the lowest two social classes were the only ones frequenting such housing.

Other British research shows that perceived neighborhood problems of noise, crime, air quality, rubbish/litter, traffic, and graffiti are predictive of poorer health for elderly persons, but positive perceptions about neighborhoods such as good health services, closeness to shops, rubbish collection, nice areas for walks, and friendly neighbors are predictive of good health for the aged (Bowling et al. 2006). When it comes to weather, the health of the aged in their neighborhoods is not only affected by heat waves, but also by extreme cold. Old age pensioners have been found to be more likely to die in Glasgow, for example, than elsewhere in Scotland or other cold weather locales like Finland, Canada, and even Siberia (Paterson 2004). This is because excess winter deaths by people who cannot afford to heat their homes are directly linked to poverty and Glasgow has a particularly high concentration of the poor in some of its neighborhoods. Although designated the 1999 UK City of Design, Glasgow has an abundance of old, dilapidated housing badly in need of repair that house the poor.

According to a Glasgow newspaper account, one such resident is a 58-year-old woman who lives with her cat in a second-floor flat consisting of one room and a kitchen (Johnstone 1999: 13). There is no hot water and no bathroom, just a toilet in a small space. It has been two years since she last had a bath during a hospital stay. Instead, she washes herself daily in front of the fireplace. She seldom goes out and needs a stick to help her walk because of osteoporosis. It has been a month since she left her flat. There's no space for a bed, so she sleeps on an old settee. Because of continual funding cuts, the local housing association has no plans to upgrade her flat. She only pays £66 monthly for rent, which seems cheap until you see her accommodation.

Macintyre and her colleagues Laura McKay and Anne Ellaway (2005) interviewed residents in two socioeconomically distinct neighborhoods in Glasgow to determine whether the residents believed if rich people or poor people were most likely to become ill. They conducted this research because prior studies suggested that people in lower social classes and from poorer neighborhoods were less likely than people from higher classes and nicer neighborhoods to agree that the poor had worse health and life expectancy. They cited examples from an earlier English study by Michael Calnan (1987: 79) in which a working-class woman stated that she did not believe in class differences in health:

> No, I shouldn't think it makes any difference myself. I mean, it's like people with money, they get the same illnesses as we get. So I shouldn't think that would make any difference . . .

Another working-class woman even thought that being affluent was dangerous for a person's health because of the stress from job responsibilities or overindulgence on the part of the rich. This woman stated:

> No, I think the rich are less healthy, yes, I do – they are much more greedy than we are, aren't they? (Calnan 1987: 78)

In contrast, a middle-class woman said this about the health of lower classes:

> There are bound to be [differences]. Bound to be because of diets, differences in diet, and the opportunities for seeking medical help, I mean an environment as well, things like housing. I mean, if you live in a home that is damp and cold all the time, you are more likely to suffer from illnesses than the person who is not, so yes, there are differences. (Calnan 1987: 78)

Calnan supported earlier work arguing that health policies which emphasize the role of the individual being in control of his or her health are inappropriate when lay persons believe the causes of disease have little to do with their behavior. In a subsequent study, Blaxter

(1997) found the people most exposed to disadvantaged environments were least likely to say they were less healthy than people in the classes above them. Macintyre et al. (2005) confirmed these findings when they found that individuals in the lower classes and living in poorer localities were significantly less likely to believe that rich people are healthier and live longer. Since a person's health is part of his or her social identity, socially and economically disadvantaged persons apparently do not wish to degrade their social standing further by maintaining they are also likely to be less healthy. The reason this finding is important is that it shows the population most at risk for poor health is least likely to acknowledge the social gradient in health and, in doing so, imply that their health is not especially worse than anyone else's when collectively this is not the case.

Physical Health and Neighborhood Disadvantage in the US

The study of the health effects of neighborhood disadvantage in the United States has taken on greater importance in recent years. As Terrence Hill, Catherine Ross, and Ronald Angel (2005: 170) observe: "Neighborhoods where a high percentage of residents are poor, poorly educated, unemployed, and single mothers who receive more public assistance, have little or no wealth or savings, and rent rather than own their homes adversely impact on the health of people who live in them." Hill et al. note that such neighborhoods are characterized by high levels of crime, vandalism, drug use, unsupervised youth, abandoned buildings, garbage, graffiti, and noise. While it is obvious that living in unpleasant and threatening neighborhoods causes anxiety, depression, and demoralization, it is less obvious, state Hill et al., how neighborhood disorder affects physical health.

They sought to answer this question by studying the health of low-income women receiving welfare benefits in disadvantaged neighborhoods in Chicago, Boston, and San Antonio. These women had lived in the neighborhoods an average of seven years and therefore most had long-term exposure to neighborhood effects. Hill et al. suggest that chronic exposure to dangerous and disagreeable environments produces frequent physiological stress responses (the "fight or flight" response) that promote poor health. They observe that physiological changes in the body as the result of stress situations primarily involve the autonomic and neuroendocrine systems that prepare the individual to cope with threats. Heart rate, blood pressure, and gastrointestinal functions are affected, while hormone secretions by the endocrine glands increase. Unless the stress is satisfactorily resolved, frequent and general stressors can impair health over time in a number of ways, such as increasing susceptibility to disease, reducing resistance to infections and cancers, and exacerbating chronic health conditions like cardiovascular problems. "Whatever the name," state Hill et al. (2005: 172), "when violence, crime, dilapidation, and decay are experienced as a way of life, people's bodies may pay the price."

Not surprisingly, Hill et al. found that women in disadvantaged neighborhoods had much greater psychophysiological stress and reported significantly worse physical health. Symptoms included dizziness, chest pains, trouble breathing, nausea, upset stomachs, and weakness. Poor health was especially characteristic of women who had lived in these neighborhoods for more than three years as compared to women with less time as residents. Not only did these women have poorer health, but their living circumstances also influenced heavy drinking as seen in high rates of alcohol consumption (Hill and Angel 2005). Other studies have linked neighborhood influences to adolescent smoking and drinking, with parental and peer influences being important factors as well (Chuang et al. 2005). Research in New York City finds that exposure to deteriorated housing and low social cohesion in neighborhoods significantly increased the odds of suffering from asthma (Rosenbaum 2008). Another study using a national data set further illustrates the significance of neighborhood environments for health by finding an association with heart disease in women and cancer for both men and women (Freedman, Grafova, and Rogowski 2011). Even obesity may have a connection to neighborhood disadvantage as a nationwide study by Jason Boardman and his colleagues (2005) found that people in such neighborhoods have significantly greater obesity, and greater neighborhood obesity, in turn, signified that other people living there were also at greater risk for obesity. Boardman et al. (2005: 239) conclude that neighborhood "context must be considered in conjunction with individual risk factors to more fully understand obesity, a major contributor to ill health and shortened life among US adults."

In yet other research, Liam Downey and Marieke van Willigen (2005) found in a nationwide study that residential proximity to industrial activity – which is most likely for the poor, the working class, and racial minorities – is stressful for the inhabitants, adding yet another category to the list of stress-promoting neighborhood variables. Conversely, in Chicago, residents of affluent neighborhoods rated their health significantly better compared to people in disadvantaged neighborhoods (Browning and Cagney 2003). This is not surprising since these neighborhoods have healthier living conditions and better access to quality medical care. Access to services like medical care may be one of the multiple pathways through which neighborhood structure influences health outcomes in either a positive or negative direction. Living in a disadvantaged neighborhood, for example, reduces the likelihood of having a regular source of health services and obtaining preventive care, while increasing the possibility of having unmet health needs (Kirby and Kaneda 2005). Overall, these studies illustrate the harmful health effects of the structural characteristics of neighborhoods on the people that live in them.

As Leonard Pearlin and his associates (2005: 208) conclude: "the pattern of status attainments can funnel people into contexts that surround their lives, most conspicuously the neighborhoods in which they come to reside. When neighborhoods are predominantly populated by people possessing little economic or social capital, they have a notable impact on health independent of individual-level socioeconomic status."

Mental Health and Neighborhood Disadvantage in the US

There is, of course, a long history of research in American sociology on the effects of urban conditions on the mental health of a city's inhabitants, including its neighborhoods (Cockerham 2010b). This research began in Chicago in the mid-1930s with the classic study of Robert Faris and H. Warren Dunham. They used maps of the city and hospital records to identify the home addresses of some 35,000 people who lived in Chicago and received psychiatric care between 1922 and 1931 at area mental hospitals. The highest rates of schizophrenia, the most disabling of all mental disorders, were clustered in the slum neighborhoods of town. Faris and Dunham (1939) hypothesized that people living in poverty were isolated from normal social contacts and therefore more likely to develop what they called a "seclusive personality" that they believed was the key trait of schizophrenia. Being socially isolated, in their view, prompted hallucinations, delusions, and inappropriate behavior common in schizophrenic people since the usual social controls that enforced normality were missing. "If the various types of unconventional behavior observed in different schizophrenic patients can be said to result from one condition," concluded Faris and Dunham (1939: 173–4), "it appears that extreme seclusiveness may be that condition."

However, Faris and Dunham were clearly mistaken because we now know that much more is involved in schizophrenia than simply living an isolated life. Social isolation is typically a result rather than a cause of schizophrenia. Commenting nearly 40 years later, Dunham (1977: 61–2) points out that he and Faris were too young and enthusiastic at the time to see that their conclusion, while consistent with the notion that the poor are more likely to be schizophrenic, overlooks the opposite notion that schizophrenics tend to be or become poor. But what was important about the Faris and Dunham study is that they found rates of schizophrenia in Chicago could be arranged into definitive neighborhood patterns that closely matched the ecological structure of the city. The greatest concentration was in the central district where the rate for schizophrenia was 700 or more per 100,000 of the 1927 estimated population. The areas around the center and the south of the city had the next highest rates, while the affluent neighborhoods (at that time) had the lowest. For a person from the lower class, as evidenced by living in neighborhoods with the least attractive living arrangements, the greater the risk that person had for schizophrenia.

Leo Levy and Louis Rowitz (1973) later replicated the Faris and Dunham study in Chicago with addresses on 10,653 city residents admitted to area mental hospitals during 1960 and 1961. They confirmed the results of the Faris and Dunham study with respect to the distribution of mental disorder in Chicago's neighborhoods, with the exception that people diagnosed as schizophrenic were not as concentrated in the inner city. Levy and Rowitz concluded that the prevalence of serious psychiatric problems, especially schizophrenia and alcohol-related disorders, was located primarily in lower-class neighborhoods.

The major research projects that followed, like the New Haven study of August Hollingshead and Frederick Redlich (1958) and the Midtown Manhattan study of Leo Srole and his associates (1962), focused on confirming the link between class position and mental disorder. It eventually became a truism that the lower class has the greatest prevalence of mental disorder generally and schizophrenia and personality disorders in particular. Depressive and anxiety disorders, in turn, tend to be more common in the middle and upper classes. While a large literature evolved on the class–mental health relationship, medical sociologists did not start a serious examination of the social psychological effects of living conditions until they started investigating overcrowding in the 1970s and neighborhood disadvantage in the 1990s.

One particular feature of urban living that caught the attention of social scientists rather early was the density of living conditions in large cities and the possible effects of overcrowding on health. These studies attempted to test the theory that people living in large communities find themselves in a locale that is confining in relation to the number of other people present and the amount of space available. The greater the density, the more "crowded" people feel. It was thought that the tension brought on by this situation could become so stressful that physical or mental problems would result.

The preponderance of research on this topic suggested that overcrowding in neighborhoods produces little evidence of stress, but overcrowding in the home is more pathological because relationships in the home are more meaningful to the individual (Gove, Hughes, and Galle 1979). This is because disruption of relationships in the home is more central to a person's well-being. However, studies of overcrowding in the home have often been either inconclusive or only produced modest results. Overcrowding was seen to produce poor interpersonal relationships, but not poor mental health (Baldassare 1978). Finally, in the well-designed study in Chicago by Gove et al. (1979) on objective crowding (persons per room) and subjective crowding (excessive social demands and lack of privacy), it was found that overcrowding was indeed distressing. They suggested that overcrowding could result in feeling "washed out," poor planning behavior, and physical withdrawal from others. Whether overcrowding leads to mental problems is still not clear, although it is likely that overcrowding exacerbates negative interpersonal relationships and is perhaps harder on women than men.

The research literature on neighborhood disadvantage and mental health has produced findings that are significantly more robust than those found in studies of household crowding. For example, Ross (2000) compared advantaged and disadvantaged neighborhoods in Illinois and found significantly higher levels of depression in the latter. She asked whether individuals who live in disadvantaged neighborhoods suffer psychologically because of their environment and found the answer to be yes. Although more than half of the depression was linked to traits of the individuals themselves – female sex, younger age, low education and incomes, unemployment, and being unmarried – the remainder resulted from living in a poor neighborhood. The daily stressors of disorder, crime, and danger were associated with feeling run-down, tired, hopeless, and sad – all symptoms of depression. People living in neighborhoods that were clean and safe showed low levels of depression.

In Detroit, Amy Schulz and her colleagues (2000) found psychological distress highest among blacks and whites living in high poverty areas. The findings suggested that individual demoralization was not only associated with socioeconomic status, but also with neighborhood poverty and slum living conditions. Another study in Baltimore likewise found that neighborhoods with stressful living conditions had high levels of depression (Latkin and Curry 2003). Additional research in Detroit by Boardman et al. (2001) showed both psychological distress and adult drug use associated with neighborhood disadvantage.

These studies do not claim that neighborhood disadvantage drives people crazy, but they do show that poor, run-down neighborhoods can depress people who live in them and also create fear by harboring dangerous people that make particular locales threatening places. The research literature shows, accordingly, that the adverse features of such neighborhoods can be psychologically distressing.

Conclusion

The health effects of living conditions involve much more than the quality of housing, water, air, and the like, but also include the structural conditions of disadvantaged neighborhoods in cities. Fear, crime, and a lack of personal safety that promote anxiety, and substandard housing, lack of heating on cold days or air-conditioning on hot days, trash and litter on streets and alleys, lack of shops, restaurants, and other amenities, and features of concentrated poverty that promote depression and demoralization – all function as multiple social mechanisms to harm physical and mental health. The finding that overcrowding has only modest effects on mental health does not subtract from the strong evidence that neighborhood disadvantage causes depression and poor health over and above the characteristics of the individuals in these neighborhoods.

This outcome speaks to the importance of structure in health matters. These findings show that structural conditions elicit illness responses. It is not the case that either structure or agency is unimportant, for both are relevant in explaining the onset and course of health and disease. Rather, the issue is one of recognizing that both are central to explaining human social behavior and it is time to fully account for the effects of structural conditions on health. Future studies are likely to go beyond neighborhoods and focus increasingly on higher-level social units through the use of multilevel statistical methods, so the amount of variance explained by each level can be successfully determined.

Suggested Further Reading

Klinenberg, Eric. 2002. *Heat Wave: A Social Autopsy of Disaster in Chicago*. Chicago: University of Chicago Press.
A comparative history of selected Chicago neighborhoods, including those with the most heat casualties in a 1995 heat wave and the various factors (plant closings, lost jobs, degraded infrastructures, rise in crime, and family dispersion) that made older residents more susceptible to social isolation and risk of heat-related mortality.

8

Health and Social Capital

Recognition of the potential of macro-level social variables in determining health outcomes has also helped stimulate another relatively new area of research: social capital. The notion of capital, especially economic capital, has a long history in sociology, but the concept of social capital is recent and still in a state of development. Robert Putnam (2000) describes social capital as a community-level resource seen in social relationships involving networks of people, norms, and levels of trust. In medical sociology, Bryan Turner (2004: 13) refers to social capital as "investments" that people make in society, such as their membership in formal and informal groups, networks, and institutions. The more people invest socially, the more they are integrated into society and the better their health and well-being. Social isolation, depression, and illness are most likely among persons with little or no social capital.

Social capital is generally described in the research literature as a characteristic of social structures consisting of a network of cooperative relationships between residents of particular neighborhoods and communities that are reflected in the levels of interpersonal trust and norms of reciprocity and mutual aid. In effect, social capital refers to a supportive social atmosphere in specific places where people look out for one another and interact positively with a sense of belonging. Charles Lemert (2005: xi) provides us with an example of how such feelings were lost in his New York City neighborhood when one of the residents was tragically murdered:

Just around the corner from our apartment in Brooklyn there is a small deli we visit for milk and the morning papers. Until recently, the owner kept such long hours that we could drop in late Saturday evenings for the early sections of the Sunday *Times*. Since the sports and front pages are not available in that neighborhood until the morning, I would return for them the next morning. Being by nature always a little unsure of myself, I would on those occasions prepare in my mind a small account of why I was now taking more paper. "It was I who last night. . . ." But before I could finish, he'd wave me home. Though he never knew my name, he knew who I was. Once I came out in the bitter cold without my money. Again, as I fiddled through empty pockets, he sent me along with my milk for breakfast. He trusted me to pay the next time. Then one day he was gone. Murdered for the Friday night receipts, probably for drug money. Thereafter, life was changed – grotesquely for his wife and seven children, but also for me and my wife and everybody in the neighborhood. It was not just that we suddenly felt ourselves at a risk we had ignored until then but that this kind man, nameless to most of us on the block, was lost forever. His violent disappearance made life less than it had been.

Lemert (2005: 180) continues:

The last I heard (from his oldest son, who took over the deli), no one knows for certain who killed him or why. Still, everyone – the cops, the neighbors, the newspapers, probably the family for all I know – assume he was killed for drug money. This terrible little story changed and charged the little worlds in and around DeGraw and Henry Streets in Cobble Hill of Brooklyn of New York of the many, many wider worlds that come together on that corner as they do on most. We who lived there thought the murderer just had to have been an invader from the outer worlds. One reason we thought that way is that everyone who lived there, especially the Italian Americans, knew that several of *the* families [Mafia] lived nearby. No one of right mind would dare to commit a crime in our neighborhood. Screw around with one of *the* families and, as Annie puts it, you'll be a goner.

In this example, it was not just individuals who were harmed, but the neighborhood itself as the social capital generated collectively by its residents suffered a terrible loss. In another, more violent and less orderly neighborhood with low social capital, the man's death might not have been felt so deeply. Social capital is a positive product of social interaction that exists to varying degrees as a public good. And in doing so, we are now finding out that social capital has likely benefits for health, although its potential for offering new insights has been criticized for various methodological and theoretical shortcomings.

This has caused some researchers to question its relevance (Carpiano 2006). Nevertheless, as will be discussed, the concept has become increasingly popular among researchers in medical sociology and public health as they are finding that – while more extensive research and clarification is needed – health benefits may indeed be generated by social capital.

Canadian medical sociologist Gerry Veenstra and his colleagues (2005) point out, for example, that social capital has the potential to affect health in three major ways. First, it may influence health directly through the extension of a community's or social network's resources to an individual, such as through the provision of quality medical services or caregiving. Second, it may influence health indirectly through its effects on the larger social, economic, political, and physical environment that serve as health determinants for the population. And third, social capital may interact with other health determinants at the individual or group level to promote health. For example, education may be able to promote healthy lifestyles more readily in communities with high levels of social capital, than in locales lacking such capital.

The importance of social capital in health outcomes captured the attention of researchers in the Roseto study begun in the 1950s (Lasker, Egolf, and Wolf 1994). Roseto is a small mostly Italian American community in Pennsylvania. Mortality from heart disease in this town was 50 percent less than in surrounding communities and the only difference between Roseto and these other towns was that Roseto had a tradition of strong family and social ties, church participation, and marriage within the same ethnic group. The level of community support and social cohesion was so strikingly high that it was the only significant variable detected promoting less heart disease compared to otherwise similar communities nearby. "The lower incidence of heart disease in Roseto," states Bryan Turner (2004: 14–15), "is an interesting illustration of the unintended consequences of communal solidarity, arising from high levels of intermarriage, church membership, and social participation." However, once the upwardly mobile younger generation in Roseto started departing from local traditions, mortality from heart disease actually surpassed that of the other communities. Ethnic intermarriage and church and club membership declined, while many younger people left the community to seek higher paying and more rewarding jobs elsewhere.

The results of this study and others that followed indicated that people embedded in supportive social relationships had better health and longevity. Turner (2003, 2004) suggests that theories about such outcomes can be regarded as a contemporary application of

Durkheim's ([1897] 1951) theory of suicide in which individuals were protected from suicide by their close integration into society. Suicide rates were low when social integration and regulation were strong and rates were higher when social ties had eroded. Thus society existed above the individual (as a social fact) to foster social relationships that kept that person from feeling alone and isolated. Turner observed that Durkheim never used the term social capital, but maintains that his concepts of social solidarity and social facts are still valid in illustrating how social capital is protective of the health of the individual. Turner is correct on this point because social capital refers to levels of social support that a person has and feelings of belonging that promote a sense of well-being similar to Durkheim's views on social solidarity.

However, Durkheim's views on social capital have been rarely acknowledged in sociology, despite their potential (B. Turner 2003). It has fallen to other theorists to advance the concept. Four major theories have been formulated in recent years to provide a more modern interpretation of social capital and each of these theories – formulated by Robert Putnam, Nan Lin, Pierre Bourdieu, and Robert Sampson – will be reviewed before examining the research literature on social capital.

Robert Putnam: Bowling Alone

Putnam is a leading proponent of the social capital thesis. In his seminal work, *Bowling Alone,* Putnam (2000: 19) states that: "Whereas physical capital refers to physical objects and human capital refers to properties of individuals, social capital refers to connections among individuals – social networks and the norms of reciprocity and trustworthiness that arise from them." Much of Putnam's book is about his claim that American society has experienced a downturn in civic engagement since the 1970s that represents a decline in social capital. He notes, however, that levels of community involvement have fluctuated in American culture throughout its history and he promotes its revival to facilitate the growth of healthy communities in the twenty-first century.

Putnam suggests there are two types of social capital: bonding and bridging. Bonding social capital ties people together from the same social background and examples include ethnic fraternal organizations, church-based women's groups, and fashionable country clubs. Bonding tends to create strong in-group loyalty, but also can create strong out-group antagonism. Bridging social capital, in contrast, links people of different social backgrounds together. Examples of bridging social capital include the civil rights movement, youth service groups, and ecumenical religious organizations.

Each type of social capital has its own particular social function. Putnam (2000: 23) says that "bonding social capital constitutes a kind of sociological superglue, whereas bridging social capital provides a sociological WD-40 [a lubricant]." That is, bonding causes social reciprocity and solidarity to be stronger, while bridging links communities and individuals to resources and information. Individuals or communities may possess both types of social capital but do so in varying amounts. This means that the social networks providing social capital are not solely bonding or bridging; rather, they reflect more or less of each type of capital. "In short," states Putnam (2000: 23), "bonding and bridging are not 'either-or' categories into which social networks can be neatly divided, but 'more or less' dimensions along which we can compare different forms of social capital."

Putnam also suggests various ways to measure social capital. Bonding social capital can be measured by three key variables: religious social capital, group participation or civic engagement, and social trust and reciprocity. In the United States, religious social capital is particularly important because of the heavy volume of religious activity. Putnam estimates that approximately one-half of all group memberships, as well as charitable donations and volunteer work, are church-related. Churches are incubators for civic norms, skills, and recruitment, along with shaping community interests. Group participation, or what Putnam calls "civic engagement," is determined by affiliations with groups like the PTA (Parent–Teacher Association), National Wildlife Federation, Junior League, and other voluntary organizations. Those groups that have regular face-to-face contact provide significantly greater social capital than groups that never bring its members together – so groups vary in the amount of social capital they produce. Nevertheless, they provide a useful measure of community integration.

Finally, there is social trust and reciprocity that represent normative rather than behavioral standards. Putnam believes that a generalized sense of reciprocity is the touchstone or benchmark of social capital. Social reciprocity is the sense of obligation to help others with the understanding that they or someone else will help you at some point in the future. Raking one's leaves before they blow into a neighbor's yard, giving coins to a stranger for a parking meter, buying a round of drinks at a local bar, keeping an eye on a friend's house, and taking snacks to Sunday school are all examples of a generalized sense of reciprocity. Social trust is the expectation that such reciprocity is generally available. Social trust, however, is trust in other people, and is different from trust in institutions or politicians, which is why it is a measure of social capital. As Putnam (2000: 137) explains:

> In short, people who trust others are all-round good citizens, and those more engaged in community life are both more trusting and more trustworthy. Conversely, the civically disengaged believe themselves to be surrounded by miscreants and feel less constrained to be honest themselves. The causal arrows among civic involvement, reciprocity, honesty, and social trust are as tangled as well-tossed spaghetti. Only careful, even experimental research will be able to sort them apart indefinitely. For the present purposes, however, we need to recognize that they form a coherent syndrome.

Putnam argues that social capital is important for an individual's health. While the specific mechanisms by which this occurs are not fully known, he makes several suggestions about how this is likely to happen: (1) first, social networks furnish tangible assistance to people like money, convalescent care, and transportation that reduces stress and provides a safety net; (2) social networks reinforce healthy norms with respect to smoking, drinking alcohol, diet, and the like that promote health; (3) socially cohesive communities are most able to organize quality medical services; and (4), especially intriguing in Putnam's view, is his assertion that social capital may serve as a physiological triggering mechanism stimulating the immune systems of individuals to block stress and fight disease. Social connectedness, Putnam claims, is one of the most powerful determinants of an individual's health. "Of all the domains in which I have traced the consequences of social capital," states Putnam (2000: 236), "in none is the importance of social connectedness so well established as in the case of health and well-being." Beginning with Durkheim's ([1897] 1951) study of suicide, Putnam reviews the literature on social integration and finds that several studies, such as the well-known Alameda County study in California (Berkman and Breslow 1983), demonstrate the importance of social integration for health. Social networks of families and friends provide important resources and reinforce healthy behavior, while rejecting unhealthy practices. Putnam determined, after analyzing several studies, that people who are socially disconnected are between two to five times more likely to die from all causes when compared with similar individuals having close ties to family, friends, and community. He concludes that the more people are socially integrated, the better their health and longevity.

Nan Lin: Social Capital as Structure

Lin's (2001) concept of social capital is grounded in classical Marxist sociology and especially Marx's analysis of how capital emerges from social relations between capitalists (the bourgeoisie) and workers through the process of commodity production and consumption. He observes how the formation of economic capital in Marx's view results from the production and exchange of commodities as a process that entails social activity on the part of all concerned, and notes more recent micro-level interpretations of the manner in which workers in capitalist societies evolved into investors in the companies they worked for through stock options. "The confrontation and struggle between classes [in this situation]," states Lin (2001: 13), "becomes a cooperative enterprise – 'What's good for the company is good for the worker, and vice versa.'"

This led Lin to characterize social capital as relationships embedded in social structures. Lin (2001: 19) says that the premise underlying "the notion of social capital is relatively simple and straightforward: *investment in social relations with expected returns in the marketplace* [italics in original]." Thus social capital is formed through social relations and is seen as an asset by virtue of the connections between people and access to resources in the group or social network to which they belong. People are viewed as actively engaging in specific activities intended to increase their level of social capital received from their networks for the purpose of achieving their targeted goals. People in isolated situations have little or no social capital because they lack the social networks providing such capital.

Social capital in Lin's view consists of three components: structure, opportunity, and action. Lin sees social capital as a product of positions within a hierarchal social structure that stretches beyond the individual. Individuals may change positions within this structure, but social capital remains associated with the position rather than the person. Individuals do have capital, what Lin calls human capital, that they have the freedom to use as they will, but social capital consists of resources entrenched in networks and associations. As Lin (2001: 41) indicates, "social capital is rooted in social networks and social relations and is conceived as resources embedded in a social structure that are accessed and/or mobilized in purposive actions." Opportunity is also related to positions in a social structure, with persons in higher social positions having an advantage in accessing and mobilizing social ties with better resources. Consequently, social capital is not uniformly distributed in society as certain groups have access to more and better capital than others. Obviously, people in lower social class positions have less access to social capital and the capital that might be available has fewer resources. Differences may also exist between men and women and racial groups if their respective social positions are unequal.

Lin's emphasis on socioeconomic differences in social capital differs from Putnam who does not consider this type of variation (Song, Son, and Lin 2010). Whereas Putnam concentrates on how group participation and civic engagement builds social capital at the community level that individuals can draw on, Lin is more concerned with explaining the relationship between social structure and social capital. In doing so, Lin applies more of a sociological perspective to the social capital phenomenon. Putnam, however, provides a more extensive consideration of the effects of social capital on health, which might be considered surprising given Lin's long career as a medical sociologist. His work on social capital represents a departure from his usual focus, although much of his past research is somewhat related as it dealt with the role of social support (feelings of being loved, accepted, cared for, and needed by others) as a buffer against stress, feelings of tension, and depression (Lin, Ye, and Ensel 1999). Lijun Song and Lin (2009) have found, however, that social capital contributes to health beyond and independently of social support, thereby demonstrating "that social capital is a social determinant of health."

Pierre Bourdieu: A Social Form of Capital

Bourdieu was the first sociologist to formulate a concept of social capital. He did so in 1983 in a chapter published in an edited volume in Germany that was subsequently translated into English for a handbook on the sociology of education (Bourdieu 1986). However, his ideas did not reach a large audience until he started making references to different forms of capital in his better known works like *Distinction* (1984). Bourdieu (1986: 243) said that capital can present itself in three fundamental forms: (1) *economic capital*, which can be converted into money and institutionalized in property rights; (2) *cultural capital*, which can be converted, in certain situations, into economic capital and institutionalized in educational credentials; and (3) *social capital*, which consists of social obligations (connections), convertible in certain conditions to economic capital, and institutionalized in formal titles (like doctor, general, president/prime minister, or those of the nobility). Bourdieu (1986: 248) defines social capital as "the aggregate of the actual or potential resources which are linked to possession of a durable network of more or less institutionalized relationships of mutual acquaintance and recognition – or in other words, to membership in a group – which provides each of its members with the backing of the collectively-owned capital, a 'credential' which entitles them to credit, in the various sense of the word."

Additionally, Bourdieu (1986) adds the term symbolic capital to refer to the legitimation of power relations through symbolic forms which is derived from the successful use of the other capitals (Swartz 1997). However, symbolic capital and social capital are inextricably linked, as Bourdieu (1986: 257) notes "that social capital is so totally governed by the logic of knowledge and acknowledgment that it always functions as symbolic capital." Yet much of Bourdieu's (1984) interest in capital is to show how cultural resources arbitrate class differences, particularly in relation to tastes and lifestyles. In this regard, economic and especially cultural capital take up most of his attention on the topic of capital (Swartz 1997). Nevertheless, in recent years, as medical sociologists have turned their attention increasingly toward the relationship between social capital and health, his concept of social capital has received greater scrutiny.

Bourdieu views economic and cultural capital as owned by the person; social capital is a resource that accrues to individuals through their membership in particular groups or networks. Consequently, social capital is a characteristic of social networks from which individuals draw benefits. As Bourdieu (1993: 32) states: "Take social capital, for example: one can give an intuitive idea of it by saying that it is what ordinary language calls 'connections'." Bourdieu's perspective on this is similar to that of Lin who likewise locates social capital in social structures, but differs from Putnam who depicts such capital as a community-level resource reflected in networks, norms, and trust in specific geographic locales. Bourdieu emphasizes the resources of networks, while Putnam emphasizes the cohesion of networks (Carpiano 2006). Like Lin, Bourdieu also recognizes class disparities in social capital. He maintains that the amount of social capital a person possesses depends on (1) the size of the network whose connections the person can effectively mobilize and (2) the volume of capital possessed by the person that he or she can claim through connections to those networks.

American medical sociologist Richard Carpiano (2006: 167) points out that it is this twofold conceptualization of social capital that makes Bourdieu's theory useful for studying health. This is because Bourdieu requires us to consider not only the existence of community networks, but the type and volume of resources possessed by that network and the individual's ability to draw on those resources. Not all networks and individuals are equal in this process, as some networks have better resources than others and certain individuals may be excluded from particular networks.

However, Bourdieu takes an extra step by linking social capital to economic (financial) and cultural (education, taste) capital, showing how they are all interrelated – with economic capital at the root of all other types of capital. The different forms of capital can be used in concert or separately. One can also be converted into another. In *Distinction*, Bourdieu (1984: 122) refers to social capital as a "capital of social connections, honourability and respectability" that can be converted into economic, political, and social advantages. For example, people with economic capital can convert that capital into social and cultural capital. Social capital, in turn, may enhance cultural or economic capital and vice versa. Bourdieu says that the convertibility of the different types of capital is the basis of strategies aimed at ensuring the reproduction of that capital. He also maintains that the existence of a social network of connections outside the family is not a natural given, but must be cultivated and developed so that it contains social relationships that are durable and directly usable in either the long or short term.

Bourdieu did not address health concerns in his discussion of social capital and few studies in medical sociology utilize his approach. Bourdieu's work is not as well-known in American medical sociology and translations from French are often difficult to read because of his writing style. Almost all studies of social capital and health have instead relied more or less exclusively on Putnam's theory. However, Bourdieu provides a framework of analysis for conceptualizing social capital that some researchers have described as having considerable potential (Carpiano 2006). For example, public health researcher Anna Ziersch (2005) observed in her research in Adelaide, Australia, how formal and informal networks – what she called infrastructures – produced social capital resources in the form of social support, social cohesion, and civic activities. Thus the source of social capital was social structures and the outcome was resources that could be used by individuals consistent with Bourdieu's approach. "The findings," states Ziersch (2005: 2130), "suggest that Bourdieu's notion of [social capital] is clearly part of the jigsaw puzzle of health inequities in the way it links the everyday social lives of individuals to the broader structural factors that have an impact on health."

Robert Sampson: Collective Efficacy

Another concept of social capital that has recently appeared is collective efficacy theory developed by Robert Sampson and his colleagues (Sampson 2003; Sampson, Morenoff, and Earls 1999; Sampson, Raudenbush, and Earls 1997). Sampson takes the position that the nature of cities and the meaning of community have changed. There is no longer a strong norm of neighborhood ties in many urban areas. People generally have fewer intimate connections due to less frequent face-to-face social interaction. Consequently, the notion that neighborhoods serve as a primary group that possesses the usual intimate and affective relationships that characterize other primary groups like the family is a false assumption. Sampson and his associates, however, say that the decline in personal ties notwithstanding, there has nevertheless been the emergence of a large body of research findings showing links between the social characteristics of communities and the health of the individuals that live there. Typically, the health of residents in low-income and low-status communities is poor in comparison to residents elsewhere. In short, says Sampson (2003: S55), research in social and behavioral science has established a reasonably consistent set of findings showing the relevance of community characteristics for health.

The question thus arises as to how communities and larger collectives might be important for health. Sampson (2003: S56) therefore proposes: "If multiple and seemingly disparate health outcomes are linked together empirically across communities and are predicted by similar characteristics, there may be common underlying causes or mediating mechanisms." The neighborhood effects of concentrated poverty, for example, likely involve collective aspects of neighborhood life like social cohesion, spatial diffusion, local support networks, informal social control, and subcultures of violence. The challenge is to measure their effects at the community level to determine the collective-level pathways to poor health. Sampson and his associates undertook this challenge by analyzing data from the 1994–5 Community Survey of the Project on Human Development in Chicago Neighborhoods. The researchers organized the city's census tracts into 343 relatively homogeneous neighborhood clusters and interviewed a sample of some 8,782 residents representing all clusters. They also used videotaping equipment to observe micro-community environments that affect health like unsafe housing, garbage in the streets, and public intoxication, and interviewed some 2,800 city leaders in religion, politics, business, law enforcement, education, and community organizations.

They used their data to test a theory of "collective efficacy" that reflects levels of mutual trust and shared expectations for intervening on behalf of a neighborhood's common good by the people who live there. Sampson (2003: S58) states: "Moving away from a focus on private ties, the term collective efficacy is meant to signify an emphasis on shared beliefs in a neighborhood's conjoint capability for action to achieve an intended effect, and hence an active sense of engagement on the part of residents." As part of their study, Sampson and his colleagues wanted to know if the respondents felt their neighbors could be counted on to take action if (1) children were skipping school and hanging out on a street corner; (2) children were spray-painting graffiti on a local building; (3) children were showing disrespect to an adult; (4) a fight broke out in front of their house; and (5) the fire station closest to home was threatened with budget cuts. Using these items, they were able to construct measures of social cohesion and informal social control that were combined into a global scale of collective efficacy.

Collective efficacy theory emphasizes the capacity of neighborhoods to mobilize social action for positive outcomes. It was found that neighborhood clusters ranking high in collective efficacy showed significantly lower rates of violence, homicide, and low birth-weights than those neighborhoods low in such efficacy, leading Sampson to suggest that collective efficacy has implications for health generally. He argues that neighborhood effects are not confined to single neighborhoods but that spatially proximate neighborhoods interact with one another to extend those effects to larger areas. Obviously, the notion of collective efficacy requires more extensive testing on a variety of health problems to determine the theory's validity.

One such study, also using the same Chicago data, is that of Christopher Browning and Kathleen Cagney (2002) who found that individuals living in neighborhoods with higher levels of collective efficacy reported better overall physical health. They found that education was strongly associated with self-rated physical health, but this effect largely disappeared in neighborhoods with low collective efficacy. In other words, in neighborhoods lacking in collective action to improve local conditions, the benefits of education for the health of the residents was not strong. "These findings suggested," state Browning and Cagney (2002: 395), "that the benefits of education for health – which have proved robust and substantial across a range of studies – are dependent on social context." If this finding holds in future studies, it would help illustrate why low education and poor health are synonymous: poorly educated people find it difficult to rise above the effects of low social capital to improve their health.

Research Applications of Social Capital

Using data from the same Community Survey of the Project on Human Development in Chicago Neighborhoods as Sampson et al. (1997, 1999) and Browning and Cagney (2002), Kimberly Lochner and her colleagues (2003) investigated whether the social organization of neighborhoods – not just their physical environment – affected mortality rates. They constructed a hierarchical linear model to examine the association of social capital with race and sex in Chicago's neighborhood clusters. The analysis showed that high neighborhood social capital as measured by reciprocity, trust, and civic engagement was linked to lower neighborhood death rates after adjusting for neighborhood material deprivation. Thus social capital affected mortality rates even after the effects of run-down, physically dilapidated neighborhood environments were taken into account.

Specifically, higher neighborhood social capital was linked to lower neighborhood mortality rates for total mortality, heart disease, and other causes of death for whites of both sexes and to a somewhat lesser extent for blacks. An exception was cancer mortality that was not associated with social capital for either sex or race. Other than cancer, this study produced evidence of relatively strong effects of social capital on mortality at the neighborhood level.

While it might be argued that this particular Chicago data set provides especially positive and friendly results for researchers – like Lochner et al., Sampson et al., and Browning and Cagney – whose studies advance the social capital thesis, the Lochner et al. findings are also consistent with those of Ichiro Kawachi et al. (1997, 1999) using different data at the state level. Kawachi et al. (1997) found that social capital – as indicated by interpersonal trust, norms of reciprocity, and memberships in associations – explained a significant portion of mortality across the 50 American states. This link remained after controlling for state differences in median income and poverty rates. Moreover, subsequent research by Kawachi et al. (1999) on self-reported health status and social capital at the state level produced similar findings supporting the importance of social capital for health.

Other studies that have successfully used the social capital concept include research by Drentea and Moren-Cross (2005), discussed in chapter 6, who investigated an Internet site for young mothers that served as a virtual online community for support and the exchange of information about caring for babies and children. They agreed with the theoretical line advanced by Lin (2001) who maintains cybernetworks constitute a form of social capital. They found that the website they studied created a source of feminine thinking, thereby establishing a circle of women that took the power to influence them away from an exclusive reliance on the masculine medical establishment and placed it in a realm of women. The Internet helped young mothers establish links with other women like themselves, as urban neighborhoods are often empty of working mothers and their offspring during the workday. "In this case," state Drentea and Moren-Cross (2005: 939), "we find a virtual community of mothers with young children increases social capital during a time when women are [often socially] isolated as new mothers."

Another recent study of social capital is that of Gerry Veenstra and his colleagues (2005) who conducted a telephone survey of a randomly selected sample of adults in the mid-sized city of Hamilton, Canada. Social capital was measured by the number and depth of involvement in voluntary organizations by the respondents. These organizations included the YMCA, YWCA, labor unions, Kiwanis, Rotary Club, Ladies Auxiliary, Optimist Club, Neighborhood Watch, Francophone Community Center, volunteer at hospital and old age home, and various church and synagogue memberships and activities. The study sought to determine if this form of social capital in four diverse neighborhoods influenced self-rated health, body mass, emotional distress, health behaviors, and various chronic health conditions like arthritis, asthma, high blood pressure, and diabetes. Veenstra et al. hypothesized that social capital, as determined by participation in organizations, will (1) be more strongly related to health in some neighborhoods than in others, (2) have greater effect in disadvantaged neighborhoods where other types of resources are not readily available, and that (3) some forms of civic engagement will be more strongly related to health than others.

They found that overall involvement in voluntary organizations had positive but not overwhelmingly strong effects on well-being, but was strongest in relation to self-related health, emotional distress, and body mass index scores. Memberships in such associations were believed to foster positive health behaviors and coping skills because of their behavioral codes (norms) and awareness of the availability of their resources that served to reduce stress. The first two hypotheses about neighborhood differences, however, were not supported by the data. While the neighborhood of residence had effects on health, social capital affected health independently of the neighborhood people lived in. Veenstra et al. speculated that this outcome was due to the fact that the associations the respondents belonged to spanned many neighborhoods causing similar effects throughout all neighborhoods and reducing the strength of neighborhood-specific associations. The third hypothesis was supported in that associations with work colleagues and religious groups involving socialization and feelings of closeness were more important for health than other forms of civic participation.

While their results were mixed with respect to the social capital–health relationship in that social capital was related to some but all not measures of health, Veenstra et al. argue that it would be premature to discard social capital as an important health determinant. More extensive research is needed to ascertain its exact contributions. They called for additional research, particularly research that treats social capital as a form of power giving persons and groups the ability to carry out their will even when opposed by others, rather than only treating social capital as a reflection of consensus for accomplishing goals that everyone shares. Theoretically they favor Bourdieu's (1984) approach of using the various forms of social, economic, and cultural capital to identify cultural distinctions and the social class groupings that underlie these distinctions to show how such capital affects the social space people live in.

Elsewhere, in Sweden, Jan Sundquist and his associates (2006) used voting participation as a measure of social capital in a nationwide study consisting of all 2.8 million persons in the country between the ages of 45 and 74 years at the end of 1997. The experiences of this age cohort with respect to coronary heart disease were recorded over the next two years. Social capital was measured by the number of people who voted in the 1998 *local* government elections divided by the number of people in their neighborhood who were eligible to vote. The neighborhoods were subsequently categorized as having low, medium, or high levels of social capital, depending on their voter turnout. Sundquist et al. justified this approach on the basis of Putnam's (2000) recommendation that voting is a proxy of empowerment and political participation, and they deliberately chose voting in local rather than national elections to obtain neighborhood-relevant data. They found a significant difference between neighborhoods as those with low social capital (voting participation) had a much higher incidence of coronary heart disease. "Without denying or detracting from the importance of individual action," state Sundquist et al. (2006: 960), "the social capital perspective pulls the spotlight back to light up a wider stage, illuminating individuals and their actions in the larger context of society."

British researcher Wouter Poortinga (2006), in contrast, suggests that variables at the individual level are more important than variables measuring collective factors when it comes to the effects of social capital on health. He examined data from 22 European countries and argues, contrary to Lin (2001), that social capital is more embedded in individuals than social structures. This finding, however, is likely due to the way social capital was measured. Poortinga aggregated the average scores of individuals on questionnaire items about trusting other people (social trust) and their total number of memberships in voluntary organizations (civic participation) as representative of social capital at the collective level. Consequently, his collective measures were derived from summing individual characteristics and were therefore not the properties of collectivities whose strength he was allegedly testing.

Other researchers have taken the same approach of aggregating individual responses to represent measures of social capital. One such study summed the average time of volunteer service work by college students as a measure of campus-level volunteering (Weitzman and Kawachi 2000). Campuses with high aggregate scores for such volunteering had less binge drinking. But whether or not the summed scores of individual students reflect campus-level properties is a matter of conjecture. The effects of structures are best determined by measuring characteristics that are independent of individuals. Given the variety of measures of social capital and the lack of consensus about its precise meaning, it is clear that exact concepts and measurement strategies – having general applicability for researchers – are required.

Conclusion

Despite the obvious difficulty in measuring a variable like social capital that operates at multiple – individual, group, neighborhood, community, etc. – conceptual levels, the general concept has grown in popularity as an explanation for structural influences on health outcomes. At present, however, there is no generally accepted definition of social capital as ideas about what constitutes the concept are relatively new. But there does seem to be a general understanding that social capital is a feature of social structures consisting of a network of cooperative relationships between people in communities involving high levels of interpersonal trust and strong norms of reciprocity and mutual aid that facilitate action for shared benefits (Coleman 1988; Veenstra et al. 2005). Such features can further the goals of individuals and also exist as resources for social groups and communities (Lin 2001).

However, low or nonexistent social capital fashioned by a neighborhood or a community obviously has a negative impact on the quality of life of its residents. As Vicky Cattell (2001) determined in a qualitative study of a low-income community in London: neighborhood characteristics influence the forms of social capital created. She found that a neighborhood's history, work opportunities, resources, opportunities, norms of cooperation and reciprocity, patterns of mutual aid, information exchange, perception of safety, and stability are preconditions for the development of social capital. Thus, Cattell concludes that community context is key to understanding the genesis of social capital.

The social capital concept has both subjective and objective components, or what some might call cognitive and structural elements. Its subjective aspect is the positive feeling stemming from awareness of belonging to a community that offers social support for problems. Such feelings promote a sense of well-being. The objective component is the actual provision of assistance when in need, such as advice, looking out for one another, help when sick, law enforcement, options for emergency financial support, and the establishment of community medical and social welfare services. The notion of social capital, consequently, is that of resources embedded in a neighborhood or community structure beyond the level of the individual that the person can draw on to improve his or her life situation, including health. Social capital may be able to enhance health and extend longevity not only through the provision of mutual aid and social support, but also through the maintenance of social norms promoting positive health lifestyles with respect to smoking, alcohol use, diet, exercise, and the like (Berkman and Kawachi 2000; Lochner et al. 2003). Consequently, social capital is of interest to medical sociologists because of its potential for serving as a social mechanism linking inequality to health or, conversely, enhancing the health of people in neighborhoods and communities with high levels of it.

Most researchers, as noted, use Putnam's work as their starting point, but in sociology others favor Lin or Bourdieu, while some are utilizing the collective efficacy theory of Sampson. The proposition that structural dimensions of communities can affect health and longevity is fundamentally different from the usual studies of socioeconomic status that have been conducted in the past several decades (Young and Lyson 2001). Part of its popularity may not only be due to it allowing researchers to open a new area of inquiry, but also to promote movement toward constructing more complete and thorough explanations of social causes of health.

Conversely, full acceptance of the role of social capital in causing health outcomes is not universal in medical sociology or other health-related fields. Some studies find the effects of social capital in some situations to be weak. The message of social capital research, however, is not to claim individual-level characteristics are unimportant or are superseded by such capital (although that might be the case in some circumstances), but that structural variables like communities can have a causal impact on health. The extent to which this is precisely the case needs to determined. It is clear, for example, that we do not fully understand the connection between health and well-being in individuals with social capital by way of feelings of trust, social support, happiness, confidence, self-esteem, and sense of belonging (B. Turner 2003). So although considerable work needs to done, the relationship between social capital and health is another promising avenue of research showing how social factors cause health and disease.

Suggested Further Reading

Lin, Nan. 2001. *Social Capital: A Theory of Social Structure and Action.* Cambridge, UK: Cambridge University Press.
An advanced book in which the author, a leading medical sociologist, presents his theory of social capital that he sees as investments in social relations that people can use as a cushion against stress.
Song, Lijun, Joonmo Son, and Nan Lin. 2010. "Social Capital and Health." In *The New Blackwell Companion to Medical Sociology*, ed. William Cockerham, 184–210. Oxford, UK: Wiley-Blackwell.
Reviews the various theories of social capital, including those by Bourdieu, Lin, Putnam, and Coleman. Discusses the theoretical development of the concept and the empirical evidence supporting it, followed by a discussion of major challenges and future directions. Lin and two of his former students co-author the work.

Concluding Remarks

The purpose of this book has been to call attention to the capability of social factors to cause health and disease. The basic thesis is that such factors have *direct* causal effects on physical health and are not just background or secondary variables in the hunt for causation. Recognition of the causal properties of social variables in health matters has been slow in coming, but there is growing evidence that this is indeed the case. This development will require a paradigm shift away from methodological individualism to a more balanced conceptual approach that includes a renewed focus on structural effects. As discussed, methodological individualism refers to research centered on the individual attitudes and behaviors, thereby making the individual the focal point of the researcher's attention. Variables beyond the level of individuals and small groups in determining health outcomes are thus ignored, even though people can find their health and longevity directly influenced – either positively or negatively – by social structures. A comprehensive understanding of health and disease is therefore impossible without considering the role of macro-level structures.

The Return of Structure

As Bryan Turner (2003) points out, one might argue that much of the influential research in medical sociology in the second half of the twentieth century, namely symbolic interaction and the vast volume of literature on stress, has been predominately social psychological. Turner finds that even Parsons, who attempted to develop a sociology of sickness with his concept of the sick role, produced an area of research that became typically psychological. Durkheim's theory of suicide is depicted as a self-consciously sociological theory as it locates the causes of suicide in social forces rather than the psychology of individuals. But, as we have seen, Durkheim did not become a strong influence in medical sociology and theories of causal structures in health matters have languished.

Acknowledgment of the causal role of social factors and conditions in sickness and mortality has been slowed not only because of the priority given to the individual in social science research, but also results from prior methodological difficulties in determining the direct effects of macro-level variables on the health of individuals. With the increasing use of multilevel forms of statistical analysis in medical sociology like hierarchical linear modeling, random coefficient models, and mixed models, the way is open to simultaneously determine the effects of sequentially higher and multiple structures on health.

For example, in hierarchical linear models, lower-level units that are nested or contained within higher ones can be analyzed to take account of their interdependence within higher-level units. This is seen in the research of Kirby and Kaneda (2005) who used hierarchical linear modeling to analyze data on individuals nested within block groups (approximations of neighborhoods) nested within primary health care service areas nested in counties. They determined that living in socioeconomically disadvantaged neighborhoods is associated with (1) a decreased likelihood of having a usual source of health care, (2) an increased likelihood of experiencing unmet health needs, and (3) a decreased likelihood of obtaining recommended preventive care. Kirby and Kaneda suggest that when disadvantaged individuals are concentrated into specific geographic areas, disadvantage becomes an "emergent characteristic" of those areas that affects the ability of its residents to obtain needed health care. Thus we see an example of how structure (neighborhood disadvantage) serves as a social mechanism adversely affecting the health needs of individuals and ultimately their health.

It is important to note once again, however, that structural variables should not be treated as an aggregation of individual-level variables, but as direct measures of the structures themselves. For example, measures of neighborhoods should reflect the characteristics of the neighborhood (i.e., home values, businesses, recreational facilities, parks, banks, health care, crime rates, and public safety) not the individuals who reside there. This is necessary to avoid confounding structural characteristics with individual characteristics, so the precise effects of neighborhoods on individual health can be determined.

While some multilevel studies may show that agency and individual-level variables in some circumstances are more important for health than structural variables, structure is nevertheless always present and its effects still need to be taken into account in order to provide complete explanations of the social phenomena being studied. Agency and structure operate on a continuum in which agency is stronger in the social conditions on the lower end and structure on the upper end (Cockerham 2006b). Yet there is no hypothetical moment in which agency is totally free of structure (Emirbayer and Mische 1998: 1004). Structure is always with the individual. Consequently, the argument here is that the relative contributions of *both* agency and structure need to be considered when analyzing health and disease and that structure is capable of exerting a direct causal effect.

Overlooking the influence of social structures on people removes an ever present and vital variable from the analysis of their social behavior. Moreover, when the relative strengths of structure and agency are considered it is the case that the effects of structure cannot only outweigh agency, but render it relatively powerless (G. Williams 2003). People with jobs carrying high risks to their health, for example, may have little or no choice or option about exercising agency because they need the money the jobs pay.

Agency, in turn, does not seem to be capable of exerting a similar smothering effect on structure, although agency may at times be more important than structure in particular social scenarios than in others. For instance, an individual may decide to change physicians when the attending doctor is uncommunicative, brusque, or makes a mistake and this behavior may have little or nothing to do with structure. Everyday human social behavior incorporates the exercise of both agency and structure in its calculation and researchers need to do likewise. They also need to recognize that agency and structure are not equal in their influence on that behavior – as one or the other is likely to be dominant.

Structure–Agency Interface

The capability to determine the relative effects of hierarchical structures on individuals should not signal the demise of qualitative studies that put a human face on quantitative results or what was described earlier as a narrative of numbers. Qualitative studies that provide first-hand observations and reports of social life at the micro-level deepen our understanding of the effects of structure on the everyday lives of people in their natural social environment – provided such studies are alert to and observant of the effects of structure on the people in the study. Qualitative studies, like participant observation, must therefore be especially attentive to structural influences that go beyond and act on the small group.

Unfortunately, few qualitative studies consider structural influences and instead focus solely on agency and the face-to-face interaction of individuals in constructing and maintaining their specific social world. A distinct exception is the study of diabetes clinics in Chicago by Lutfey and Freese (2005) who included the organizational features of the clinics, structural constraints on patients like incomes, job demands, and private health insurance, and external influences on patient motivation such as wait times, the cost of compliance to their health regimen, and lifestyle adjustments to their observations and interviews. In doing so, they were able to show how structural variables either enabled or impeded the ability of diabetic patients to cope with their disease.

The availability of multiple research methodologies capable of measuring the effects of structure on agency forecasts growth in the number of studies investigating the agency–structure interface. It also forecasts changes in sociological theories, namely, the rise of a neo-structuralist approach – in which the influence of structure becomes more prominent in theoretical discourse. This does not mean a return to rigid structural theories like structural-functionalism or the French structuralism of the 1960s, but it does signify a reduced dependence on agency-oriented theories in favor of an approach that restores greater consideration to structure. Thus, the antiquated notion that people are essentially automatons – a contrivance whose actions are fixed, routine, and mechanical with little or no indication of active thought – who are driven down particular behavioral pathways by the larger social order remains as erroneous today as it was in the past. As Giddens (1984: 179) reminds us, there is no such entity as a distinctive type of purely "structural explanation" in the social sciences, since all explanations now involve at least an implicit reference to the purposive, reasoning behavior of agents and the intersection of that reasoning with the constraining and enabling features of the social and material contexts of that behavior.

Bourdieu, whose concept of habitus has been labeled by Jeffrey Alexander (1995: 136) as "a Trojan horse for [structural] determinism," likewise rejects the notion of such determinism. Indeed, Bourdieu's work is heavily weighted toward structure. However, in taking up the Aristotelian notion of *hexis*, that Bourdieu (1996: 179) finds converted by scholastic tradition into *habitus*, he wanted to show his negative reaction to structuralism and what he regarded as its strange philosophy of action that made the agent disappear by reducing it to the role of a supporter or bearer (*Träger*) of structure. Bourdieu's use of the German word "*Träger*" in this instance is instructive because its literal meaning conveys a sense of the individual being subjected to the weight of a very heavy burden (structure) like a porter or bearer on a safari or a furniture mover going up the stairs of a dwelling. He therefore wanted to demonstrate the active, inventive, and creative capacities of the habitus and the agent, which he felt were not adequately expressed by the term "habit." "It seemed to me," states Bourdieu (1996: 180), "that the concept of habitus – long outmoded, despite a number of occasional usages – was the best one to signify that desire to escape from the philosophy of consciousness without annulling the agent in its true role of practical operator of constructions of the real."

So agency does appear in Bourdieu's sociology, just as structure surfaces in the work of Giddens. For example, Giddens's (1984) structuration theory is weighted most heavily toward agency, but it makes a major contribution to theory generally through its notion of the duality of structure depicting structure as either constraining or enabling for the individual. Thus we see considerations of both agency and structure in the composition of both sociological approaches. But neither approach provides a balanced version in which agency and structure are equal partners, and that is likely the case in real life as well.

French social theorist Bruno Latour (2005: 215) uses the example of the relationship between the puppeteer (social structure) and his or her puppets (individuals) to discuss the agency–structure divide. Of course, the puppets are bound to the puppeteer by strings or threads, but if the puppets are agency and the puppeteers are structure, it is simply implausible that domination is transported through the strings without translation. In this metaphor, the puppets may in fact indicate the direction of movement to puppeteer, although the puppeteer continues to hold the strings. Latour maintains that current sociological theories cause us to do "double-entry accounting" in that whatever influence comes from the outside (structure) is deducted from the total sum of action allocated to originating from the inside (agency). Latour (2005: 215) describes the situation this way:

> With that type of balance sheet, the more threads you added in order to *make you act* from the outside, the *less* you *yourself* acted: the conclusion

of this accounting procedure was inescapable. And if you wished, for some moral or political reason, to save the actor's intention, initiative, and creativity, the only way left was to increase the total sum of action coming from the inside by *cutting some of the threads*, thus denying the role of what is now seen as so many "bondages," "external constraints," "limits to freedom," etc. Either you were a free subject or you lived in abject subjection. And of course critical sociologists reinforced this tendency since they couldn't talk about the "outside force" of the social, except by gloating over the "narrow constraints" put by "the anonymous weight of society" over "personal freedom."

Latour concludes that it is not the sociologist's job to fix the limits of agency and structure in advance. And this should be the position of any forthcoming neo-structuralist theory or addition to existing theories. Consequently, the thrust of a new approach to structuralism should not be to advocate the outright domination of structure over agency, but to determine the situations in which structure is dominant and others in which it is less dominant or perhaps ineffectual. The basic call is for structure to be given serious consideration when analyzing social life and accorded causal significance when indeed it is a causal factor in health, disease, or other situations.

Policy Implications

Structure's role as a social determinant of health and disease carries with it policy implications, as its effects should be modifiable to a certain extent by social policies. We know that universal health insurance coverage mitigates health inequalities by ensuring people have access to medical care, but the British experience unambiguously shows that such insurance coverage is not sufficient to eliminate socioeconomic differences in mortality (Quesnel-Vallée and Jenkins 2010). Despite health care, persons on society's lower rungs still live in disadvantaged social and physical environments and have less healthy lifestyles regardless of the medical treatment they receive.

Since class differences are based upon unequal resources, an obvious proposal is a redistribution of those resources. Phelan et al. (2010: S37) note "that if we redistribute resources in the population so as to reduce the degree of resource inequality, inequalities in health should also decrease." However, requiring people to hand over some of their hard-earned assets to people with less in a democratic society would be extremely difficult or impossible to achieve for any politician or political party. Since capitalism is an inherently unequal economic system, safety nets for the poor are provided by the state in the form of welfare benefits. These benefits are intended to provide a basic level of resources for an individual's health and well-being, although they are typically not generous and subject to erosion or reduction in economic hard times. So what Phelan et al. suggest is policies that better support state intervention, such as increasing the minimum wage, boosting social security benefits, assisting low-income persons and the homeless to obtain adequate housing, reducing unemployment, and improving opportunities for universal education. Such policies, they say, are health-relevant and understanding how they are relevant is an important area for research in medical sociology. With current research methodologies better able to measure structural effects on the health of populations and individuals, medical sociology is in an improved position to make future evidence-based policy recommendations.

Conclusion

The evidence examined in this book shows that, as Link and Phelan (1995) initially suggested, social factors cause health and disease. For example, the primary variable determining the shape of an individual's health lifestyle – either positive or negative – is that person's location in a class hierarchy. Study after study confirms that the lifestyles of the upper and upper-middle classes are the healthiest and those of the lower class the least healthy. The power of class is so pervasive that it produces differences in the effects of age, gender, and race/ethnicity beyond those already produced. The effects of race in health matters generally are in fact largely determined by class. While age and gender do have some explanatory power in their own right, other structural variables like the influence of collectivities and living conditions also impact on the form of health lifestyles adopted by the individual. The end result is a pattern of lifestyle choices that typically fit a particular mode of living decisively influenced by structure. Since health lifestyles can either cause or prevent or delay the onset of disease – especially chronic conditions like heart disease, diabetes, and cancer that serve as the leading causes of human mortality – strong evidence of the critical role of social factors in determining their form makes it impossible to deny to such factors a causal role in health lifestyle-related outcomes.

While some scholars have suggested that class influence is waning or that class differences are no longer important – the so-called "end of class" thesis – we have seen that class is the strongest predictor of health, disease causation, and mortality in medical sociology. This is particularly evident when social gradients in mortality universally display a hierarchical gradient from low to high in death rates along class lines. The enduring outcome of good health at the top of society and worse health in descending order toward the bottom marks class as a "fundamental cause" of health, disease, and death. According to Link and Phelan (1995), the requirements that a social variable must meet to qualify as a fundamental cause are: (1) influencing multiple diseases through (2) multiple pathways of risk that are (3) reproduced over time, and (4) involve access to resources that can be used to avoid these risks or minimize the consequences should they occur. Class clearly meets all these requirements.

As previously noted, the social aspects of age and gender can also function in a causal role. Age acts as a social force in health matters through cohort effects on individuals and while the strength of age as an independent variable can be undercut by class and gender, there are situations in which age cohort effects can be powerful causal factors as well. Gender obviously has an important effect on health as women are sick more often than men but live longer and have been found to adopt healthier lifestyle practices as a general rule. The differential position of women in comparison to men lies largely in differences in socialization and experience, as well as biology, but the ultimate result is that gender can also be a fundamental cause of health and disease as men and women act in ways normative for their gender. Race/ethnicity is a different matter, however, as it fails to qualify as a fundamental cause – until stronger evidence is forthcoming – because its effects are so clearly undercut by the power of class position. Critics of the fundamental cause thesis typically use the weakness of race to argue that the entire causal thesis for social variables is deficient. However, this is an error because other social factors do operate as fundamental causes and race is not a proxy representing all other social determinants of health.

One social variable that is attracting considerable attention from researchers is that of neighborhood disadvantage which strongly supports the relevance of structure in eliciting poor health and illness responses. The characteristics of neighborhoods themselves, in terms of facilities, public safety, a socially supportive environment, hazards, noise and stress, and the like, that extend beyond the individual characteristics of the people who live there have been shown to affect levels of health and mortality. The literature on social capital is not as powerful, but growing numbers of studies are finding it to be relevant in determining health outcomes. More research is obviously needed and will likely follow so that the true extent to which the social capital of a community can have a causal impact on health can be ascertained. Nevertheless, it is already clear from research on other topics that the debate over whether or not social factors are fundamental causes of health and disease is essentially over. A large body of research currently shows that society can make you sick and the next step is to further refine the causes and consequences of this social fact.

References

Abel, Thomas, Esther Walter, Steffen Niemann, and Rolf Weitkunat. 1999. "The Berne-Munich Lifestyle Panel." *Sozial- und Präventivmedizin* 44:91–106.

Abercrombie, Nicholas and Alan Warde, with Rosemary Deem, Sue Penna, Keith Soothill, John Urry, Andrew Sayer, and Sylvia Walby. 2000. *Contemporary British Society*, 3rd ed. Cambridge, UK: Polity.

Adamson, Joy, Yoav Ben-Shlomo, Nish Chaturvedi, and Jenny Donovan. 2003. "Ethnicity, Socio-Economic Position and Gender – Do They Affect Reported Health-Care Seeking Behaviour?" *Social Science and Medicine* 57:895–904.

Adler, Nancy E., Thomas Boyce, Margaret A. Chesney, Sheldon Cohen, Susan Folkman, Robert L. Kahn, and S. Leonard Syme. 1994. "Socioeconomic Status and Health: The Challenge of the Gradient." *American Psychologist* 10:15–24.

Adonis, Andrew and Stephen Pollard. 1997. *A Class Act: The Myth of Britain's Classless Society*. London: Penguin.

Aesop Study Team. 2002. "Raised Incidence of All Psychosis in UK Migrant Populations." *Schizophrenia Research* 53:33.

Ainsworth, Barbara E. 2000. "Issues in the Assessment of Physical Activity in Women." *Research Quarterly for Exercise and Sport* 71:37–50.

Alexander, Jeffrey C. 1995. *Fin de Siècle Social Theory*. London: Verso.

Angel, Ronald J. and Jacqueline L. Angel. 2009. *Hispanic Families at Risk*. New York: Springer.

Angel, Ronald J., Michelle Frisco, Jacquelin L. Angel, and David Chiriboga. 2003. "Financial Strain and Health Among Elderly Mexican-Origin Individuals." *Journal of Health and Social Behavior* 44:536–51.

Annandale, Ellen. 1998. *The Sociology of Health and Medicine: A Critical Introduction.* Cambridge, UK: Polity.

——2010. "Health Status and Gender." In *The New Blackwell Companion to Medical Sociology*, ed. William Cockerham, 97–112. Oxford, UK: Wiley-Blackwell.

Annandale, Ellen and David Field. 2005. "Medical Sociology in Great Britain." In *The Blackwell Companion to Medical Sociology*, ed. William Cockerham, 246–62. Oxford, UK: Blackwell.

Antunes, Ricardo Jorge. 2011. "The Social Space of Health Inequalities in Portugal." *Social Theory and Health* 9:393–409.

Arber, Sara. 1997. "Changing Inequalities in Women's and Men's Health: Britain in the 1990s." *Social Science and Medicine* 44:773–87.

Arber, Sara and Hilary Thomas. 2005. "From Women's Health to a Gender Analysis of Health." In *The Blackwell Companion to Medical Sociology*, ed. William Cockerham, 94–113. Oxford, UK: Blackwell.

Archer, Margaret S. 1995. *Realist Social Theory: Morphogenetic Approach.* Cambridge, UK: Cambridge University Press.

——1998. "Realism and Morphogenesis." In *Critical Realism*, ed. Margaret Archer, Roy Bhaskar, Andrew Collier, Tony Lawson, and Alan Norrie, 356–81. London: Routledge.

——2003. *Structure, Agency and the Internal Conversation.* Cambridge, UK: Cambridge University Press.

Aspinall, Peter J. 2001. "Operationalising the Collection of Ethnicity Data in Studies of Health and Illness." *Sociology of Health and Illness* 23:829–62.

Avison, William R. and Stephanie S. Thomas. 2010. "Stress." In *The New Blackwell Companion to Medical Sociology*, ed. William Cockerham, 242–67. Oxford, UK: Wiley-Blackwell.

Avraamova, Elena M. 2002. "The Formation of a Middle Class in Russia: Definition, Methodology, and Quantitative Assessments." *Sociological Research* 41:57–68.

Backett, Kathryn C. and Charlie Davison. 1995. "Lifecourse and Lifestyle: The Social and Cultural Location of Health Behaviours." *Social Science and Medicine* 40:629–38.

Baldassare, Mark. 1978. *Residential Crowding in Urban America.* Berkeley: University of California Press.

Banks, James, Michael Marmot, Zoe Oldfield, and James P. Smith.

2006. "Disease and Disadvantage in the United States and England." *JAMA* 295:2037–45.

Barrett, Anne E. and R. Jay Turner. 2005. "Family Structure and Mental Health: The Mediating Effects of Socioeconomic Status, Family Process, and Social Stress." *Journal of Health and Social Behavior* 46:156–69.

Bartley, Mel. 2004. *Health Inequality*. Cambridge, UK: Polity.

Bartley, Mel, David Blane, and George Davey Smith. 1998. "Introduction: Beyond the Black Report." *Sociology of Health and Illness* 20:563–77.

Bauman, Zygmunt. 1992. *Intimations of Postmodernity*. London: Routledge.

——1999. *In Search of Politics*. Stanford, CA: Stanford University Press.

——2000. *Liquid Modernity*. Cambridge, UK: Polity.

Becker, Howard S. 1963. *Outsiders: Studies in the Sociology of Deviance*. New York: Free Press.

Becker, Howard S., Blanche Greer, Everett C. Hughes, and Anselm Strauss. 1961. *Boys in White: Student Culture in Medical School*. Chicago: University of Chicago Press.

Beckfield, Jason. 2004. "Does Income Inequality Harm Health?" *Journal of Health and Social Behavior* 45:231–48.

Beliaeva, Liudmila. 2000. "The 'New Middle Classes' in Russia." *Russian Social Science Review* 41:42–55.

Bengtsson, C., B. Nordmark, L. Klareskog, I. Lundberg, L. Alfredsson, and the EIRA Study Group. 2005. "Socioeconomic Status and the Risk of Developing Rheumatoid Arthritis: Results from the Swedish EIRA Study." *Annals of the Rheumatic Diseases* 64:1588–94.

Benoit, Cecilia, Sirpa Wrede, Ivy Bourgeault, Jane Sandall, Raymond de Vires, and Edwin R. van Teijlingen. 2005. "Understanding the Social Organisation of Maternity Care Systems: Midwifery as a Touchstone." *Sociology of Health and Illness* 27:722–38.

Berger, Peter L. and Thomas Luckmann. 1967. *The Social Construction of Reality*. New York: Anchor.

Berkman, Lisa F. and Lester Breslow. 1983. *Health and Ways of Living: The Alameda County Study*. Fairlawn, NJ: Oxford University Press.

Berkman, Lisa F. and Ichiro Kawachi (eds). 2000. *Social Epidemiology*. New York: Oxford University Press.

Bhaskar, Roy. 1998. *The Possibility of Naturalism: A Philosophical Critique of the Contemporary Human Sciences*. London: Routledge.

Blane, David. 1990. "Real Wages, the Economic Cycle, and Mortality in England and Wales, 1870–1914." *International Journal of Health Services* 20:43–52.

Blaxter, Mildred. 1990. *Health Lifestyles.* London: Routledge.

——1997. "Whose Fault Is It? People's Own Conceptions of the Reasons for Health Inequalities." *Social Science and Medicine* 44:747–56.

——2010. *Health*, 2nd ed. Cambridge, UK: Polity.

Bloom, Samuel W. 2002. *The Word as Scalpel: A History of Medical Sociology.* Oxford, UK: Oxford University Press.

Blumer, Herbert. 1969. *Symbolic Interaction.* Englewood Cliffs, NJ: Prentice Hall.

Boardman, Jason D., Brian Karl Finch, Christopher G. Ellison, David R. Williams, and James S. Jackson. 2001. "Neighborhood Disadvantage, Stress, and Drug Use among Adults." *Journal of Health and Social Behavior* 42:151–65.

Boardman, Jason D., Jarron M. Saint Onge, Richard G. Rogers, and Justin T. Denney. 2005. "Race Differentials in Obesity: The Impact of Place." *Journal of Health and Social Behavior* 46:229–43.

Bobak, Martin, Hyner Pikhart, Clyde Hertzman, Richard Rose, and Michael Marmot. 1998. "Socioeconomic Factors, Perceived Control and Self-Reported Health in Russia: A Cross-Sectional Survey." *Social Science and Medicine* 47:269–79.

Bohman, James. 1999. "Practical Reason and Cultural Constraint: Agency in Bourdieu's Theory of Practice." In *Bourdieu: A Critical Reader*, ed. Richard Schusterman, 129–52. Oxford, UK: Blackwell.

Borooah, Vani K. 1999. "Occupational Class and the Probability of Long-Term Limiting Illness." *Social Science and Medicine* 49:253–66.

Bourdieu, Pierre. 1977. *Outline of a Theory of Practice.* Trans. Richard Nice. Cambridge, UK: Cambridge University Press.

——1983. "Ökonomisches Kapital, kulturelles Kapital, soziales Kapital" ["Economic Capital, Cultural Capital, Social Capital"]. In *Soziale Ungleichheiten* [*Social Inequality*], ed. Reinhard Kreckel, 183–98. Göttingen: Schwartz.

——1984. *Distinction.* Trans. Richard Nice. Cambridge, MA: Harvard University Press.

——1986. "The Forms of Capital." Trans. Richard Nice. In *Handbook of Theory and Research for the Sociology of Education*, ed. John Richardson, 241–58. New York: Greenwood Press.

——1990. *The Logic of Practice.* Trans. Richard Nice. Stanford, CA: Stanford University Press.

——1993. *Sociology in Question.* Trans. Richard Nice. London: Sage.

——1996. *The Rules of Art.* Trans. Susan Emanuel. Cambridge, UK: Cambridge University Press.

Bourdieu, Pierre and Loïc J. D. Wacquant. 1992. *An Introduction to Reflexive Sociology.* Chicago: University of Chicago Press.

Bowling, Ann, Julie Barber, Richard Morris, and Shah Ebrahim. 2006. "Do Perceptions of Neighbourhood Environment Influence Health? Baseline Findings from a British Survey of Aging." *Journal of Epidemiology and Community Health* 60:476–83.

Bradby, Hannah and James Y. Nazroo. 2010. "Health, Ethnicity, and Race." In *The New Blackwell Companion to Medical Sociology*, ed. William Cockerham, 113–30. Oxford, UK: Wiley-Blackwell.

Brandt, Alan M. and Martha Gardner. 2000. "Antagonism and Accommodation: Interpreting the Relationship Between Public Health and Medicine in the United States During the 20th Century." *American Journal of Public Health* 90:707–15.

Bratter, Jenifer L. and Bridget K. Gorman. 2011. "Is Discrimination an Equal Opportunity Risk? Racial Experiences, Socioeconomic Status, and Health Status Among Black and White Adults." *Journal of Health and Social Behavior* 52:365–82.

Brown, Tamara L., Gregory S. Parks, Rick S. Zimmerman, and Clarenda M. Phillips. 2001. "The Role of Religion in Predicting Adolescent Alcohol Use and Problem Drinking." *Journal of Studies on Alcohol* 65:696–706.

Brown, Tony. 2003. "Critical Race Theory Speaks to the Sociology of Mental Health: Mental Health Problems Produced by Racial Stratification." *Journal of Health and Social Behavior* 44: 292–301.

Browning, Christopher R. and Kathleen A. Cagney. 2002. "Neighborhood Structural Disadvantage, Collective Efficacy, and Self-Rated Health in a Physical Setting." *Journal of Health and Social Behavior* 43:383–99.

——2003. "Moving Beyond Poverty: Neighborhood Structure, Social Processes, and Health." *Journal of Health and Social Behavior* 44:552–71.

Browning, Christopher R., Danielle Wallace, Seth L. Feinberg, and Kathleen A. Cagney. 2006. "Neighborhood Social Processes, Physical Conditions, and Disaster-Related Mortality: The Case of the 1995 Chicago Heat Wave." *American Sociological Review* 71:661–78.

Bury, Michael. 1986. "Social Constructionism and the Development of Medical Sociology." *Sociology of Health and Illness* 8:137–70.

——2001. "Illness Narratives: Fact or Fiction?" *Sociology of Health and Illness* 23:263–85.

——2005. *Health and Illness.* Cambridge, UK: Polity.

Callinicos, Alex. 1999. *Social Theory: A Historical Introduction.* Cambridge, UK: Polity.

Calnan, Michael. 1987. *Health and Illness: The Lay Perspective.* London: Tavistock.

Cannadine, David. 1999. *The Rise and Fall of Class in Britain.* New York: Columbia University Press.

Carlson, Elwood and Rasmus Hoffman. 2011. "The State Socialist Mortality Syndrome." *Population Research and Policy Review* 30:355–79.

Carpiano, Richard M. 2006. "Toward a Neighborhood Resource-Based Theory of Social Capital for Health: Can Bourdieu and Sociology Help Us?" *Social Science and Medicine* 62:165–75.

Carpiano, Richard M., Bruce G. Link, and Jo C. Phelan. 2008. "Social Inequality and Health: Future Directions for the Fundamental Cause Explanation." In *Social Class*, ed. Annette Lareau and Dalton Conley, 232–63. New York: Russell Sage.

Carr, Deborah and Michael A. Friedman. 2005. "Is Obesity Stigmatizing? Body Weight, Perceived Discrimination, and Psychological Well-Being in the United States." *Journal of Health and Social Behavior* 46:244–59.

Cattell, Vicky. 2001. "Poor People, Poor Places, and Poor Health: The Mediating Role of Social Networks and Social Capital." *Social Science and Medicine* 52:1501–16.

Centers for Disease Control and Prevention. 2002. "Annual Smoking-Attributable Mortality, Years of Potential Life Lost, and Economic Costs – United States, 1995–1999." *Mortality and Morbidity Report* 51:300–2.

Chandola, Tarani. 2000. "Social Class Differences in Mortality Using the New UK National Statistics Socio-Economic Classification." *Social Science and Medicine* 50:641–9.

Chaney, David. 1996. *Lifestyles.* London: Routledge.

Chang, Virginia W. and Diane S. Lauderdale. 2009. "Fundamental Cause Theory, Technological Innovation, and Health Disparities: The Case of Cholesterol in the Era of Statins." *Journal of Health and Social Behavior* 50:245–60.

Charmaz, Kathy. 2009. "Stories, Silences, and Self: Dilemmas in Disclosing Chronic Illness." In *Communicating to Manage Health and Illness*, ed. Dale Brashers and Daena Goldstein, 240–70. New York: Routledge.

Chuang, Ying-Chih, Susan T. Enett, Karl E. Bauman, and Vangie A. Foshee. 2005. "Neighborhood Influences on Adolescent Cigarette and Alcohol Use: Mediating Effects Through Parent and Peer Behaviors." *Journal of Health and Social Behavior* 46: 187–204.

Clair, Jeffrey Michael, Colin Clark, Brian P. Hinote, Caroline O. Robinson, and Jason A. Wasserman. 2007. "Developing, Integrating, and Perpetuating New Ways of Applying Sociology to Health, Policy, and Everyday Life." *Social Science and Medicine* 64:248–58.

Clarke, Adele E., Janet K. Shim, Laura Mamo, Jennifer Ruth Fosket, and Jennifer R. Fishman. 2003. "Biomedicalization: Technoscientific Transformations of Health, Illness, and U.S. Biomedicine." *American Sociological Review* 68:161–94.

Coburn, David. 2004. "Beyond the Income Inequality Hypothesis: Class, Neo-Liberalism, and Health Inequalities." *Social Science and Medicine* 58:41–56.

——2009. "Inequality and Health." In *Morbid Symptoms: Health Under Capitalism*, ed. L. Panitch and C. Leys, 39–58. New York: Monthly Review Press.

Cockerham, William C. 1997. "The Social Determinants of the Decline of Life Expectancy in Russia and Eastern Europe: A Lifestyle Explanation." *Journal of Health and Social Behavior* 38:131–48.

——1999. *Health and Social Change in Russia and Eastern Europe*. London: Routledge.

——2000a. "The Sociology of Health Behavior and Health Lifestyles." In *Handbook of Medical Sociology*, ed. Chloe Bird, Peter Conrad, and Allen Fremont, 159–72. Upper Saddle River, NJ: Prentice Hall.

——2000b. "Health Lifestyles in Russia." *Social Science and Medicine* 51:1313–24.

——2004. "Health as a Social Problem." In *Handbook of Social Problems: A Comparative International Perspective*, ed. George Ritzer, 281–97. Thousand Oaks, CA: Sage.

——2005. "Health Lifestyle Theory and the Convergence of Agency and Structure." *Journal of Health and Social Behavior* 46:51–67.

——2006a. "Class Matters: Health Lifestyles in Post-Soviet Russia." *Harvard International Review* (Spring):42–5.

——2006b. *Society of Risk-Takers: Living Life on the Edge.* New York: Worth.

——2007a. "Health Lifestyles and the Absence of the Russian Middle Class." *Sociology of Health and Illness* 29:457–73.

——2007b. "A Note on the Fate of Postmodern Theory and its Failure to Meet the Basic Requirements for Success in Medical Sociology." *Social Theory and Health* 5:285–96.

——2009. "Understanding the Russian Health Crisis: A Sociological Perspective. *Sociology Compass* 3:327–40.

——2010a. "Health Lifestyles: Bringing Structure Back." In *The New Blackwell Companion to Medical Sociology*, ed. William Cockerham, 159–83. Oxford, UK: Wiley-Blackwell.

——2010b. *Sociology of Mental Disorder*, 8th ed. Upper Saddle River, NJ: Pearson Prentice Hall.

——2012. *Medical Sociology*, 12th ed. Upper Saddle River, NJ: Pearson Prentice Hall.

Cockerham, William C., Thomas Abel, and Günther Lüschen. 1993. "Max Weber, Formal Rationality, and Health Lifestyles." *Sociological Quarterly* 34: 413–35.

Cockerham, William C., Hiroyuki Hattori, and Yukio Yamori. 2000. "The Social Gradient in Life Expectancy: The Contrary Case of Okinawa in Japan." *Social Science and Medicine* 51: 115–22.

Cockerham, William C., Brian P. Hinote, Geoffrey B. Cockerham, and Pamela Abbott. 2006. "Health Lifestyles and Political Ideology in Belarus, Russia, and Ukraine." *Social Science and Medicine* 62:1799–809.

Cockerham, William C., Alfred Rütten, and Thomas Abel. 1997. "Conceptualizing Contemporary Health Lifestyles: Moving Beyond Weber." *Sociological Quarterly* 38:321–42.

Cockerham, William C. and Graham Scambler. 2010. "Medical Sociology and Sociological Theory." In *The New Blackwell Companion to Medical Sociology*, ed. William Cockerham, 3–26. Oxford, UK: Wiley-Blackwell.

Cockerham, William C., M. Christine Snead, and Derek F. DeWaal. 2002. "Health Lifestyles in Russia and the Socialist Heritage." *Journal of Health and Social Behavior* 43:42–55.

Coleman, James S. 1988. "Social Capital in the Creation of Human Capital." *American Journal of Sociology* 94:S95–121.

Colen, Cynthia G., Arline T. Gernomimus, John Bound, and Sherman A. James. (2006). "Maternal Upward Socioeconomic Mobility and Black–White Disparities in Infant Birth Weight." *American Journal of Public Health,* 96:2032–9.

Collini, Stefan. 1978. "Sociology and Idealism in Britain, 1880–1920." *European Journal of Sociology* 19:3–50.

——1979. *Liberalism and Society*. Cambridge, UK: Cambridge University Press.

Collins, Patricia Hill. 2000. *Black Feminist Thought: Knowledge, Consciousness, and Politics of Empowerment*. New York: Routledge.

——2005. *Black Sexual Politics*. New York: Routledge.

Conley, Dalton, Kate W. Strully, and Neil G. Bennett. 2003. *The*

216

References

Starting Gate: Birth Weight and Life Chances. Berkeley: University of California Press.
Conrad, Peter. 2007. *The Medicalization of Society.* Baltimore: Johns Hopkins University Press.
Cooper, Helen. 2002. "Investigating Socio-Economic Explanations for Gender and Ethnic Inequalities in Health." *Social Science and Medicine* 54:693–706.
Coser, Lewis. 1979. "American Trends." In *A History of Sociological Analysis*, ed. Tom Bottomore and Robert Nisbet, 287–320. London: Heinemann.
Crawford, Robert. 1984. "A Cultural Account of Health: Control, Release, and the Social Body." In *Issues in the Political Economy of Health Care*, ed. John McKinley, 60–103. New York: Tavistock.
Crenshaw, Kimberlé. 1989. "Demarginalizing the Intersection of Race and Sex: A Black Feminist Critique of Antidiscrimination Doctrine, Feminist Theory and Antiracist Politics." *University of Chicago Legal Forum* 139:139–67.
Crompton, Rosemary. 2008. *Class and Stratification*, 3rd ed. Cambridge, UK: Polity.
Cummins, Steven and Sally Macintyre. 2006. "Food Environments and Obesity – Neighbourhood or Nation?" *International Journal of Epidemiology* 35:100–4.
Dahrendorf, Ralf. 1979. *Life Chances.* Chicago: University of Chicago Press.
——1990. *The Modern Social Conflict.* Berkeley: University of California Press.
Davey Smith, George, Mel Bartley, and David Blane. 1990. "The Black Report on Socioeconomic Inequalities in Health 10 Years On." *British Medical Journal* 301:373–7.
Delormier, Treena, Katherine L. Frohlich, and Louise Potvin. 2009. "Food and Eating as Social Practice: Understanding Eating Patterns as Social Phenomena and Implications for Public Health." *Sociology of Health and Illness* 31:215–28.
De Maio, Fernando. 2010. *Health and Social Theory.* London: Palgrave Macmillan.
Demers, Andrée, Jocelyn Bisson, and Jézabelle Palluy. 1999. "Wives' Convergence with Their Husbands' Alcohol Use: Social Conditions as Mediators." *Journal of Studies of Alcohol* 60:368–77.
Demers, Andrée, Sylvia Kairouz, Edward M. Adlaf, Louis Glickman, Brenda Newton-Taylor, and Alain Marchand. 2002. "Multilevel Analysis of Situational Drinking Among Canadian Undergraduates." *Social Science and Medicine* 55:415–24.

Dennis, Mike. 1985. *German Democratic Republic*. London: Pinter.

Denton, Margaret and Vivienne Walters. 1999. "Gender Differences in Structural and Behavioral Determinants of Health: An Analysis of the Social Production of Health." *Social Science and Medicine* 48:1221–35.

Denzin, Norman K. 1992. *Symbolic Interactionism and Cultural Studies*. Oxford, UK: Blackwell.

d'Houtaud, A. and Mark G. Field. 1984. "The Image of Health: Variations in Perception by Social Class in a French Population." *Sociology of Health and Illness* 6:30–59.

Diez-Roux, Ana V., F. Javier Nieto, Carles Muntaner, Herman A. Tyroler, George W. Comstock, Eyal Shahar, Lawton S. Cooper, Robert L. Watson, and Moyses Szkio. 1997. "Neighborhood Environments and Coronary Heart Disease: A Multilevel Analysis." *American Journal of Epidemiology* 146:48–63.

Dmitrieva, Elena. 2005. "The Russian Health Care Experiment: Transition of the Health Care System and Rethinking the Sociology of Medicine." In *The Blackwell Companion to Medical Sociology*, ed. William Cockerham, 320–33. Oxford, UK: Blackwell.

Dolan, Alan. 2007. " 'Good Luck to Them if They Get It.' Exploring Working Class Men's Understandings and Experiences of Income Inequality and Material Standards." *Sociology of Health and Illness* 29:711–29.

——2011. " 'You Can't Ask for a Dubonnet and Lemonade!': Working Class Masculinity and Men's Health Practices." *Sociology of Health and Illness* 33:586–601.

Doll, Richard, Richard Peto, Jillian Boreham, and Isabelle Sutherland. 2004. "Mortality in Relation to Smoking: 50 Years' Observations on Male British Doctors." *British Medical Journal* 328:1519–28.

Downey, Liam and Marieke van Willigen. 2005. "Environmental Stressors: The Mental Health Impacts of Living Near Industrial Activity." *Journal of Health and Social Behavior* 46:289–305.

Drentea, Patricia and Jennifer L. Moren-Cross. 2005. "Social Capital and Social Support on the Web: The Case of an Internet Mother Site." *Sociology of Health and Illness* 27:920–43.

Drever, F. and M. Whitehead. 1997. *Health Inequalities: Decennial Supplement*. London: HMSO.

Dubos, René. 1959. *Mirage of Health*. New York: Harper & Row.

Dunham, H. Warren. 1977. "Schizophrenia: The Impact of Sociocultural Factors." *Hospital Practice* 12:61–8.

Dunn, Andrea L., Bess H. Marcus, James B. Kampert, Melissa E. Garcia, Harold W. Kohl III, and Steven N. Blair. 1999.

"Comparison of Lifestyle and Structural Interventions to Increase Physical Activity and Cardiovascular Fitness." *JAMA* 281:327–34.

Durkheim, Emile. [1893] 1964. *The Division of Labor in Society*. New York: Free Press.

——[1895] 1950. *The Rules of Sociological Method*. New York: Free Press.

——[1897] 1951. *Suicide: A Study in Sociology*. New York: Free Press.

Eberstadt, Nicolas and Sally Satel. 2004. *Health and the Income Inequality Hypothesis: A Doctrine in Search of Data*. Washington, DC: AEI Press.

Edwards, R., P. McElduff, R. A. Harrison, K. Watson, G. Butler, and P. Elton. 2006. "Pleasure or Pain? A Profile of Smokers in Northern England." *Public Health* 120:760–8.

Ellison, G. 2002. "Letting the Gini Out of the Bottle? Challenges Facing the Relative Income Hypothesis." *Social Science and Medicine* 54:561–76.

Emirbayer, Mustafa and Ann Mische. 1998. "What is Agency?" *American Journal of Sociology* 103:962–1023.

Epstein, Helen. 1998. "Life and Death on the Social Ladder." *New York Review of Books* (July 16):26–30.

Erickson, Robert E. and John H. Goldthorpe. 1992. *The Constant Flux: A Study of Class Mobility in Industrial Society*. Oxford, UK: Clarendon Press.

Evans, Robert G., Morris L. Barer, and Theodore R. Marmor (eds). 1994. *Why Are Some People Healthy and Others Not? The Determinants of the Health of Populations*. New York: Aldine de Gruyter.

Ezzati, Majid, Ari B. Friedman, Sandeep C. Kulkarni, and Christopher J. L. Murray. 2008. "The Reversal of Fortunes: Trends in County Mortality and Cross-Country Mortality Disparities in the United States." *PloS Medicine* 5:e66/001–0011.

Faris, Robert E. and H. Warren Dunham. 1939. *Mental Disorders in Urban Areas*. Chicago: University of Chicago Press.

Farmer, Melissa and Kenneth F. Ferraro. 2005. "Are Racial Disparities in Health Conditional on Socioeconomic Status?" *Social Science and Medicine* 60:191–204.

Fenwick, Rudy and Mark Tausig. 1994. "The Macroeconomic Context of Job Stress." *Journal of Health and Social Behavior* 35:266–82.

Ferraro, Kenneth F. and Melissa M. Farmer. 1999. "Utility of Health Data from Social Surveys: Is There a Gold Standard for Measuring Morbidity?" *American Sociological Review* 64:303–15.

Field, Mark. 2000. "The Health and Demographic Crisis in Post-

Soviet Russia." In *Russia's Torn Safety Nets*, ed. Mark Field and Judith Twigg, 11–42. New York: St. Martin's Press.

Finkelstein, Murray M., Michael Jerrett, and Malcolm R. Sears. 2004. "Environmental Inequality and Circulatory Disease Mortality Gradients." *Journal of Community Health* 59:481–7.

Fitzpatrick, Kevin and Mark LaGory. 2000. *Unhealthy Places: The Ecology of Risk in the Urban Landscape.* New York: Routledge.

——2011. *Unhealthy Cities: Poverty, Race, and Place in America.* New York: Routledge.

Ford, Earl S., Robert K. Merritt, Gregory W. Heath, Kenneth E. Powell, Richard A. Washburn, Andrea Kriska, and Gwendolyn Halle. 1991. "Physical Activity in Lower and Higher Socioeconomic Status Populations." *American Journal of Epidemiology* 133:1246–56.

Foucault, Michel. 1973. *Birth of the Clinic.* London: Tavistock.

——1979. *History of Sexuality*, vol. 1. London: Allen Lane.

Fox, A. J. and P. Goldblatt. 1982. *Socio-Demographic Differentials in Mortality: The OPCS Longitudinal Study.* London: HMSO.

Fox, Nick, Katie Ward, and Alan O'Rourke. 2005. "Pro-Anorexia, Weight-Loss Drugs, and the Internet: An 'Anti-Recovery' Exploratory Model of Anorexia." *Sociology of Health and Illness* 27:944–72.

Freedman, Vicki A., Irina B. Grafova, and Jeanette Rogowski. 2011. "Neighborhoods and Chronic Disease Onset in Later Life." *American Journal of Public Health* 101:79–86.

Freidson, Eliot. 1970a. *Professional Medicine: A Study of the Sociology of Applied Knowledge.* New York: Dodd, Mead.

——1970b. *Professional Dominance.* Chicago: Aldine.

Frohlich, Katherine L., Ellen Corin, and Louise Potvin. 2001. "A Theoretical Proposal for the Relationship Between Context and Disease." *Sociology of Health and Illness* 23:776–97.

Gabe, Jonathan, Mike Bury, and Mary Ann Elston. 2004. *Key Concepts in Medical Sociology.* London: Sage.

Gallagher, K. 2000. "Dietary Practices and Nutrition Knowledge of Adolescents from Contrasting Social Backgrounds." *Journal of Consumer Studies and Home Economics* 24:207–11.

Gallo, William T., Hsun-Mei Teng, Tracy A. Falba, Stanislav V. Kasl, Harlan V. Krumholz, and Elizabeth H. Bradley. 2006. "The Impact of Late-Career Job Loss on Myocardial Infarction and Stroke: A 10-Year Follow-up Using the Health and Retirement Study." *Occupational and Environmental Medicine* 63:683–87.

Gane, Mike. 2003. *French Social Theory.* London: Sage.

George, Valerie A. and Paulette Johnson 2001. "Weight Loss Behaviors and Smoking in College Students of Diverse Ethnicity." *American Journal of Health Behavior* 25:115–24.

Giddens, Anthony. 1984. *The Constitution of Society: Outline of a Theory of Structuration*. Berkeley: University of California Press.

——1987. *Social Theory and Modern Sociology*. Stanford, CA: Stanford University Press.

——1991. *Modernity and Self-Identity: Self and Society in the Late Modern Age*. Stanford, CA: Stanford University Press.

Giddens, Anthony and Christopher Pierson. 1998. *Conversations with Anthony Giddens: Making Sense of Modernity*. Stanford, CA: Stanford University Press.

Glaser, Barney G. and Anselm M. Strauss. 1965. *Awareness of Dying*. Chicago: Aldine.

——1967. *The Discovery of Grounded Theory*. Chicago: Aldine.

——1968. *Time for Dying*. Chicago: Aldine.

Glassner, Barry. 2007. *The Gospel of Food: Everything You Think You Know About Food is Wrong*. New York: Ecco/HarperCollins.

Gochman, David S. 1997. "Health Behavior Research, Cognate Disciplines, Future Identity, and an Organizing Matrix: An Integration of Perspectives." In *Handbook of Health Behavior*, vol. 4, ed. David Gochman, 395–425. New York: Plenum.

Goffman, Erving. 1961. *Asylums*. New York: Anchor.

——1963a. *Behavior in Public Places: Notes on the Social Organization of Gatherings*. Glencoe, IL: Free Press.

——1963b. *Stigma: Notes on the Management of Spoiled Identity*. Englewood Cliffs, NJ: Prentice Hall.

Goldthorpe, John H. 2007. *On Sociology; Critique and Program*, 2nd ed., vol. 1. Stanford, CA: Stanford University Press.

Goldthorpe, John H. with Richard Breen. 2000. "Explaining Educational Differentials: Towards a Formal Rational Action Theory." In John Goldthorpe, *On Sociology: Numbers, Narratives, and the Integration of Research and Theory*, 183–205. Oxford, UK: Oxford University Press.

Gorman, Bridget K. and Jen'nan Ghazal Read. 2006. "Gender Disparities in Adult Health: An Examination of Three Measures of Morbidity." *Journal of Health and Social Behavior* 47:95–110.

Gove, Walter R., Michael Hughes, and Omer R. Galle. 1979. "Overcrowding in the Home: An Empirical Investigation of its Possible Pathological Consequences." *American Sociological Review* 44:59–80.

Grant, Struan F. A., Gudmar Thorleifson, Inga Reynisdottir, et al.

2005. "Variant of Transcription Factor 7-like 2 (TCLF7L2) Gene Confers Risk of Type 2 Diabetes." *Nature Genetics* 38:320–3.

Greenland, Philip, Maria Deloria Knoll, Jeremiah Stamler, James D. Neaton, Alan R. Dyer, Daniel B. Garside, and Peter W. Wilson. 2003. "Major Risk Factors as Antecedents of Fatal and Nonfatal Coronary Heart Disease Events." *JAMA* 290:891–7.

Gregory, Susan. 2005. "Living with Chronic Illness in the Family Setting." *Sociology of Health and Illness* 27:372–92.

Grzywacz, Joseph G. and Nadine F. Marks. 2001. "Social Inequalities and Exercise During Adulthood: Toward an Ecological Perspective." *Journal of Health and Social Behavior* 42:202–20.

Hadfield, Philip M. 2006. *Bars Wars: Contesting the Night in Contemporary British Cites.* Oxford, UK: Oxford University Press.

Haines, Rebecca J., Blake D. Poland, and Joy L. Johnson. 2009. "Becoming a 'Real' Smoker: Cultural Capital in Young Women's Accounts of Smoking and Other Substance Use." *Sociology of Health and Illness* 31:66–80.

Hall, Wayne. 2005. "British Drinking: A Suitable Case for Treatment?" *British Medical Journal* 331:527–8.

Halsey, A. H. 2004. *A History of Sociology in Britain.* Oxford, UK: Oxford University Press.

Hamilton, Lee V., Clifford Broman, William Hoffman, and Deborah Renner. 1990. "Hard Times and Vulnerable People: Initial Effects of Plant Closings on Autoworkers." *Journal of Health and Social Behavior* 31:123–40.

Hankivsky, Olena. 2012. "Women's Health, Men's Health, and Gender and Health: Implications of Intersectionality." *Social Science and Medicine* 74:1712–20.

Hardey, Michael. 1999. "Doctor in the House: The Internet as a Source of Lay Knowledge and the Challenge to Expertise." *Sociology of Health and Illness* 21:820–35.

Harrison, Eric and David Rose. 2010. "From Derivation to Validation: Evidence from the UK." In *Social Class in Europe*, ed. David Rose and Eric Harrison, 39–60. London: Routledge.

Hattery, Angela and Earl Smith. 2011. "Health, Nutrition, Access to Healthy Food and Well-Being among African Americans." In *Handbook of African American Health*, ed. Anthony Lemelle, Wornie Reed, and Sandra Taylor, 47–59. New York: Springer.

Hayward, Mark D., Eileen M. Crimmins, Tom P. Miles, and Yu Yang. 2000. "The Significance of Socioeconomic Status in Explaining the Racial Gap in Chronic Health Conditions." *American Sociological Review* 65:910–30.

Hedström, Peter and Richard Swedberg. 1998. "Social Mechanisms." In *Social Mechanisms*, ed. Peter Hedström and Richard Swedberg, 1–30. Cambridge, UK: Cambridge University Press.

Hemström, Örjan. 1999. "Explaining Differential Rates of Mortality Decline for Swedish Men and Women: A Time-Series Analysis, 1945–1992." *Social Science and Medicine* 49:1759–77.

Herzlich, Claudine and Janine Pierret. 1987. *Illness and Self in Society*. Trans. E. Forster. Baltimore: Johns Hopkins University Press.

Hill, Terrence D. and Ronald J. Angel. 2005. "Neighborhood Disorder, Psychological Distress, and Heavy Drinking." *Social Science and Medicine* 61:965–75.

Hill, Terrence D., Christopher G. Ellison, Amy M. Burdette, and Marc A. Musick. 2007. "Religious Involvement and Healthy Lifestyles: Evidence from a Survey of Texas Adults." *Annals of Behavioral Medicine* 34:217–22.

Hill, Terrence D., Catherine E. Ross, and Ronald J. Angel. 2005. "Neighborhood Disorder, Psychophysiological Distress, and Health." *Journal of Health and Social Behavior* 46:170–86.

Hollingshead, August B. and Frederick C. Redlich. 1958. *Social Class and Mental Illness: A Community Study*. New York: John Wiley.

Holtz, Timothy H., Seth Holmes, Scott Stonington, and Leon Eisenberg. 2006. "Health is Still Social: Contemporary Examples in the Age of Genome." *PLoS Medicine* 3:e419–25.

House, James S. 2002. "Understanding Social Factors and Inequalities in Health: 20th Century Progress and 21st Century Prospects." *Journal of Health and Social Behavior* 43:124–42.

Hughes, Jason. 2003. *Learning to Smoke: Tobacco Use in the West*. Chicago: University of Chicago Press.

Humphries, Karin H. and Eddy van Doorslaer. 2000. "Income-Related Inequality in Canada." *Social Science and Medicine* 50:663–71.

Hurt, Richard D. 1995. "Smoking in Russia: What do Stalin and Western Tobacco Companies Have in Common?" *Mayo Clinic Proceedings* 70:1007–11.

Husserl, Edmund. [1952] 1989. *Ideas Pertaining to a Pure Phenomenology and to a Phenomenological Philosophy*. Trans. R. Rojecwicz and A. Schuwer. London: Kluwer Academic.

Idler, Ellen L. 2010. "Health and Religion." In *The New Blackwell Companion to Medical Sociology*, ed. William Cockerham, 133–58. Oxford, UK: Wiley-Blackwell.

Illsley, Raymond. 1975. "Promotion to Observer Status." *Social Science and Medicine* 9:63–7.

Issacs, Stephen L. and Steven A. Schroeder. 2004. "Class – The

Ignored Determinant of the Nation's Health." *New England Journal of Medicine* 351:1137–42.

James, Veronica and Jonathan Gabe (eds). 1996. *Health and the Sociology of Emotions*. Oxford, UK: Blackwell.

Janečková, Hana. 2005. "Transformation of the Health Care System in the Czech Republic – A Sociological Perspective." In *The Blackwell Companion to Medical Sociology*, ed. William Cockerham, 347–64. Oxford, UK: Blackwell.

Jarvis, Martin and Jane Wardle. 1999. "Social Patterning of Individual Health Behaviours." In *Social Determinants of Health*, ed. Michael Marmot and Richard Wilkinson, 240–55. Oxford, UK: Oxford University Press.

Johnson, Joy L., Joan L. Bottorff, Barbara Moffat, Pamela A. Ratner, Jean A. Shoveller, and Chris Y. Lovato. 2003. "Tobacco Dependence: Adolescents: Perspectives on the Need to Smoke." *Social Science and Medicine* 56:1481–92.

Johnson, Malcolm. 1975. "Medical Sociology and Sociological Theory." *Social Science and Medicine* 9:227–32.

Johnson, Robert A. and John P. Hoffman. 2000. "Adolescent Cigarette Smoking in the U.S. Racial/Ethnic Subgroups: Findings from the National Education Longitudinal Study." *Journal of Health and Social Behavior* 41:392–407.

Johnston, David Cay. 2005. "Richest Are Leaving Even the Rich Far Behind." *New York Times* (June 5):1, 16–17.

Johnstone, Anne. 1999. "Cold Comfort: Anne Johnstone Investigates Victorian Living Conditions in Glasgow; Time to Put Our Houses in Order." *The Herald* (February 18): 13.

Jones, Rees Ian, Olia Papocosta, Peter H. Whincup, S. Goya Wannamethee, and Richard W. Morris. 2011. "Class and Lifestyle 'Lock-in' among Middle-Aged and Older Men: A Multiple Correspondence Analysis of the British Regional Heart Study." *Sociology of Health and Illness* 33:399–419.

Judge, Ken, Jo-Ann Mulligan, and Michael Benzeval. 1998. "Income Inequality and Population Health." *Social Science and Medicine* 46:567–79.

Judt, Tony. 2005. *Postwar: A History of Europe Since 1945*. New York: Penguin Press.

Kahn, Joan R. and Leonard I. Pearlin. 2006. "Financial Strain over the Life Course and Health Among Older Adults." *Journal of Health and Social Behavior* 47:17–31.

Kalberg, Stephen. 1994. *Max Weber's Comparative Historical Sociology*. Chicago: University of Chicago Press.

Karlsen, Saffron and James Y. Nazroo. 2002. "Agency and Structure: The Impact of Ethnic Identity and Racism on the Health of Ethnic Minority People." *Sociology of Health and Illness* 24:1–20.

Kawachi, I., B. P. Kennedy, K. Lochner, and D. Prothrow-Smith. 1997. "Social Capital, Income Inequality, and Mortality." *American Journal of Public Health* 87:1491–8.

Kawachi, Ichiro, Bruce P. Kennedy, and Richard G. Wilkinson (eds). 1999. *The Society and Population Health Reader: Income Inequality and Health.* New York: The New Press.

Kelly, Michael J. and Sherry Weitzen. 2010. "The Association of Lifetime Education with the Prevalence of Myocardial Infarction: An Analysis of the 2006 Behavioral Risk Factor Surveillance System." *Journal of Community Health* 35:76–80.

Kessler, Ronald C., Katherine A. McGonagle, Shanyang Zhao, Christopher B. Nelson, Michael Hughes, Suzann Eshleman, Hans-Ulrich Wittchen, and Kenneth S. Kendler. 1994. "Lifetime and 12-Month Prevalence of DSM-III-R Psychiatric Disorders in the United States." *Archives of General Psychiatry* 51:8–19.

Khot, Umesh N., Monica B. Khot, Christopher T. Bajzer, Shelly K. Sapp, E. Magnus Ohman, Sorin J. Brener, Stephen G. Ellis, A. Michael Lincoff, and Eric J. Topol. 2003. "Prevalence of Conventional Risk Factors in Patients with Coronary Heart Disease." *JAMA* 290:898–904.

King, Michael, James Nazroo, Scott Weich, Kwane McKenzie, Kan Bhui, Saffron Karlson, Stephen Stansfeld, Peter Tyrer, Martin Blanchard, Keith Lloyd, Sally McManus, Kerry Sproston, and Bob Erens. 2005. "Psychotic Symptoms in the General Population of England." *Social Psychiatry and Epidemiology* 40:375–81.

Kingston, Paul W. 2000. *The Classless Society.* Stanford, CA: Stanford University Press.

Kirby, James B. and Toshiko Kaneda. 2005. "Access to Health Care: Does Neighborhood Residential Instability Matter?" *Journal of Health and Social Behavior* 47:142–55.

Klatsky, Arthur L. 1999. "Moderate Drinking and Reduced Risk of Heart Disease." *Alcohol Research and Health* 23:15–23.

Kleinfield, N. R. 2006a. "Diabetes and Its Awful Toll Quietly Emerge as a Crisis." *New York Times* (January 9):A1, A18.

——2006b. "Living at an Epicenter of Diabetes, Defiance, and Despair." *New York Times* (January 10):A1, A20.

Klinenberg, Eric. 2002. *Heat Wave: A Social Autopsy of Disaster in Chicago.* Chicago: University of Chicago Press.

——2006. "Blaming the Victims: Hearsay, Labeling, and the Hazards of Quick-Hit Disaster Ethnography." *American Sociological Review* 71:689–98.

Kolata, Gina. 2006. "So Big and Healthy Nowadays, Grandpa Wouldn't Know You." *New York Times* (July 30):1, 20.

Korp, Peter. 2008. "The Symbolic Power of 'Healthy Lifestyles'." *Health Sociology Review* 17:18–26.

Kosteniuk, Julie G. and Harley D. Dickinson. 2003. "Tracing the Social Gradient in the Health of Canadians: Primary and Secondary Determinants." *Social Science and Medicine* 57:263–76.

Kozyrskyj, Anita L., Garth E. Kendall, Peter Jacoby, and Stephen R. Zubrick. 2010. "Association Between Socioeconomic Status and the Development of Asthma: Analyses of Income Trajectories." *American Journal of Public Health* 1000:540–46.

Kunitz, Stephen J. with Irena Pesis-Katz. 2005. "Morality of White Americans, African Americans, and Canadians: The Causes and Consequences for Health of Welfare State Institutions and Policies." *Milbank Quarterly* 83:5–39.

Kunst, Anton E., Feikje Gronenhof, Johan P. Mackenbach, and the EU Working Group on Socioeconomic Inequalities in Health. 1998. "Mortality by Occupational Class Among Men in 11 European Countries." *Social Science and Medicine* 46:1459–76.

Laaksonen, Mikko, Ritva Prättälä, and Eero Lahelma. 2002. "Sociodemographic Determinants of Multiple Unhealthy Behaviours." *Scandinavian Journal of Public Health* 30:1–7.

Lahelma, Eero. 2010. "Health and Social Stratification." In *The New Blackwell Companion to Medical Sociology*, ed. William Cockerham, 71–96. Oxford, UK: Wiley-Blackwell.

Lahelma, Eero, Sara Arber, Ossi Rahkonen, and Karri Silventoinen. 2000. "Widening or Narrowing Inequalities in Health? Comparing Britain and Finland from the 1980s to the 1990s." *Sociology of Health and Illness* 22:110–36.

Lantz, Paula M., James S. House, Richard P. Mero, and David R. Williams. 2005. "Stress, Life Events, and Socioeconomic Disparities in Health: Results from the Americans' Changing Lives Study." *Journal of Health and Social Behavior* 46:274–88.

Lareau, Annette and Dalton Conley (eds). 2008. *Social Class: How Does It Work?* New York: Russell Sage.

Lasker, J. N., N. P. Egolf, and S. Wolf. 1994. "Community, Social Change, and Mortality." *Social Science and Medicine* 39:53–62.

Latkin, Carl A. and Aaron D. Curry. 2003. "Stressful Neighborhoods and Depression: A Prospective Study of the Impact of Neighborhood Disorder." *Journal of Health and Social Behavior* 44:34–44.

Latour, Bruno. 2005. *Reassembling the Social: An Introduction to Actor-Network-Theory*. Oxford, UK: Oxford University Press.

Lau, Richard R., Marilyn Jacobs Quadrel, and Karen A. Hartman. 1990. "Development and Change of Young Adults' Preventive Health Beliefs and Behavior: Influence from Parents and Peers." *Journal of Health and Social Behavior* 31:240–59.

Laumann, Edward O. and Yoosik Youm. 2001. "Racial/Ethnic Group Differences in the Prevalence of Sexually-Transmitted Diseases in the United States: A Network Explanation." In *Sex, Love, and Health in America: Private Choices and Public Policies*, ed. Edward Laumann and Robert Michaels, 327–51. Chicago: University of Chicago Press.

Lemelle, Anthony, Wornie Reed, and Sandra Taylor (eds). 2011. *Handbook of African American Health*. New York: Springer.

Lemert, Charles. 2005. *Social Things: An Introduction to the Sociological Life*, 3rd ed. Lanham, MD: Rowman and Littlefield.

Leon, D. A. and J. McCambridge. 2006. "Liver Cirrhosis Mortality Rates in Britain from 1950 to 2002: An Analysis of Routine Data." *Lancet* 367:52–6.

Levy, Leo and Louis Rowitz. 1973. *The Ecology of Mental Disorder*. New York: Behavioral Publications.

Lin, Nan. 2001. *Social Capital: A Theory of Social Structure and Action*. Cambridge, UK: Cambridge University Press.

Lin, Nan, Xiaolan Ye, and Walter W. Ensel. 1999. "Social Support and Depressed Mood: A Structural Analysis." *Journal of Health and Social Behavior* 40:344–59.

Lindquist, Christine, William C. Cockerham, and Sean-Shong Hwang. 1999. "Drinking Patterns in the American South." *Journal of Studies on Alcohol* 60:663–6.

Link, Bruce G. and Jo Phelan. 1995. "Social Conditions as Fundamental Causes of Disease." *Journal of Health and Social Behavior* (Extra Issue):80–94.

——2000. "Evaluating the Fundamental Cause Explanation for Social Disparities in Health." In *The Handbook of Medical Sociology*, 5th ed., ed. Chloe Bird, Peter Conrad, and Allen Fremont, 33–46. Upper Saddle River, NJ: Prentice Hall.

Lleras-Muney, Adriana. 2005. "The Relationship Between Education and Adult Mortality in the United States." *Review of Economic Studies* 72:189–221.

Lochner, Kimberly A., Ichiro Kawachi, Robert T. Brennan, and Stephen L. Buka. 2003. "Social Capital and Neighborhood Mortality Rates in Chicago." *Social Science and Medicine* 56:1797–805.

Lomas, Jonathan. 1998. "Social Capital and Health: Implications for Public Health and Epidemiology." *Social Science and Medicine* 47:1181–8.

Lopez-Gonzalez, Lorena, Veronica C. Aravena, and Robert A. Hummer. 2005. "Immigrant Acculturation, Gender, and Health Behavior: A Research Note." *Social Forces* 84:581–93.

Lostao, Lourdes, Enrique Regidor, Pierre Aïach, and Vincente Dominguez. 2001. "Social Inequalities in Ischaemic Heart and Cerebrovascular Disease Mortality in Men: Spain and France, 1980–1982 and 1988–1990." *Social Science and Medicine* 52:1879–87.

Lupton, Deborah (ed.). 1999. *Risk and Sociocultural Theory: New Directions and Perspectives*. Cambridge, UK: Cambridge University Press.

——2003. *Medicine as Culture: Illness, Disease, and the Body in Western Societies*. Thousand Oaks, CA: Sage.

Lutfey, Karen and Jeremy Freese. 2005. "Toward Some Fundamentals of Fundamental Causality: Socioeconomic Status and Health in the Routine Clinic Visit for Diabetes." *American Journal of Sociology* 110:1326–72.

Macintyre, Sally. 1997. "The Black Report and Beyond: What are the Issues?" *Social Science and Medicine* 44:723–45.

Macintyre, Sally, Anne Ellaway, and Steven Cummins. 2002. "Place Effects on Health: How Can We Conceptualise, Operationalise, and Measure Them?" *Social Science and Medicine* 55:125–39.

Macintyre, Sally, Laura McKay, and Anne Ellaway. 2005. "Are Rich People or Poor People More Likely to Be Ill? Lay Perceptions, by Social Class and Neighbourhood, of Inequalities in Health." *Social Science and Medicine* 60:313–17.

Manning, Nick and Nataliya Tikhonova. 2009. *Health and Health Care in the New Russia*. Farnham, UK: Ashgate.

Marmot, Michael. 1996. "The Social Pattern of Health and Disease." In *Health and Social Organizations*, ed. David Blane, Eric Brunner, and Richard Wilkinson, 42–70. London: Routledge.

——2004. *The Status Syndrome*. New York: Times Books.

Marmot, Michael, George Davey Smith, Stephen Stansfield, Chandra Patel, Fiona North, Jenny Head, Ian White, Eric Brunner, and Amanda Feeney. 1991. "Health Inequalities Among British Civil Servants: The Whitehall II Study." *Lancet* 337:1387–92.

Marmot, M. G., M. J. Shipley, and Geoffrey Rose. 1984. "Inequalities in Death – Specific Explanations of a General Pattern." *Lancet* 83:1003–6.

Martin, Paul A. and Robert Dingwall. 2010. "Medical Sociology and

Genetics." In *The New Blackwell Companion to Medical Sociology*, ed. William Cockerham, 511–29. Oxford, UK: Wiley-Blackwell.

Matthews, Sharon and Chris Power. 2002. "Socio-economic Gradients in Psychological Distress: A Focus on Women, Social Roles and Work–Home Characteristics." *Social Science and Medicine* 54:799–810.

McIntire, Charles. 1894. "The Importance of the Study of Medical Sociology." *Bulletin of the American Academy of Medicine* 1:425–34.

McKee, Martin, Martin Bobak, Richard Rose, Vladimir Shkolnikov, Laurent Chenet, and David Leon. 1998. "Patterns of Smoking in Russia." *Tobacco Control* 70:22–6.

McKeown, Thomas. 1979. *The Role of Medicine*. Oxford, UK: Blackwell.

McKie, Linda, Susan Gregory, and Sophie Bowlby. 2002. "Shadow Times: The Temporal and Spatial Frameworks and Experiences of Caring and Working." *Sociology* 36:897–924.

——2004. "Starting Well: Gender, Care and Health in Family Settings." *Sociology* 38:593–611.

McLeod, Jane D. and Elbert P. Almazan. 2003. "Connections Between Childhood and Adulthood." In *Handbook of the Life Course*, ed. Jeylan Mortimer and Michael Shanahan, 391–411. New York: Kluwer.

McLeod, Jane D. and James M. Nonnemaker. 2000. "Poverty and Child Emotional and Behavioral Problems: Racial/Ethnic Differences in Processes and Effects." *Journal of Health and Social Behavior* 41:137–61.

McLeod, Jane D., James M. Nonnemaker, and Kathleen Theide Call. 2004. "Income Inequality, Race, and Child Well-Being: An Aggregate Analysis in the 50 United States." *Journal of Health and Social Behavior* 45:249–64.

McLeod, Jane D. and Michael J. Shanahan. 1996. "Trajectories of Poverty and Children's Mental Health." *Journal of Health and Social Behavior* 37:207–20.

Mead, George Herbert. 1934. *Mind, Self, and Society*. Chicago: University of Chicago Press.

——1982. *The Individual and the Social Self*, ed. D. L. Miller. Chicago: University of Chicago Press.

Merton, Robert K., George G. Reader, and Patricia Kendall. 1957. *The Student Physician*. Cambridge, MA: Harvard University Press.

Meslé, France, Jacques Vallin, Véronique Hertrich, Evgueni Andreev, and Vladimir Shkolnikov. 2003. "Causes of Death in Russia: Assessing the Trends since the 1980s." In *Population of Central and*

Eastern Europe: Challenges and Opportunities, ed. I. Kotowska and J. Jozwiak, 389–414. Warsaw: Statistical Publishing Establishment.

Mielck, Andreas, Adrienne Cavelaars, Uwe Helmert, Karl Martin, Olaf Winklehake, and Anton E. Kunst. 2000. "Comparison of Health Inequalities Between East and West Germany." *European Journal of Public Health* 10:262–7.

Mirowsky, John and Catherine E. Ross. 1989. *Social Causes of Psychological Distress.* New York: Aldine de Gruyter.

——2003a. *Education, Social Status, and Health.* New York: Aldine de Gruyter.

——2003b. *Social Causes of Psychological Distress*, 2nd ed. New York: Aldine de Gruyter.

Mirowsky, John, Catherine E. Ross, and John Reynolds. 2000. "Links Between Social Status and Health Status." In *Handbook of Medical Sociology*, 5th ed., ed. Chloe Bird, Peter Conrad, and Allen Fremont, 47–67. Upper Saddle River, NJ: Prentice Hall.

Mokdad, Ali H., James S. Marks, Donna F. Stroup, and Julie L. Gerberding. 2004. "Actual Causes of Death in the United States, 2000." *JAMA* 291:1238–45.

Morris, Stephen, Matthew Sutton, and Hugh Gravelle. 2005. "Inequity and Inequality in the Use of Health Care in England: An Empirical Investigation." *Social Science and Medicine* 60:1251–66.

Murphy, Barbara. 2004. *Why Women Bury Men: The Longevity Gap in Canada.* Winnipeg, Canada: Shillingford.

Naess, Øyvind, Alastair H. Leyland, George Davey Smith, and Bjorgulf Claussen. 2006. "Contextual Effect on Mortality of Neighbourhood Level Education Explained by Earlier Life Deprivation." *Journal of Community Health* 59:1058–9.

Narcisse, Marie-Rachelle, Nicole Dedobbeleer, Andre-Pierre Contandriopoulos, and Antonio Ciampi. 2009. "Understanding the Social Patterning of Smoking Practices: A Dynamic Typology." *Sociology of Health and Illness* 31:583–601.

National Center for Health Statistics. 2002. *Health, United States, 2002.* Washington, DC: US Government Printing Office.

——2010. *Health, United States, 2010.* Washington, DC: US Government Printing Office.

Navarro, Vicente. 1976. *Medicine Under Capitalism.* New York: Prodist.

Nazroo, James Y. 1997. *The Health of Britain's Ethnic Minorities.* London: Policy Studies Institute.

Nettleton, Sarah. 2006. *The Sociology of Health and Illness*, 2nd ed. Cambridge, UK: Polity.

——2010. "The Sociology of the Body." In *The New Blackwell Companion to Medical Sociology*, ed. William Cockerham, 47–68. Oxford, UK: Wiley-Blackwell

Nettleton, Sarah, Roger Burrows, and Lisa O'Malley. 2005. "The Mundane Realities of the Everyday Lay Use of the Internet for Health, and Their Consequences for Media Convergence." *Sociology of Health and Illness* 27:972–92.

Nettleton, Sarah, Jo Neale, and Lucy Pickering. 2011. " 'I Don't Think There's Much of a Rational Mind in a Drug Addict When They Are in the Thick of It.' Towards an Embodied Analysis of Recovering Heroin Users." *Sociology of Health and Illness* 33:341–55.

Oliver, M. Norman and Carles Muntaner. 2005. "Researching Health Inequalities Among African Americans: The Imperative to Understand Social Class." *International Journal of Health Services* 35:485–98.

Orpana, Heather M. and Louise Lemyre. 2004. "Explaining the Social Gradient in Health in Canada: Using the National Population Health Survey to Examine the Role of Stressors." *International Journal of Behavioral Medicine* 11:143–51.

Ostrowska, Nina. 2005. "In and Out of Communism: The Macrosocial Context of Health in Poland." In *The Blackwell Companion to Medical Sociology*, ed. William Cockerham, 334–46. Oxford, UK: Blackwell.

Pakulski, Jan and Malcolm Waters. 1996. *The Death of Class*. London: Sage.

Pampel, Fred C. 2008. "Racial Convergence in Cigarette Use from Adolescence to the Mid-Thirties." *Journal of Health and Social Behavior* 49:484–98.

——2009. "The Persistence of Educational Disparities in Smoking." *Social Problems* 56:526–42.

Pampel, Fred C. and Richard G. Rogers. 2004. "Socioeconomic Status, Smoking, and Health: A Test of Competing Theories of Cumulative Advantage." *Journal of Health and Social Behavior* 45: 306–21.

Parsons, Talcott. 1951. *The Social System*. New York: Free Press.

Paterson, Stewart. 2004. "Glasgow OAPS Most Likely to Die in Winter; Old Folk at More Risk Than in Siberia as They Can't Pay to Heat Homes." *Evening Times* (January 22):4.

Pearlin, Leonard I. 1989. "The Sociological Study of Stress." *Journal of Health and Social Behavior* 30:241–56.

Pearlin, Leonard I., Scott Schieman, Elena M. Fazio, and Stephen C. Meersman. 2005. "Stress, Health, and the Life Course: Some

Conceptual Perspectives." *Journal of Health and Social Behavior* 46:205–19.

Pederson, M., S. Jackson, M. Klarlund, and M. Frisch. 2006. "Socioeconomic Status and Risk of Rheumatoid Arthritis." *Journal of Rheumatology* 33:1069–74.

Pescosolido, Bernice A., Jane McLeod, and Margarita Alegría. 2000. "Confronting the Second Contract: The Place of Medical Sociology in Research and Policy for the Twenty-First Century." In *Handbook of Medical Sociology*, 5th ed., ed. Chloe Bird, Peter Conrad, and Allen Fremont, 411–26. Upper Saddle River, NJ: Prentice Hall.

Pescosolido, Bernice A. and Beth A. Rubin. 2000. "The Web of Group Affiliations Revisited: Social Life, Postmodernism, and Sociology." *American Sociological Review* 65:52–76.

Petersen, Alan. 2005. "Securing Our Genetic Benefits: Engendering Trust in UK Biobank." *Sociology of Health and Illness* 27:271–92.

Phelan, Jo C., Bruce G. Link, Ana Diez-Roux, Ichiro Kawachi, and Bruce Levin. 2004. "'Fundamental Causes' of Social Inequalities in Mortality: A Test of the Theory." *Journal of Health and Social Behavior* 45:265–85.

Phelan, Jo C., Bruce G. Link, and Parisa Tehranifar. 2010. "Social Conditions as Fundamental Causes of Health Inequalities: Theory, Evidence, and Policy Implications." *Journal of Health and Social Behavior* 51:S28–S40.

Pilgrim, David and Anne Rogers. 1999. *A Sociology of Health and Mental Illness*, 2nd ed. Buckingham, UK: Open University Press.

Pilnick, Alison. 2002a. *Genetics and Society: An Introduction.* Buckingham, UK: Open University Press.

——2002b. " 'There Are No Rights and Wrongs in These Situations': Identifying Interactional Difficulties in Genetic Counseling." *Sociology of Health and Illness* 24:66–88.

Plummer, Ken. 2000. "Symbolic Interactionism in the Twentieth Century." In *The Blackwell Companion to Social Theory*, ed. Bryan Turner, 193–222. Oxford, UK: Blackwell.

Poortinga, Wouter. 2006. "Social Capital: An Individual or Collective Resource for Health?" *Social Science and Medicine* 62:292–302.

Popay, Jennie and Gareth Williams. 2009. "Equalizing the People's Health: A Sociological Perspective." In *The New Sociology of the Health Service,* ed. Jonathan Gabe and Michael Calnan, 222–44. London: Routledge.

Porter, Roy. 1997. *The Greatest Benefit to Mankind: A Medical History of Humanity*. New York: Norton.

Power, C. and S. Matthews. 1997. "Origins of Health Inequalities in a National Population Sample." *Lancet* 350:1584–9.

Power, C., S. Matthews, and O. Manor. 1996. "Inequalities in Self Rated Health in the 1958 Birth Cohort – Lifetime Social Circumstances or Social Mobility." *British Medical Journal* 313:449–53.

Power, Elaine M. 2005. "Determinants of Healthy Eating Among Low-Income Canadians." *Canadian Journal of Public Health* 96:S37–43.

Putnam, Robert D. 2000. *Bowling Alone: The Collapse and Revival of American Community*. New York: Touchstone.

Quah, Stella. 2010. "Health and Culture." In *The New Blackwell Companion to Medical Sociology*, ed. William Cockerham, 27–46. Oxford, UK: Wiley-Blackwell.

Quesnel-Vallée, Amélie and Tania Jenkins. 2010. "Social Policies and Health Inequalities." In *The New Blackwell Companion to Medical Sociology*, ed. William Cockerham, 455–83. Oxford, UK: Wiley-Blackwell.

Rahkonen, Ossi, Eero Lahelma, P. Martikainan, and K. Silventoinen. 2002. "Determinants of Health Inequalities by Income from the 1980s to the 1990s in Finland." *Journal of Epidemiology and Public Health* 56:442–3.

Raudenbush, Stephen W. and Anthony S. Bryk. 2002. *Hierarchical Linear Models: Applications and Data Analysis Methods*, 2nd ed. Thousand Oaks, CA: Sage.

Redelmeier, Donald A. and Jeffrey C. Kwong. 2004. "Death Rates of Medical School Class Presidents." *Social Science and Medicine* 58:2437–543.

Redelmeier, Donald A. and Sheldon M. Singh. 2001. "Survival in Academy Award Winning Actors and Actresses." *Annals of Internal Medicine* 134:955–62.

Regidor, Enrique, Elena Ronda, David Martinez, M. Elisa Calle, Pedro Navarro, and Vincente Dominguez. 2005. "Occupational Social Class and Mortality in a Population of Men Economically Active: The Contribution of Education and Employment Situation." *European Journal of Epidemiology* 20:501–8.

Reid, Ivan. 1989. *Social Class Differences in Britain*, 3rd ed. Glasgow, UK: Fontana Press.

——1998. *Class in Britain*. Cambridge, UK: Polity.

Reynolds, Paul Davidson. [1971] 2007. *A Primer in Theory Construction*. Boston: Allyn and Bacon.

Ridge, Damien, Carol Emslie, and Alan White. 2011. "Understanding How Men Experience, Express and Cope with Mental Distress: Where Next?" *Sociology of Health and Illness* 33:145–59.

Riley, Matilda White. 1987. "On the Significance of Age in Sociology." *American Sociological Review* 52:1–14.

Ringer, Fritz. 2004. *Max Weber*. Chicago: University of Chicago Press.

Ritzer, George. 2011. *Sociological Theory*, 8th ed. New York: McGraw-Hill.

Ritzer, George and William Yagatich. 2012. "Contemporary Sociological Theory." In *The Wiley-Blackwell Companion to Sociology*, ed. George Ritzer, 98–118. Oxford, UK: Wiley-Blackwell.

Robert, Stephanie A. 1998. "Community-Level Socioeconomic Status Effects on Adult Health." *Journal of Health and Social Behavior* 39:18–37.

Robert, Stephanie A. and James S. House. 2000. "Socioeconomics Inequalities in Health: An Enduring Sociological Problem." In *Handbook of Medical Sociology*, 5th ed., ed. Chloe Bird, Peter Conrad, and Allen Fremont, 79–97. Upper Saddle River, NJ: Prentice Hall.

Robert, Stephanie and Eric N. Reither. 2004. "A Multilevel Analysis of Race, Community Disadvantage, and Body Mass Index Among Adults in the U.S." *Social Science and Medicine* 59:2421–34.

Roos, Eva, Eero Lahelma, Mikko Virtanen, Ritva Prättälä, and Pirjo Pietinen. 1998. "Gender, Socioeconomic Status and Family Status as Determinants of Food Behavior." *Social Science and Medicine* 46:1519–29.

Rose, David and Eric Harrison (eds.). 2010. *Social Class in Europe*. London: Routledge.

Rosenbaum, Emily. 2008. "Racial/Ethnic Differences in Asthma Prevalence: The Role of Housing and Neighborhood Environments." *Journal of Health and Social Behavior* 49:131–45.

Rosenfield, Sarah. 1989. "The Effects of Women's Employment: Personal Control and Sex Differences in Mental Health." *Journal of Health and Social Behavior* 33:77–91.

——1999. "Gender and Mental Health: Do Women Have More Psychopathology, Men More, or Both the Same (and Why?)." In *A Handbook for the Study of Mental Health: Social Contexts, Theories, and Systems*, ed. Allan Horowitz and Teresa Scheid, 348–60. Cambridge, UK: Cambridge University Press.

Ross, Catherine E. 2000. "Neighborhood Disadvantage and Adult Depression." *Journal of Health and Social Behavior* 41:177–87.

Ross, Catherine E. and Chloe E. Bird. 1994. "Sex Stratification and Health Lifestyle: Consequences for Men's and Women's Perceived Health." *Journal of Health and Social Behavior* 35:161–78.

Ross, Catherine E. and John Mirowsky. 2001. "Neighborhood Disadvantage, Disorder, and Health." *Journal of Health and Social Behavior* 42:258–76.

Ross, Catherine E. and Chia-ling Wu. 1995. "The Links Between Education and Health." *American Sociological Review* 60: 719–45.

Rubin, Lillian Breslow. 1976. *Worlds of Pain: Life in Working Class Families*. New York: Basic Books.

Saint Onge, Jarron M. and Patrick M. Krueger. 2011. "Education and Racial-Ethnic Differences in Types of Exercise in the United States." *Journal of Health and Social Behavior* 52:197–211.

Sampson, Robert J. 2003. "The Neighborhood Context of Well-Being." *Perspectives in Biology and Medicine* 46:S53–64.

Sampson, Robert J., Jeffrey D. Morenoff, and Felton Earls. 1999. "Beyond Social Capital: Social Dynamics of Collective Efficacy for Children." *American Sociological Review* 64:633–60.

Sampson, Robert J., Stephen W. Raudenbush, and Felton Earls. 1997. "Neighborhoods and Violent Crime: A Multilevel Study of Collective Efficacy. *Science* 277:918–24.

Sanders, Teela. 2004. "A Continuum of Risk? The Management of Health, Physical and Emotional Risks by Female Sex Workers." *Sociology of Health and Illness* 26:557–74.

Santora, Marc. 2006. "East Meets West, Adding Pounds and Peril." *New York Times* (January 12):A1, A20.

Satterthwaite, D. 1993. "The Impact on Health of Urban Environments." *Environment and Urbanization* 2:87–111.

Scambler, Graham. 2002. *Health and Social Change*. Buckingham, UK: Open University Press.

Scheff, Thomas. [1966] 1999. *Being Mentally Ill*, 3rd ed. Chicago: Aldine.

Schilling, Chris. 2003. *The Body and Social Theory*, 2nd ed. London: Sage.

Schnittker, Jason. 2004. "Education and the Changing Shape of the Income Gradient in Health." *Journal of Health and Social Behavior* 45:386–405.

Schulz, Amy, David Williams, Barbara Israel, Adam Becker, Edith Parker, Sherman A. James, and James Jackson. 2000. "Unfair Treatment, Neighborhood Effects, and Mental Health in the Detroit Metropolitan Area." *Journal of Health and Social Behavior* 41:314–32.

Scott, Janny. 2005. "Life at the Top in America Isn't Just Better, It's Longer." *New York Times* (May 16):A1, A18–19.

Scott, John. 1996. *Stratification and Power: Structures of Class, Status, and Command.* Cambridge, UK: Polity.

Seccombe, Karen and Cheryl Amey. 1995. "Playing by the Rules and Losing: Health Insurance and the Working Poor." *Journal of Health and Social Behavior* 36:168–81.

Sewell, William H. 1992. "A Theory of Structure: Duality, Agency, and Transformation." *American Journal of Sociology* 98:1–29.

Shankina, A. I. 2004. "The Middle Class in Russia: Hunting Nessie." *Russian Social Science Review* 45:26–41.

Shaw, Mary, Danny Dorling, and Nic Brimblecombe. 1998. "Changing the Map: Health in Britain 1951–91." *Sociology of Health and Illness* 20:694–709.

Shifflett, Peggy A. 1987. "Future Time Perspective, Past Experiences, and Negotiation of Food Use Patterns Among the Aged." *Gerontologist* 27:611–15.

Shifflett, Peggy A. and William A. McIntosh. 1986–7. "Food Habits and Future Time: An Exploratory Study of Age-Appropriate Food Habits Among the Elderly." *International Journal of Aging and Human Development* 24:1–17.

Shishehbor, Mehdi H., David Litaker, Claire E. Pothier, and Michael S. Lauer. 2006. "Association of Socioeconomic Status with Functional Capacity, Heart Rate Recovery, and All-Cause Mortality." *JAMA* 295:784–92.

Shkolnikov, Vladimir M., David A. Leon, Sergey Adamets, Eugeniy Andreev, and Alexander Deev. 1998. "Educational Level and Adult Mortality in Russia: An Analysis of Routine Data 1979 to 1994." *Social Science and Medicine* 47:357–69.

Shkolnikov, Vladimir M. and Alexander Nemstov. 1997. "The Anti-Alcohol Campaign and Variations in Russian Mortality." In *Premature Mortality in the New Independent States*, ed. J. Bobadilla, C. Costello, and E. Mitchell, 39–68. Washington, DC: National Academy Press.

Sibeon, Roger. 2004. *Rethinking Social Theory.* London: Sage.

Siegrist, Johannes. 2010. "Stress in the Workplace." In *The New Blackwell Companion to Medical Sociology*, ed. William Cockerham, 268–87. Oxford, UK: Wiley-Blackwell.

Sihvonen, Ari-Pekka, Anton E. Kunst, Eero Lahelma, Tapani Valkonen, and John P. Mackenbach. 1998. "Socioeconomic Inequalities in Health Expectancy in Finland and Norway in the Late 1980s." *Social Science and Medicine* 47:303–15.

Simmons, L. and H. Wolff. 1954. *Social Science and Medicine.* New York: Russell Sage.

Sitnikov, A. 2000. "Is a 'Middle Class' Forming?" *Russian Social Science Review* 41:66–80.

Smaje, Chris. 2000. "Race, Ethnicity, and Health." In *Handbook of Medical Sociology*, 5th ed., ed. Chloe Bird, Peter Conrad, and Allen Fremont, 114–28. Upper Saddle River, NJ: Prentice Hall.

Smelser, Neil. 1997. *Problematics of Sociology*. Berkeley: University of California Press.

Snead, M. Christine and William C. Cockerham. 2002. "Health Lifestyles and Social Class in the Deep South." *Research in the Sociology of Health Care* 20:107–22.

Song, Lijun and Nan Lin. 2009. "Social Capital and Health Inequality: Evidence from Taiwan." *Journal of Health and Social Behavior* 50:149–63.

Song, Lijun, Joonmo Son, and Nan Lin. 2010. "Social Capital and Health." In *The New Blackwell Companion to Medical Sociology*, ed. William Cockerham, 184–210. Oxford, UK: Wiley-Blackwell.

Splawski, I., K. Timothy, M. Tateyama, C. Clancy, A. Malhorta, A. Beggs, F. Cappuccio, G. Sagnella, R. Kass, and M. Keating. 2002. "Variant of SCH5A Sodium Channel Implicated in Risk of Cardiac Arrhythmia." *Science* 297:1333–6.

Srole, Leo, T. S. Langner, S. T. Michael, M. K. Opler, and T. A. C. Rennie. 1962. *Mental Health in the Metropolis: The Mid-Town Manhattan Study*, vols. 1 and 2. Revised and enlarged ed. New York: McGraw-Hill.

Stacey, Claire. 2005. "Finding Dignity in Dirty Work: The Constraints and Rewards of Low-Wage Home Care Labour." *Sociology of Health and Illness* 27:831–54.

Stacey, Margaret, with Hilary Homans. 1981. "The Sociology of Health and Illness: Its Present State, Future Prospects, and Potential for Health Research." *Sociology of Health and Illness* 3:281–307.

Stafford, M., S. Cummins, S. Macintyre, A. Ellaway, and M. Marmot. 2005. "Gender Differences in the Associations Between Health and Neighbourhood Environment." *Social Science and Medicine* 60:1681–92.

Stead, Martine, Laura McDermott, Anne Marie MacKintosh, and Ashley Adamson. 2011. "Why Healthy Eating is Bad for Young People's Health: Identity, Belonging and Food." *Social Science and Medicine* 72:1121–39.

Strauss, Anselm, Leonard Schatzman, Danuta Ehrlich, Rue Bucher, and Melvin Sabshin. 1963. "The Hospital and its Negotiated Order." In *The Hospital in Modern Society*, ed. Eliot Friedson, 147–69. New York: Free Press.

Sundquist, Jan and Sven-Erik Johansson. 1997. "Indicators of Socioeconomic Position and Their Relation to Mortality in Sweden." *Social Science and Medicine* 45:1757–66.

Sundquist, Jan, Sven-Erik Johansson, Min Yang, and Kristina Sundquist. 2006. "Low Linking Social Capital as a Predictor of Coronary Heart Disease in Sweden: A Cohort Study of 2.8 Million People." *Social Science and Medicine* 62:954–63.

Swartz, David. 1997. *Culture and Power: The Sociology of Pierre Bourdieu*. Chicago: University of Chicago Press.

Sweat, Michael D. and Julie A. Denison. 1995. "Reducing HIV Incidence in Developing Countries with Structural and Environmental Interventions." *AIDS* 9:S251–7.

Tausig, Mark and Rudy Fenwick. 1999. "Recession and Well-Being." *Journal of Health and Social Behavior* 40:1–16.

Taylor, John and R. Jay Turner. 2001. "A Longitudinal Study of the Role and Significance of Mattering to Others for Depressive Symptoms." *Journal of Health and Social Behavior* 42: 310–25.

Thisted, Ronald A. 2003. "Are There Social Determinants of Health and Disease?" *Perspectives in Biology and Medicine* 46:S65–73.

Thoits, Peggy A. 1995. "Stress, Coping, and Social Support Processes: Where Are We? What Next?" *Journal of Health and Social Behavior* (Extra Issue):53–79.

——2010. "Stress and Health: Major Findings and Implications." *Journal of Health and Social Behavior* 51:S41–S53.

Tocqueville, Alexis de. [1835] 1958. *Journeys to England and Ireland*, ed. K. Mayer and trans. G. Lawrence and K. Mayer. New Haven, CT: Yale University Press.

Trivedi, Amal N., Alan M. Zaslavsky, Eric C. Schneider, and John Z. Ayanian. 2005. "Trends in the Quality of Care and Racial Disparities in Medicare Managed Care." *New England Journal of Medicine* 353:692–700.

Tuchman, Barbara W. 1979. *A Distant Mirror: The Calamitous 14th Century*. New York: Random House.

Tung, Jenny, Luis B. Barreiro, Zachery P. Johnson, Kasper D. Hansen, Vasiliki Michopoulos, Donna Toufexius, Katelyn Michelini, Mark E. Wilson, and Yoav Gilad. 2012. "Social Environment is Associated with Gene Regulatory Variation in the Rhesus Macaque Immune System." *Proceedings of the National Academy of Sciences*. www.pnas.org/cgi/doi/10.1073/pnas.1202734109.

Turner, Bryan S. [1984] 2008. *The Body and Society*, 3rd ed. London: Sage.

——1992. *Regulating Bodies: Essays in Medical Sociology*. London: Routledge.

——1995. *Medical Power and Social Knowledge*, 2nd ed. London: Sage.

——2003. "Social Capital, Inequality and Health: The Durkheimian Revival." *Social Therapy and Health* 1:4–20.

——2004. *The New Medical Sociology: Social Forms of Health and Illness*. London: Norton.

Turner, Bryan S. and Steven P. Wainwright. 2003. "Corps de Ballet: The Case of the Injured Dancer." *Sociology of Health and Illness* 25:269–88.

Turner, R. Jay and William R. Avison. 2003. "Status Variations in Stress Exposure: Implications for the Interpretation of Research on Race, Socioeconomic Status, and Gender." *Journal of Health and Social Behavior* 44:488–505.

Turner, R. Jay, John Taylor, and Karen van Gundy. 2004. "Personal Resources and Depression in the Transition to Adulthood: Ethnic Comparisons." *Journal of Health and Social Behavior* 45:34–52.

Van Gundy, Karen, Scott Schieman, Margaret S. Kelley, and Cesar J. Rebellion. 2005. "Gender Role Orientations and Alcohol Use Among Moscow and Toronto Adults." *Social Science and Medicine* 61:2317–30.

Vartanian, Thomas P. and Linda Houser. 2010. "The Effects of Childhood Neighborhood Conditions on Self-Reports of Adult Health." *Journal of Health and Social Behavior* 51:291–306.

Veblen, Thorstein. [1899] 1994. *Theory of the Leisure Class*. New York: Dover.

Veenstra, Gerry, Issac Luginaah, Sarah Wakefield, Stephen Birch, John Eyles, and Susan Elliott. 2005. "Who You Know, Where You Live: Social Capital, Neighbourhood and Health." *Social Science and Medicine* 60:2799–818.

Waitzkin, Howard. 1983. *The Second Sickness: Contradictions of Capitalist Health Care*. New York: Free Press.

Walsh, Diana Chapman, Glorian Sorensen, and Lori Leonard. 1995. "Gender, Health, and Cigarette Smoking." In *Society and Health*, ed. Benjamin Amick, Alvin Tarlov, Sol Levine, and Diana Walsh, 131–71. New York: Oxford University Press.

Wamala, Sarah P., Murray A. Mittleman, Myriam Horsten, Karin Schenck-Gustafsson, and Kristina Orth-Comér. 2000. "Job Stress and the Occupational Gradient in Coronary Heart Disease Risk in Women: The Stockholm Female Coronary Risk Study." *Social Science and Medicine* 51:481–9.

Warren, John Robert. 2009. "Socioeconomic Status and Health across the Life Course: A Test of the Social Causation and Health Selection Hypothesis." *Social Forces* 87:125–54.

Warren, Mary Guptill, Rose Weitz, and Stephen Kulis. 1998. "Physician Satisfaction in a Changing Health Care Environment: The Impact of Challenges to Professional Autonomy, Authority, and Dominance." *Journal of Health and Social Behavior* 39: 356–67.

Wasserman, Jason Adam and Jeffrey Michael Clair. 2010. *At Home on the Street: People, Poverty, and a Hidden Culture of Homelessness.* Boulder, CO: Lynne Rienner.

Weber, Max. [1922] 1978. *Economy and Society.* 2 vols. Trans. and ed. Guenther Roth and Claus Wittich. Berkeley: University of California Press.

——1946. *From Max Weber: Essays in Sociology.* Trans. and ed. Hans Gerth and C. Wright Mills. New York: Oxford University Press.

——1949. *The Methodology of the Social Sciences.* Trans. and ed. E. Shils and H. Finch. New York: Free Press.

——1958. *The Protestant Ethic and the Spirit of Capitalism.* Trans. Talcott Parsons. New York: Scribners.

Weitzman, E. R. and I. Kawachi. 2000. "Giving Means Receiving: The Protective Effect of Social Capital on Binge Drinking on College Campuses." *American Journal of Public Health* 90:1936–9.

Wermuth, Laurie. 2003. *Global Inequality and Human Needs: Health and Illness in an Increasingly Unequal World.* Boston: Allyn and Bacon.

White, Kevin. 2006. *The Sage Dictionary of Health and Society.* London: Sage.

Whitehead, Margaret. 1990. "The Health Divide." In *Inequalities in Health*, ed. P. Townsend and N. Davidson, 222–356. London: Penguin Books.

Wickrama, K. A. S., Rand D. Conger, Lora Ebert Wallace, and Glen H. Elder, Jr. 1999. "The Intergenerational Transmission of Health-Risk Behaviors: Adolescent Lifestyles and Gender Moderating Effects." *Journal of Health and Social Behavior* 40:258–72.

——2003. "Linking Early Social Risks to Impaired Health During the Transition to Adulthood." *Journal of Health and Social Behavior* 44:61–74.

Wilkinson, Richard G. 1992. "Income Distribution and Life Expectancy." *British Medical Journal* 304:165–8.

——1996. *Unhealthy Societies.* London: Routledge.

Wilkinson, Richard G. and Kate E. Pickett. 2006. "Income Inequality and Population Health: A Review and Explanation of the Evidence." *Social Science and Medicine* 62:1768–84.

Williams, David. 1999. "Race, Socioeconomic Status, and Health: The Added Effects of Racism and Discrimination." *Annals of the New York Academy of Science* 896:173–88.

Williams, David and Chiquita Collins. 1995. "U.S. Socioeconomic and Racial Differences in Health: Patterns and Explanations." *Annual Review of Sociology* 21:349–86.

Williams, David R., Harold W. Neighbors, and James S. Jackson. 2003. "Racial/Ethnic Discrimination and Health: Findings from Community Studies." *American Journal of Public Health* 93:200–8.

Williams, David R. and Michelle Sternthal. 2010. "Understanding Racial-Ethnic Disparities in Health: Sociological Contributions." *Journal of Health and Social Behavior* 51:S15–S27.

Williams, Gareth. 2003. "The Determinants of Health: Structure, Context and Agency." *Sociology of Health and Illness* 25:131–54.

Williams, Kristi. 2003. "Has the Future of Marriage Arrived? A Contemporary Examination of Gender, Marriage, and Psychological Well-Being." *Journal of Health and Social Behavior* 44:470–87.

Williams, Simon J. 1995. "Theorising Class, Health and Lifestyles: Can Bourdieu Help Us?" *Sociology of Health and Illness* 25:131–54.

——1999. "Is Anybody There? Critical Realism, Chronic Illness and the Disability Debate." *Sociology of Health and Illness* 21:797–919.

——2003. *Medicine and the Body*. London: Sage.

Williams, Simon J. and Gillian Bendelow. 1996. "Emotions, Health and Illness: The 'Missing Link' in Medical Sociology." In *Health and the Sociology of Emotions*, ed. V. James and Jonathan Gabe, 25–53. Oxford, UK: Blackwell.

Williams, Simon J., Jonathan Gabe, and Peter Davis. 2008. "The Sociology of Pharmaceuticals: Progress and Prospects." *Sociology of Health and Illness* 3:813–23.

Williams, Simon J., Paul Martin, and Jonathan Gabe. 2011. "The Pharmaceuticalisation of Society? A Framework for Analysis." *Sociology of Health and Illness* 33:710–25.

Wilson, William Julius. 1987. *The Truly Disadvantaged*. Chicago: University of Chicago Press.

Winkelby, Marilyn A., Daruis E. Jatulis, Erica Frank, and Stephen P. Fortmann. 1992. "Socioeconomic Status and Health: How Education, Income, and Occupation Contribute to Risk Factors for Cardiovascular Disease." *American Journal of Public Health* 82:816–20.

Wong, Mitchell D., Tomoko Tagawa, Hsin-Ju Hsieh, Martin F.

Shapiro, W. John Boscardin, and Susan L. Ettner. 2005. "Differences in Cause-Specific Mortality Between Latino and White Adults." *Medical Care* 43:1058–62.

Wray, Linda A., A. Regula Herzog, Robert J. Willis, and Robert W. Wallace. 1998. "The Impact of Education and Heart Attack on Smoking Cessation Among Middle-Age Adults." *Journal of Health and Social Behavior* 39:271–94.

Young, Frank W. and Thomas A. Lyson. 2001. "Structural Pluralism and All-Cause Mortality." *American Journal of Public Health* 91:136–8.

Zborowski, Mark. 1952. "Cultural Components in Responses to Pain." *Journal of Social Issues* 8:16–30.

Zerubavel, Eviatar. 1997. *Social Mindscapes*. Cambridge, MA: Harvard University Press.

Ziersch, Anna M. 2005. "Health Implications of Access to Social Capital: Findings from an Australian Study." *Social Science and Medicine* 61:2119–31.

Zola, Irving K. 1966. "Culture and Symptoms – An Analysis of Patients' Presenting Complaints." *American Sociological Review* 31:615–30.

Author index

Subject index